TRADE UNIONS AND THE GLOBAL CRISIS

LABOUR'S VISIONS, STRATEGIES AND RESPONSES

edited by

Melisa Serrano, Edlira Xhafa and Michael Fichter

INTERNATIONAL LABOUR OFFICE • GENEVA

Serrano, Melisa; Xhafa, Edlira; Fichter, Michael (eds)

Trade unions and the global crisis: Labour's visions, strategies and responses

Geneva: International Labour Office, 2011

trade union / trade union role / labour relations / collective bargaining / decent work / workers rights / role of ILO / economic recession / developed countries / developing countries

1 v.

13.06.3

ISBN: 978-92-2-124926-9

ILO Cataloguing in Publication Data

Typeset by Magheross Graphics, France & Ireland *www.magheross.com*
Printed in Switzerland

FOREWORD

Four years after the Great Recession, a catastrophe has been avoided, but few real lessons have been drawn and nothing has been fixed. Indeed, in many cases the crisis is being used as another opportunity to subordinate individual workers, governments and entire societies to the sway of unaccountable global capital markets. After a short revival of corporatist social dialogue in some countries, more workers are being pushed into precarious employment, and austerity packages are making working people, their families and pensioners pay for the crisis. Trade unions are at a crossroads, and the status quo is no longer an option.

Turning the tide is as much a battle of ideas as it is a question of mobilizing public protest. *Trade unions and the global crisis* looks at both: alternative ideas as well as strategies of mobilization and resistance against employer unilateralism and market-driven fundamentalism. While the volume does not claim to provide all the answers, it rejects self-defeating pessimism and nostalgic reminiscences of a golden age of post-war capitalism. It looks at a wide range of trade union initiatives, debates and struggles that give priority to human dignity, workers' rights, productive work and solidarity as opposed to abstract notions such as market efficiency, perfect competition and general equilibrium.

Researching, studying and debating the challenges for labour policies in the age of globalization is the motivation for the Global Labour University, a partnership of universities, trade unions and the ILO. This book is the product of this worldwide network committed to an open debate on the future of labour.

We are grateful to the Berlin School of Economics and Law, in particular Hansjörg Herr, Trevor Evans, Birgit Mahnkopf, Eckhard Hein, Miriam Klessen and Harald Kröck, for hosting and organizing last year's Global Labour

University conference, at which drafts of the contributions here were presented and discussed. Special thanks go to the contributors, as well as to Melisa Serrano, Edlira Xhafa and Michael Fichter for their superb editorial work. Thanks are also due to the anonymous peer reviewers for their invaluable feedback, and to Chris Edgar at the ILO for his professionalism in overseeing the production of this volume.

Dan Cunniah
Director, Bureau for Workers' Activities, ILO

CONTENTS

LIST OF TABLES

LIST OF FIGURES

PREFACE

Just 1 per cent of the world's population owns 40 per cent of the world's wealth, while 60 per cent have to share just 1.9 per cent of it. Most workers have no employment security and billions earn less than a dollar a day. The pursuit of profit trumps the health of people and the future of the planet. Economic growth does not translate into common prosperity. Billions of workers have no say in their working conditions; many are threatened, intimidated, fired and in the worst cases thrown into prison or killed by hired gunmen when they demand their basic human rights of freedom of association, collective bargaining and industrial democracy.

Those who profit from this world disorder tell us that these are the inevitable side-effects of market dynamism, which in turn is the most effective mechanism to create growth and wealth. It would just be too depressing to imagine that this were true and that humankind could not improve on such a world. Change is necessary – indeed, it is inevitable, as the current system is unsustainable; but it remains difficult, as vested interests constitute a huge and dangerous obstacle on the path to more equitable solutions.

The history of trade unions is a history of struggles for greater social justice and against dictatorship, both in societies and at the workplace. Often accused by their opponents of being unreasonable, unable to understand economics, and dinosaurs of the industrial past, there can be no doubt in retrospect that in most battles trade unions have been on the right side of history. While business has unhesitatingly engaged with dictatorships around the world in its pursuit of profit, trade unions were and are at the forefront of bringing about democratic change in countries from South Africa, Brazil and the Republic of Korea to Poland and most recently Egypt. The right to strike, a minimum wage, the eight-hour working day, paid vacations, social security – all are milestones in the long struggle of trade unions for social justice.

The privileged few and their servants in academia, who have from the beginning resisted these struggles for universal and basic workers' rights, accuse trade unions of representing only the privileged minority of workers who enjoy "insider" benefits at the expense of less fortunate workers. It is true that in some instances the "insider–outsider" problem exists – to a degree that depends largely on how far trade unions have succeeded in extending the concept of solidarity. Where the problem does exist, this is because, despite unions' aspiration to universal rights and protection for workers, they have not been strong enough to overcome resistance to universal solutions and have had to settle for "second best" solutions. But it ill behoves those who resist even signing a collective bargaining agreement at enterprise level in order to ensure at least equity and justice among workers within a single firm to accuse trade unionists of a lack of solidarity and inclusiveness.

Solidarity often begins on a personal level among work colleagues, and it is a constant challenge to extend its boundaries beyond the workplace. Building solidarity among workers within an enterprise, within an industry, within a country, across borders and throughout global companies is a difficult task. Those of us in leading positions in the trade union movement are asking a lot from our members. We are asking them to overcome their fear of – sometimes very aggressive – employers, to show solidarity not only with their colleagues on the shop-floor or in the office but with workers elsewhere whom they don't know, whom they will probably never meet and whose language they don't understand. We are asking them to hand over 1 per cent of their often meagre pay to fund a global labour movement. In view of this, and given that most people normally care first and foremost for their family, friends and neighbours, it is quite amazing that more than 175 million people are voluntary members of an independent and free trade union movement.

It cannot be denied that, while more workers than ever before now enjoy political freedom, aggressive resistance to industrial democracy and collective bargaining on the part of employers has also grown over recent decades. Governments in many countries, influenced by aggressive lobbying from business, have tilted the balance of power between capital and labour even more steeply in favour of the privileged few. Trade unions in many countries have been losing members and influence – and if they are to remain relevant, they have to turn the tide. This requires change both in the rules of the game and in the unions themselves.

This book focuses primarily on the latter challenge – that is, the changes required of trade unions themselves. Trade unions today face simultaneously a wide range of often contradictory tasks. They need to change, and are changing, in order to meet both new and persistent challenges to their advancement of social justice, income security and industrial democracy. Their members want them to be organized in an efficient, strategic and effective fashion; they also want them to be transparent, democratic and inclusive. Running a business is simple compared to running a trade union. Business has one objective – maximizing profit – and anyone who doesn't function in accordance with that end gets fired. Trade unions are voluntary organizations of millions of individuals with a huge diversity of interests, views and experiences. Their membership has become much more diverse over the last 50 years and needs to broaden its appeal even further to reach out to high-skilled workers and workers in the informal economy alike. To achieve simultaneously both diversity and unity is a challenge and certainly incompatible with the command and control culture of state or business machineries.

The key question any voluntary organization needs to answer is: What makes a movement move? It would be short-sighted to believe that institutional merger, sophisticated organizing tactics, skilful use of social networking or other innovative techniques are adequate to drive change. Far more radical, substantive and strategic responses are required.

The conferences run by Global Labour University provide forums in which these issues can be discussed in depth. This book presents a thought-provoking selection of essays, based on papers presented to one such conference, that examine how trade unions are responding to the current process of globalization and why trade unions in different contexts have carried out different responses. It sets out a wide range of views, thereby demonstrating that the search for answers to today's challenges needs to be an open process. While trade unions may have different and context-specific strategies in addressing economic and political changes at different levels (local, national, regional and international/global), this does not preclude finding common threads in labour discourse, strategies and struggles. It is imperative that trade union debates about priorities and strategies be grounded on a better understanding of the crisis-prone tendencies of the dominant economic paradigm.

There can be no doubt that the current globalization regime, driven by uncontrolled global capital markets and free trade, has been instrumental in putting pressure on workers throughout the world and responsible for the greatest economic crisis for a century. Trade unions' responses to this situation have to stretch from the local to the global. In this process trade unions will themselves have to change in order to be the successful agents of change towards a new social and economic development paradigm. These are challenging tasks, but the message from Tahrir Square to the world is also clear: change is possible, and it is done by ordinary people, when they come together in unity.

Michael Sommer
President, ITUC

NOTES ON CONTRIBUTORS

Lee Adler teaches public sector labour collective bargaining and labour law at the School of Industrial and Labor Relations, Cornell University, United States. His responsibilities include teaching leadership, legal strategy and other workplace skills to teacher, firefighter and police unions. He represented the rank and file and top leaders of the United Mine Workers (1975–2001), and currently represents firefighter unions throughout New York.

Chandra D. Bhatta works for the Friedrich Ebert Stiftung Nepal office. He was trained at the London School of Economics and University of Birmingham, United Kingdom, and was a Research Fellow on Civic Service at the George Warren Brown School of Social Work, Washington University, St Louis, United States. His areas of expertise include state building, civil society, civic service and citizenship building. He has published books, articles and monographs on these areas. He frequently writes for the news media on a variety of topical issues.

Maya Bhullar currently works in Canada as the research coordinator for Service Employees International Union (SEIU), Local 2 Canada, and is part of the larger labour movement initiatives in her community to build organizing campaigns. Her previous positions were research coordinator of SEIU's Global Division, project coordinator at the AFL-CIO with "Working America" and project coordinator for the International Labor Affairs Bureau at the US Department of Labor. She has an MA in international development, with a focus on urban planning and development and sub-Saharan Africa.

Conor Cradden is a research fellow in the Department of Sociology at the University of Geneva and a partner in Public World, a London-based research and policy consultancy. He was formerly head of research for a British public sector trade union. He has a PhD in social and political sciences from the European University in Florence and is the author of *Repoliticizing management: A theory of corporate legitimacy* (Ashgate, 2005).

Bill Dunn teaches in the Department of Political Economy at the University of Sydney, Australia. He is the author of *Global restructuring and the power of labour* (2004) and *Global political economy: A Marxist critique* (2009), and co-editor with Hugo Radice of *100 years of permanent revolution* (2006).

Michael Fichter is a senior lecturer in political science and labour relations at the Free University Berlin, where he also received his doctorate. Since 2004 he has taught at the Global Labour University in Berlin. He has published extensively on German and European labour relations and is currently co-director of an international research project on international framework agreements.

José Ricardo Barbosa Gonçalves is a professor at the State University of Campinas, Brazil. He is the author of *The utopia of the social order*. With Maria Alejandra Caporale Madi he has co-authored the following essays: "Corporate social responsibility and market society: Credit and banking inclusion in Brazil" in *Reading Karl Polanyi for the 21st century: Market economy as a political project* (Palgrave Macmillan, 2007), "Financialization, employability and their impacts on bank workers' union movement in Brazil (1994–2004)" in *Radical economics and labour* (Routledge, 2009), and "International economics" in *The handbook of pluralist economics education* (Routledge, 2009).

Laura Horn is a post-doctoral researcher at the Department of Political Science, VU University, Amsterdam. Her monograph on the transformation of EU corporate governance regulation is forthcoming in 2011. She has also co-edited a volume on critical political economy perspectives on European integration: *Limits and contradictions of neoliberal European governance* (Palgrave, 2008).

Maria Alejandra Caporale Madi is a professor at the State University of Campinas, Brazil. She is the author of *Monetary policy in Brazil: A post-Keynesian interpretation*. With José Ricardo Barbosa Gonçalves she has co-authored the following essays: "Corporate social responsibility and market society: Credit and banking inclusion in Brazil" in *Reading Karl Polanyi for the 21st century: Market economy as a political project* (Palgrave Macmillan, 2007), "Financialization, employability and their impacts on bank workers' union movement in Brazil

(1994–2004)" in *Radical economics and labour* (Routledge, 2009), and "International economics" in *The handbook of pluralist economics education* (Routledge, 2009).

Özgür Müftüoğlu completed his MA and PhD in the Department of Labour Economics and Industrial Relations at Marmara University, Istanbul, Turkey, where he is currently an assistant professor. He has published widely on labour studies and political economy.

Yasemin Özgün completed her MA in the Department of Government at the University of Essex, United Kingdom, and her PhD in the Faculty of Political Sciences at Ankara University, Turkey. She is now an assistant professor in political science at Anadolu University, Eskisehir, Turkey. She has published widely on Turkish politics, labour studies, educational policies and feminist politics.

Devan Pillay is an associate professor in the Department of Sociology, University of the Witwatersrand, South Africa. After his experience as a political prisoner under apartheid, he worked at the South African Labour and Development Research Unit at the University of Cape Town, and went on to receive his PhD in sociology from the University of Essex, United Kingdom, in 1989. Thereafter he become a staff writer for the *South African Labour Bulletin*, managing editor of *Work in Progress* magazine and director of the Social Policy MA Programme at the University of Durban-Westville. In 1996 he became Head of Research in the South African National Union of Mineworkers, and then Director of Policy for South Africa's Government Communication and Information System.

Bill Rosenberg has been an economist and director of policy at the Council of Trade Unions of New Zealand since May 2009. He holds a BCom in economics, a BSc in mathematics and a PhD in mathematical psychology. Before joining the CTU, Bill had worked in universities for 26 years, his last position being deputy director of the University Centre for Teaching and Learning at the University of Canterbury, New Zealand. He has published widely on globalization and trade and has been an active trade unionist for over 30 years, including three terms as national president of the Association of University Staff, the main union for university staff in New Zealand.

Jason Russell is an assistant professor at Empire State College, State University of New York, where he teaches in and coordinates undergraduate and graduate labour studies programmes. He received his PhD from York University in Toronto, Canada, and specializes in North American labour and working-class history since the Second World War.

Isabelle Schömann is a senior researcher at the European Trade Union Institute (ETUI), a labour lawyer, and coordinator of the European network of trade union legal experts (NETLEX). Her main fields of research are European social dialogue and European and comparative labour law; corporate governance; transnational trade union rights; and the constitutional law of the European Union.

Melisa Serrano is a PhD candidate in labour studies at the Graduate School in Social, Economic and Political Sciences, University of Milan, Italy. She is also a researcher and training specialist at the School of Labor and Industrial Relations, University of the Philippines, and co-author of *Building unions in Cambodia: History, challenges, strategies* (Friedrich Ebert Stiftung, 2010). She is a graduate of the Master in Labour Policies and Globalization programme of the Global Labour University in Germany.

Mark P. Thomas is an associate professor in the Department of Sociology and co-director of the Centre for Research on Work and Society at York University, Toronto, Canada. His research interests are in the areas of political economy and economic sociology, with a primary focus on the regulation of labour standards at local, national and transnational levels. He is the author of *Regulating flexibility: The political economy of employment standards* (McGill-Queen's University Press, 2009), co-editor (with N. Pupo) of *Interrogating the new economy: Restructuring work in the 21st century* (University of Toronto Press, 2010) and co-editor (with D. Brock and R. Raby) of *Power and everyday practices* (Nelson, 2011).

Edward Webster is a professor emeritus at the Society, Work and Development Institute, University of the Witwatersrand, South Africa. He is the co-author of *Grounding globalization: Labour in the age of insecurity* (Wiley-Blackwell), which won the American Sociological Association award for the best scholarly publication on labour in 2008. During 2009, he was the first Ela Bhatt Professor at the International Centre for Development and Decent Work, Kassel, Germany. He currently co-directs a South–South interdisciplinary research project examining how Governments in Brazil, India and South Africa are responding to economic insecurity through innovative social protection and public work programmes.

Ju Wenhui is an associate professor in the Department of Public Management, China Institute of Industrial Relations, Beijing. He has a PhD in population and employment. He is the author of "An econometric analysis of the impact of social networks on rural labor transfer", which appeared in *The Population and Economy*, No. 4 (2005).

Edlira Xhafa is a PhD candidate in labour studies at the Graduate School in Social, Economic and Political Sciences, University of Milan, Italy. Between 2000 and 2005, she was with the Albanian Trade Union Centre for Education and Research, which she later headed (2003–05). She is a graduate of the Master in Labour Policies and Globalization programme of the Global Labour University in Germany.

Lin Yanling is a professor in the Department of Employment Relations of the China Institute of Industrial Relations, Beijing. Her responsibilities include teaching senior trade unionists and teachers. She is the author of *International labour standards* (Chinese Workers, 2002) and *30 years of reform and opening up: The evolution and cultivation of Chinese workers' rights awareness* (Chinese Social Sciences Press, 2009). She co-authored *Factory tour of Germany* (Chinese Bookstore, 2010), which has been translated into German for publication.

LIST OF ABBREVIATIONS

ACFTU	All-China Federation of Trade Unions
AES	Alternative Economic Strategy (New Zealand)
AFL-CIO	American Federation of Labor–Congress of Industrial Organizations (United States)
AFSCME	American Federation of State, County and Municipal Employees
AKP	Justice and Development Party (Turkey)
ALBA	Bolivarian Alliance for the Americas
ANC	African National Congress
BLS	Bureau of Labor Statistics (United States)
BRICs	Brazil, Russian Federation, India, China
BSEIU	Building Service Employees International Union (Canada)
BVCA	British Private Equity and Venture Capital Association
CDL	Conference of the Democratic Left (South Africa)
COSATU	Congress of South African Trade Unions
CSEA	Civil Service Employees Association
CSR	corporate social responsibility
CTE	career and technical education
CTU	Council of Trade Unions (New Zealand)
CTW	Change-to-Win Coalition (United States)
CWP	Community Work Programme (South Africa)
DİSK	Confederation of Progressive Trade Unions of Turkey
DLF	Democratic Left Front (South Africa)
EFA	European framework agreement
EFCA	Employee Free Choice Act (United States)
EMF	European Metalworkers' Federation

ETUC	European Trade Union Confederation
ETUF	European Trade Union Federation
ETUI	European Trade Union Institute
EU	European Union
EWC	European Works Council
FOC	flag of convenience
GDP	gross domestic product
GFC	global financial crisis
GHG	greenhouse gas
GLU	Global Labour University
GM	General Motors
GSD	global social democracy
GUF	Global Union federation
IBF	International Bargaining Forum
ICEM	International Federation of Chemical, Energy, Mine and General Workers' Unions
IEO	International Employers' Organization
IFA	international framework agreement
IFBWW	International Federation of Building and Wood Workers
IFME	International Federation of Municipal Engineering
ILO	International Labour Organization
ILWU	International Longshore and Warehouse Union
IMEC	International Maritime Employers' Committee
IMF	International Monetary Fund
IOE	International Organisation of Employers
IPO	initial public offering
ISEG	International Seafarers Employers' Group
ITF	International Transport Workers' Federation
ITUC	International Trade Union Confederation
IUF	International Union of Food, Agricultural, Hotel, Restaurant, Catering, Tobacco and Allied Workers' Association
J4J	Justice for Janitors
KESK	Confederation of Public Employees (Turkey)
KSA	Korea Shipowners' Association
MGNREGS	Mahatma Gandhi National Rural Employment Guarantee Scheme
MNC	multinational corporation
NEDLAC	National Economic Development and Labour Council
NGO	non-governmental organization
NGP	New Growth Path (South Africa)

NLRB	National Labor Relations Board (United States)
NUMSA	National Union of Metalworkers of South Africa
NYSUT	New York State Union of Teachers
OECD	Organisation for Economic Co-operation and Development
PEF	private equity fund
PSI	Public Services International
SACP	South African Communist Party
SAP	Structural Adjustment Programme
SE	European Company Statute
SEIU	Service Employees International Union (Canada)
SEWA	Self Employed Women's Association
SHARE	Shareholder Association for Research and Education
TFA	transnational framework agreement
TLA	Textile Labour Association
TNC	transnational corporation
TUAC	Trade Union Advisory Committee to the OECD
UAW	United Auto Workers (United States)
UFCW	United Food and Commercial Workers (United States)
UFT	United Federation of Teachers (New York)
UNCTAD	United Nations Conference on Trade and Development
UNI	Union Network International and UNI Global Union (post-2009)
WFIW	World Federation of Industry Workers
WTO	World Trade Organization

INTRODUCTION

Melisa Serrano, Edlira Xhafa and Michael Fichter

Within three years of the outbreak of the latest global financial crisis, the economic mood appeared to have gone back to business as usual. Thanks to the massive bail-outs from state coffers, the big banks and financial institutions – which have defended their interests vigorously – are again reaping profits. Little has been done to address the root causes of the crisis, even in those countries, such as Germany, where trade unions were part of a relatively successful crisis management strategy.

For many countries in Europe (among them Greece, Ireland, Portugal, Spain and the United Kingdom) and North America (Canada and the United States), what has followed – and indeed resulted – from the huge bail-outs are soaring budget deficits. The political response has produced regimes of austerity characterized by such measures as cuts in public spending on social welfare and health care, reductions in pensions, freezing of the minimum wage, capping or holding back wage increases covered by bargaining agreements in the public sector and laying off workers in the public sector. Trade union rights, particularly in the public sector, have also been targeted as part of the austerity measures. In the United States, for example, despite massive protests and demonstrations mounted by public sector unions and community organizations, Republican Governor Scott Walker in Wisconsin forced through a so-called budget repair law which stripped public sector workers of collective bargaining and other hard-won union rights. Unions in other US states are facing similar attacks. In short, governments are ignoring the protests of workers and the poor and are forcing them to foot the bill for national budget deficits by imposing austerity programmes.

To date, there has been no serious attempt to regulate and downsize global financial markets or to rebalance tax systems more equitably in favour of labour and mass consumption. Moreover, global imbalances and extreme inequalities have remained intact if not entrenched in the aftermath of the crisis. Indeed, international institutions such as the International Monetary Fund (IMF) and Organisation for Economic Co-operation and Development (OECD) have called for a further weakening of protective labour legislation and decentralization of collective bargaining in order to facilitate flexibility – measures which in turn place downward pressure on wages.

It was against this backdrop that the Global Labour University (GLU) held a conference under the rubric "Labour and the Global Crisis: Sharing the Burden(!), Shaping the Future(?)" in Berlin from 14 to 16 September 2010. The conference brought together practitioners and academics to engage in a broad dialogue on how labour can respond to the existing highly unequal, crisis-prone and unsustainable world economic order. At the core of this effort were four main questions:

- What caused the crisis?
- What can and needs to be done as an immediate policy response?
- What are the medium and long-term policies and visions for a fairer and more inclusive global society?
- How can a recovery be organized which also helps to address the ecological challenges currently faced by the world?

Drawing on papers presented to the conference, this volume presents a selection of essays addressing these questions (with a particular focus on the latter three), focusing on the responses of trade unions and other workers' organizations. The responses vary from short-term strategies and actions to medium and long-term policies, and to alternative visions and discourses that challenge the current development paradigm.

There are three main threads of argument in this volume, reflected in the three parts into which it is divided. The first challenges mainstream analysis of the impact of the crisis on labour and proposes possible alternatives, either specifically to address the crisis or to embark on a more transformational project beyond the logic of the prevailing capitalist orthodoxy. The second thread addresses labour's international responses to the financial crisis and to the current model of globalization. The third focuses on labour responses within a variety of national settings. Together, the essays presented here build on the diversity and rich texture of the debates at the conference in exploring a broad range of topics within the overall theme of trade union responses to the global crisis. At the same time they enable the reader to consider the relevance of a number of very fundamental issues in conjunction with more specific strategic and policy questions facing labour. We will return to this point at the end of this introduction.

Advancing alternative narratives and challenging mainstream discourses

In the first part of the book, five chapters provide alternative narratives (Webster, Serrano and Xhafa) or challenge mainstream discourses on the nature of the crisis and its impact on labour (Pillay, Cradden and Dunn). These essays point to the basic structural deficits of the dominant economic order and explore fundamentally different options built on equality and solidarity, workplace democracy, socio-ecological sustainability, and the mobilization of movements, alliances and coalitions for emancipatory transformation.

In Chapter 1, Edward Webster argues that the growing recognition of what may be called a "decent work deficit logic" arises from the nature of capital accumulation in the age of globalization. This type of accumulation is eroding decent work globally. The dismantling of barriers to trade and capital flows has opened up cost-cutting competition between and within countries and companies. This allows employers to bypass labour laws, triggering a process of informalization through outsourcing and retrenchment.

Webster suggests, however, that a new labour paradigm is emerging in the global South that integrates decent work into an alternative development path. In arguing for a new labour paradigm where decent work is not seen either as an obstacle or as a mere add-on to development, Webster analyses the potential and limitations of South Africa's New Growth Path, using an alternative framework for the progressive realization of decent work which identifies a set of goals in three phases – immediate, medium-term and long-term. In pursuing this end, he emphasizes, it is imperative not only to take into account the social and economic specificities of each country, but also to recognize the importance of two conditions to the progressive realization of decent work: first, a democratic and efficient development state; and second, a broadened and autonomous labour movement that helps construct this state and is able to engage strategically with the policy-making process.

While Webster argues for political innovations grounded in successful social policy initiatives, in Chapter 2 Melisa Serrano and Edlira Xhafa construct a "dialogue" between theoretical debates on alternatives to capitalism and case studies of meso- and micro-social experiments and initiatives that challenge the capitalist canon. Arguing that the need for coherence in theoretical discourses and alternative paradigms can be addressed by approaching them through the material practice of people's struggles, they are able to link into Webster's argument that "the practice of workers' struggles and innovative organizational forms is ahead of current theories of labour". In this sense, the "alternative" to capitalism is conceptualized as an ongoing process of people's economic and political struggle to transcend the capitalist logic, whether on a macro, meso or micro scale, and thereby to change their circumstances and simultaneously transform themselves in the process. Viewed from this perspective, at the core of a desirable alternative is the full development of human potential based on equality, solidarity and sustainability, pursued through collective, democratic and participatory processes. The authors draw several lessons and insights from a number of case studies that link local social experiments with alternative theoretical paradigms. They suggest that these lessons and insights can provide material bases for alternative theoretical discourses.

The other three chapters in this group challenge mainstream discourses, each in its own way. Devan Pillay takes note of the variety of responses to the current capitalist crisis and argues in favour of a more holistic view of the impending "polycrisis" – the interconnected economic, ecological and socio-political crises – at the global level. Pillay contends that the unsustainable patterns of Western consumption and growth, particularly those prevailing in the United States, which are based on the creation of incessant wants (instead of the fulfilment of real needs), will inevitably reach an ecological limit, resulting in the "polycrisis". The author raises the fundamental question of whether a solution to the "polycrisis" can be found within capitalism. He goes on to argue that both a "green new deal" perspective and a more radical eco-socialist perspective "pose fundamental challenges to capitalism's growth-at-all-costs tendencies". In this regard, the author sees South Africa's New Growth Path as a bold attempt to place the economy on a new green growth path, but a far cry from a green new deal and even further from a radical eco-socialist alternative. He highlights the complexities of the alliance between the African National Congress (ANC), the Congress of South African Trade Unions (COSATU) and the South African Communist Party (SACP) in addressing the problem of reconciling the ecological limits to growth and the demands of the minerals–energy complex. Finding its growth proposals ignored, COSATU established its own task team outside the ruling alliance to clearly demarcate its own input into the Government's consultations on the Green Paper on climate change. The author also sees embryonic moves towards building an alternative to the ruling alliance in the newly formed Democratic Left Front (DLF), which espouses a grass-roots democratic, eco-socialist and feminist political programme as an alternative to fossil fuel based capitalism. The author reflects, however, that building this alternative movement might be a long process, given the powerful gravitational pull of the ANC.

For Conor Cradden, prioritizing the political struggle alone is not enough if the labour movement remains fixated in its response to the crisis on the traditional strategies of organizing, bargaining and regulation. In his critique of the "corporate theory of society", he argues that this theory's idea of a conflict-free economy provides the "rational" justification for the power that corporate executives wield in public policy-making with regard to the economy, to employment and to industrial relations. Instead, Cradden advocates democratizing decision-making procedures within organizations, challenging the labour movement to mount an effective critique. For him, collective bargaining is not the only possible means of achieving workplace democracy: trade unions, he argues, must look beyond this traditional mechanism to the long-term goal of developing radically democratic approaches to economic and industrial management centred on positive and equal worker participation in decision-making and the abolition of hierarchical employment relationships.

It is often argued that the unbridled capitalist development of recent decades has put labour on the defensive and even threatened its organizational survival. Bill Dunn argues against such claims. Using statistical data for the United States, he finds no evidence that there is an economic basis for a weakening of labour, at least not in connection with the rise of the new economy. Since the material bases for organization and resistance still stand, he argues, there is no need to "radically rethink notions of class or strategies for social action". Labour needs to focus more on the political causes of its weakness, for example the assaults it experienced under the Governments of Thatcher in the United Kingdom and Reagan in the United States, and the impositions it is currently suffering in the course of labour market "reforms".

Responses to the crisis: Developing international strategies

The next group of four chapters consists of contributions which pursue the second thread in this volume, critically examining labour's response at the international level to some of the pressing problems generated by the current model of globalization, particularly the deregulation of labour and financial markets. Opening the discussion is a case study by Mark P. Thomas of the labour rights strategies adopted by the International Transport Workers' Federation (ITF), a Global Union federation that represents workers in a wide range of transport industries, including seafarers and dockworkers in the international shipping industry. In particular, the essay adopts a multi-scalar approach in analysing the ITF's labour rights strategy for maritime workers, which involves transnational collective bargaining at a global level and local inspections at the worksite level. In so doing, the ITF case study illustrates how international standards may be combined with localized mechanisms of implementation and enforcement in challenging the power of transnational capital.

In another case study of a multi-level approach used by several Global Union federations, José Ricardo Barbosa Gonçalves and Maria Alejandra Caporale Madi point to the growing concern among Global Unions on the impact of private equity investment and exit deals on working conditions and workers' rights. Against this backdrop, and using a similar multi-scalar approach to that adopted by Thomas in his case study of the ITF, the authors show how Global Unions have cooperated in mobilizing efforts to reregulate private equity funds at various levels. A wide array of strategies are used to combine advocacy of policy reforms at the national and international levels, with the aim of achieving better tax regulation, greater transparency and public reporting requirements, and state protection of workers affected by private equity buy-outs, alongside the pursuit of the traditional union strategies of new organizing, collective bargaining, information and consultation.

Laura Horn focuses on the politics of corporate control and corporate governance in the European Union (EU) and the role of labour in influencing EU policies. She is critical of labour's defensiveness and its failure to advance an alternative to neoliberal restructuring. Horn's analysis of the evolution of corporate governance in the EU shows that labour regulations and provisions for workers' rights with regard to corporate control are increasingly marginalized. This conclusion calls into question the extent to which the goal of a social Europe is still achievable. To keep this possibility open, Horn argues, trade unions are increasingly using the European level – sometimes as an alternative to the national level – as a space for mobilization and for voicing their criticisms of European governance. What is required now is that they start articulating and indeed participating in a counter-hegemonic project "to overcome the neoliberal bias of European state formation".

A complementary perspective on European developments is provided by Isabelle Schömann's chapter, focusing on transnational framework agreements (TFAs) in Europe. Again taking a multi-scalar approach, Schömann highlights the contribution of TFAs in promoting labour rights absent from the global regulatory context and weakly enforced at national level. Schömann argues that these supranational instruments, inspired by national collective bargaining traditions, social dialogue and European legal structures providing for workers' information and consultation, are contributing to the Europeanization (if not internationalization) of industrial relations. She points to the potential such agreements have for facilitating the organizing of workers and exerting pressure on corporations to observe ethical approaches to the employment relationship.

Responses to the crisis: National and local perspectives

The chapters in the third part of the volume examine how labour at the national level is responding to the crisis in particular and to the prevailing political economy in general. In doing so, they turn a spotlight on the various factors and forces that influence the variety of responses undertaken by labour.

Taken together, they clearly show that there is no single set of strategies used by labour in taking on the challenges posed by the crisis and the prevailing politico-economic model.

The chapter by Lin Yanling and Ju Wenhui relates how the 2010 workers' strikes in China catapulted trade unions and the state into grappling with the conundrum of state–labour relations in the country, giving impetus to reforms of the industrial relations system in China and inside the All-China Federation of Trade Unions (ACFTU) as well. The authors argue that "trade union reform in China is closely related to the whole question of wider political reform", calling into question the double role of trade unions as an instrument of the Party on the one hand and as representatives of the workers' interests on the other.

A context of broader national change also underpins Chandra D. Bhatta's chapter, in which the author sets out to redefine labour–capital relations in Nepal in the light of multiple transitions going on in the country. The author argues in favour of a more constructive, dialogue-oriented labour–capital relationship within an inclusive socio-economic development framework, which envisages the State as active but neutral between the market and labour. The role of the trade unions, as the representatives of labour, is to mediate between State and capital and engage actively in the formulation of labour-friendly policies. Considering the current political and economic difficulties facing Nepal, the author defines the foremost objective of the unions as the creation of an environment for "decent work", to be pursued by supporting the establishment of a legal framework towards this end. Equally, she emphasizes the need for transparency in collective bargaining and the elimination of partisan interests in the trade unions.

Whereas Bhatta's chapter advocates an integrative strategy for the unions, Bill Rosenberg's chapter discusses a polarizing situation, presenting the interesting case of how New Zealand's Council of Trade Unions (CTU) handled the complex pressures on labour resulting from the aggressive neoliberal policies pursued by the Government over a long period of time. The author shows that such policies not only failed to improve the economic performance of New Zealand but caused significant deterioration of social conditions and weakened the unions. According to Rosenberg, these policies triggered an open debate among the broader labour movement which led to the development of an evidence-based Alternative Economic Strategy within the unions in 2009–10. Drawing on this alternative narrative, the CTU was able to influence the political agenda of political parties on the left.

Yasemin Özgün and Özgür Müftüoğlu argue that oppressive economic and labour policies following the military coup of 1980 in Turkey enabled the country to become integrated into the global market economy over the following years but also considerably weakened and fragmented the unions.

In the crisis of 2008 the union movement was unable to prevent further deregulation and marketization, which resulted in employment for many becoming even more precarious. The authors suggest that this inability to mount a counter-strategy may be in part attributable to the response of the global union movement to the crisis, which was based on reregulating the economy through social dialogue. Nonetheless, the authors conclude that, despite the marginalization of the unions, there is still evidence of a class-based struggle by labour in Turkey. However, they conclude that it remains an open question to what extent unions will take an active part in this struggle on the side of the working class.

As Maya Bhullar shows in her chapter, the political dimension of union strategy is a primary concern in Canada. The growth of precarious work has become a major challenge for unions in their attempts to organize labour. If the deterioration of union representation is to be prevented, circumvention by employers of highly regulated working environments for core workers must be resisted; and, as the author shows in her case studies, this is a struggle which must be waged on both a micro and a macro level. Mobilizing at the workplace is a factor in holding the line on outsourcing and flexibilization, but it needs to be flanked by strategies which address the macroeconomic dynamics of heightened market competition in a neoliberal, deregulated economy. Bhullar finds examples of such an approach in both workplace and community campaigns, which she uses to analyse union strategies in pursuit of the goal of raising standards and transforming "jobs into good jobs".

In the United States, industrial unions have been in decline for a number of years, while in the private and public service sectors unions have had some success in holding the line – even organizing significant segments of the precarious workforce, such as janitors and security guards, whose jobs had been among the first to be outsourced and privatized, stripping away any job protection and union benefits they may have had previously. At the same time, the upsurge of the political right in the wake of the economic and financial crisis in the United States, in particular the rise of the demagogical and populist Tea Party, has led to widespread attacks in particular on public service unions, as the recent conflict in Wisconsin has shown.

Jason Russell picks up on such developments in a chapter that encom - passes both public and private sector unions in the United States. In his examination of recent developments in the states of New York, Michigan and – in very timely fashion – Wisconsin, Russell shows how diverse the responses to the economic and fiscal crisis of 2008 have been, and examines the reasons why. Taking as his starting point national political developments arising from the congressional elections of 2010, he concludes from the three cases he analyses that, in the face of continuing right-wing pressure, unions will continue to decline if they are unable to develop comprehensive long-term political strategies grounded in building broadly based coalitions and social movements that reach beyond the workplace.

In his case study of the response of one union, the United Federation of Teachers in New York City, Lee Adler provides an incisive narrative of the opportunities and challenges involved in building local (and global) solidarity. Adler seeks to show how this union has parried right-wing attacks and faced problems in developing a proactive strategy which recognizes and integrates the needs of the many minority communities in New York City. As he argues, without realignment towards the needs of those communities the attempt to protect union standards and renew union organizational strength will fail.

*

On this note we come full circle in our summaries of the contributions to this volume. Starting with Webster's new paradigm for local responses in a global context, contributors pursuing all three of our threads have addressed the need to re-conceptualize "trade unionism" in order to counter the attacks being made on working people. Building solidarity locally, both to protect and improve existing working conditions and to define new, cooperative and self-determined approaches, is a crucial focus of the necessary response, as is linking the local to the national and global dimensions in the context of political, economic and environmental strategies.

As a collection of ideas, analyses and information, this volume does not represent a manifesto for a global union response to the economic and fiscal crisis of 2008 or even in a more general way to the recurring crises of capitalism. But we do regard it as a possible point of orientation and a contribution to stimulating debate, both within the labour movement and beyond.

ADVANCING ALTERNATIVE NARRATIVES AND CHALLENGING MAINSTREAM DISCOURSES

DEVELOPMENT, GLOBALIZATION AND DECENT WORK: AN EMERGING SOUTHERN LABOUR PARADIGM

1

Edward Webster

There is a widespread view that the concept of decent work has no relevance to developing societies (Standing 2009: 32–97). In these countries, with their large-scale unemployment and even larger informal economy, most workers, it is believed, are happy to have any source of income (Bhagwati 2008). Better a bad job than no job at all!

In fact, there are governments in the developing world where "decent work" is seen as a Eurocentric concept designed to protect jobs in the North (Munck 2010). By insisting on certain international labour standards, they argue, richer countries are taking away the only comparative advantage the poor have – their cheap labour. After all, this argument runs, is it not on the back of labour exploitation, including child labour, that the North industrialized (Chang 2002)? Indeed, some trade unionists from the global South argue that the demand for decent work is a form of non-tariff protection (Ganguly 1996: 45; Mahendra 1996: 49).[1]

For the Director-General of the International Labour Office, Juan Somavia, however, there is no question of having to choose between job creation and decent work. The ILO Decent Work Agenda encompasses both economic and social objectives: rights, social dialogue and social protection on the one hand, and employment and enterprise efficiency on the other (ILO 2001: 18). "Many argue that there are trade-offs between the quality and quantity of employment, and between social expenditure and investment, and that protective regulation undermines enterprise flexibility and productivity. But on the contrary, decent work may pay for itself through improved productivity. These relationships need to be examined in more detail in order to evaluate the true costs and benefits of decent work" (ILO 2001: 17).

This chapter identifies a new labour paradigm emerging in the global South that does not see decent work as an obstacle or add-on to development, but instead attempts to integrate decent work into an alternative developmental path. Work, I suggest, is the missing link in the current discourse on development; none of the dominant theories on globalization integrate the struggle for decent work into its developmental trajectory.[2] All three dominant theories of globalization – neoclassical liberalism, the social reformist or anti-capitalist/autonomist theories that underpin the current anti-globalization movement, and development statism – treat the struggle for decent work as either an obstacle or an add-on (Bowles 2010).

Part 1 of the chapter introduces the concept of a decent work deficit logic. Part 2 describes the emergence of an innovative response by labour to the decent work deficit in a developing country. Part 3 examines the response of government, taking South Africa as an example of a country attempting to reduce the decent work deficit by integrating decent work into its developmental path.

It is argued that decent work is not something that can be immediately realized in a developing country such as South Africa. Through such policy initiatives as the New Growth Path (NGP) and the Community Work Programme (CWP), the question is raised as to whether South Africa is developing a strategy for the progressive realization of decent work. Unless the State, the chapter suggests, is able to orchestrate a concrete national project and begins to address the inefficiencies in government, this potential paradigm shift will not be realized.

I conclude by arguing that no great social advances are achieved without the backing of powerful social movements in combination with state capacity. Without these two forces working in some sort of a combination, the goal of decent work will remain elusive.

Part 1: Globalization and the decent work deficit logic

The problem with the term "decent work" from the outset has been its inherent vagueness. To some, that was an advantage. To others, it left too much room for mere platitudes. Both words are difficult to define – *decency* is a normative concept, and *work* as a focus of public policy and research has been transformed over the past three decades from a mainly male activity involving stable, full-time, unionized employment to a variety of precarious forms of formal and informal employment – as well as unpaid care work, much of it done by women.

It became clear early in the era of globalization that women were taking a growing proportion of all jobs (Standing 1989). The informalization of work has created new job opportunities specifically for women due to their lower wages and greater willingness to take on flexible and part-time employment

(Moghadam 2005). This was, writes Standing, "feminisation in a double sense of more women being in jobs and more jobs being of the flexible type typically taken by women" (Standing 2011: 60). In particular, companies are recruiting women into jobs that have been traditionally filled by men, on the assumption that men require jobs that offer longer term commitment. The feminization of labour is especially widespread in the informal economy where women work as street vendors and often engage in varieties of home work.

The concept of decent work has been criticized by those on the left who see it as a "reformist" strategy designed to restore capitalism (both materially and ideologically) and by neoliberals on the right who see it as an unwarranted attempt to intervene in the market. However, the strongest challenge to the ILO's notion of decent work has come from a senior ex-employee, Guy Standing, who notes that

> the pursuit of flexible labour relations at the centre of emerging labour markets all over the world pose[s] a particular difficulty for the ILO – that of identifying employers and employees. Unless these are clear, labour law and regulations become hard to apply. Flexibility has meant a growing fuzziness, with labour externalization and a global resurgence of labour broking, employment "agencies" and labour sub-contracting. ILO Conventions began to look inapplicable for rather a lot of work statuses. (Standing 2008: 365)

One difficult challenge associated with the concept is how to measure it and assess the progress of decent work in the world (Ghai 2003). The single comprehensive attempt so far made to measure decent work and present indices for over 100 countries was shelved when it was attacked by employers (Somavia 2004; Standing 2008). In September 2008, a tripartite meeting of experts on the measurement of decent work, held in Geneva, agreed on ten indicators (ILO 2008: 1–3).

In the course of my research on working life I have seen the erosion of standard employment relationships, the growth of insecure, low paid, outsourced, temporary and part-time jobs, and the expansion of the informal economy and large-scale unemployment (Webster, Lambert and Bezuidenhout 2008). These jobs lack the characteristics of decent work as defined by the ILO; they have, in other words, a *decent work deficit*.

This deficit can be expressed in terms of the four goals of decent work: that is, as an absence of sufficient employment opportunities, inadequate social protection, the denial of rights at work, and shortcomings in social dialogue. "It is a measure of the gap between the world that we work in and the hopes that people have for a better life" (ILO 2001: 8). These absences can themselves be expressed in terms of four gaps: an employment gap; a social protection gap; a rights gap; and a social dialogue gap (ILO 2001: 8–10).

Developing societies such as India and South Africa are not creating conventional capitalist relations of production based on the separation of capital and labour. Instead, the prevalent form of labour in the informal economy is self-employment, which is different from the usual wage-based employment with a formal employer who alienates a surplus directly from the worker.

Nearly three decades ago, Theodor Shanin, introducing A.V. Chayanov's *The theory of the peasant economy*, wrote:

> While in the "developing societies" islands of pre-capitalism disappear, what comes instead is mostly not the industrial proletariat of Europe's 19th century but strata of plebeian survivors – a mixture of increasingly mobile, half employed slum-dwellers, part farmers, lumpen traders, or pimps – another extra economic existence under capitalism. (quoted in Sanyal and Bhattacharyya 2009: 35–36)

While "survivalist" types of work were emerging on the streets and backyards of the inner cities of the developing world, a second type of informalization emerged in the era of globalization: namely, the subcontracting and outsourcing of labour to sweatshops as well as small and medium-sized enterprises. Most of these micro and small enterprises are making goods for the local market, although some form links in a chain of production that begins in these small factories and ends in sales across the world.

Sanyal and Bhattacharyya argue that this process of informalization is reversing Fordist capital–labour relations. It does this in two ways: first, by expanding informal production activities within the circuit of capital – that is, the process where a sum of money is transformed into a larger sum of money – through a complex network of subcontracting and outsourcing; and second, by expanding the economic space outside the circuit of capital by destroying jobs in the formal economy (Sanyal and Bhattacharyya 2009: 36).

While both types of informalization constitute a reversal of Fordist capital–labour relations, they have different implications for the labour force in, respectively, the developed and the developing world. For the developed world, it has meant the loss of decent jobs to the developing world; for the developing world, it has meant the creation of precarious jobs. Theron describes the former as "informalization from above", as employers are transforming decent work into precarious jobs, and the latter as "informalization from below", since the unemployed are creating their own jobs (Theron 2010).

This jobs crisis is exacerbated in developing countries such as South Africa by a process of what Gillian Hart (2002) describes as "racialized dispossession" – the process of colonial conquest and dispossession of the land of the indigenous peoples, creating a marginalized labour force. The classic idea of modernization is that workers would move from the traditional to the modern economy.

Figure 1.1   The decent work deficit logic

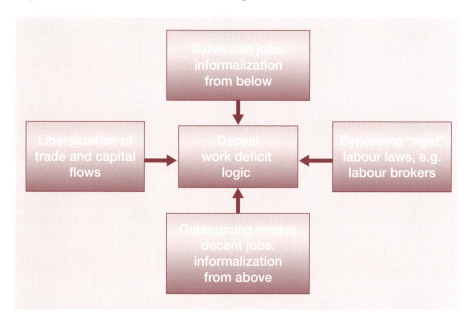

However, in countries such as South Africa the indigenous people were dispossessed of their livelihoods but were not absorbed into the modern sector (ILO 1972; Hart 1973). "As a result," Sanyal and Bhattacharyya argue, "a 'surplus' labour force emerged in developing countries consisting of dispossessed producers whose traditional livelihoods were destroyed but [who] were not absorbed in the modern sector" (Sanyal and Bhattacharyya 2009: 36). Some of this "surplus" falls back on traditional subsistence agriculture; the rest survives on petty non-traditional manufacturing and/or services activities, usually retail. Sanyal and Bhattacharyya go on to identify the following economic characteristics among this "surplus labour force": "[a] clear preponderance of self-employment largely assisted by family labour, the household as a major site of production, particularly in the case of non-agricultural activities, and community or kinship networks involving trust and reciprocity in place of impersonal exchange relations" (Sanyal and Bhattacharyya 2009: 36).

Figure 1.1 illustrates diagrammatically what I call the decent work deficit logic, a logic that arises from the nature of capital accumulation in the age of globalization. This is eroding decent work globally. The dismantling of barriers to trade and capital flows has opened up a cost-cutting competition between and within countries and companies. This both enables and encourages employers to bypass the labour laws, triggering a process of informalization through either outsourcing or retrenchment.

The economic crisis that began in late 2008 has accelerated the application of this logic, with the widespread bail-out of banks leading to austerity programmes with cutbacks to public sector jobs and benefits. Many countries no longer hire permanent public sector staff, but appoint on short-term contracts. For those in the informal economy the situation is worse: their incomes have been cut by an estimated 50 per cent (Jhabvala 2010).

Part 2: Organizing in the periphery

While the ILO was debating how to respond to its discovery of the informal economy in Kenya in 1972, in India Ela Bhatt had begun to organize the many women among these workers into a union, the Self Employed Women's Association (SEWA). Initially, SEWA's claim to be a union was rejected because their members were not seen as workers, being self-employed (Bhatt 2010: 88). From the beginning Bhatt challenged this narrow view of work and argued that the self-employed were also workers. Ironically, she said, the self-employed were the backbone of the Indian economy, in which formal jobs constituted just 7 per cent of the total (Bhatt 2010: 42).

SEWA is not a traditional trade union that aims, through collective bargaining with an employer, to improve the wages and working conditions of its members as sellers of their labour power. Instead, it aims to empower women economically in the informal economy by bringing them into the mainstream economy as owners of their labour (interview with Pratibha Pandya, 2010). Like any other trade union, SEWA does this by mobilizing its members, organizing women to come together collectively around their work issues. The union, she says, "is for collective solidarity. Poor workers individually are too weak. They need to come together on a basis of work. Women then see themselves as workers. I would not have thought of trade unionism if I had not had a background in the Textile Labour Association" (interview with Ela Bhatt, 2010).

The difference between the way SEWA operates and traditional trade unionism is that, once recruited, the women then form trade cooperatives in an effort to become owners of their labour. As a result, Bhatt suggests, SEWA "straddles the realms of both union and cooperative" (Bhatt 2010: 87). SEWA now has nearly 100 different cooperatives – rural and urban – some built around products, others around services. "There are vendors' cooperatives as well as midwives' cooperatives, rag pickers' cooperatives as well as weavers' cooperatives. There are as many trades as there are facets to a country's economy, and self-employed women can be found in every one of them" (Bhatt 2010: 87).

A second crucial difference from traditional trade unionism is that SEWA's members do not engage in only one economic activity, but rather in several income-generating activities. "Since the income of poor women from any one type of work is usually not enough to make ends meet, they must have several income-earning occupations. In fact, 80 per cent of SEWA members are engaged in multiple types of work" (Bhatt 2010: 88). It follows from their multiple economic activities that SEWA members will not have one employer. In fact, Bhatt argues, there may not be a specific employer/employee relationship at all:

> Our members perform many different forms of work. They may have been sub-contracted to do some work and may not know who the principal employer is. They may own a small farm of half an acre but also work during the harvesting season as a labourer on a neighbouring farm. You cannot categorize them as belonging to a single occupation and neither can you conceptualize the employer. The idea of a single employer has come from the conception of work in industrialized countries. (interview with Ela Bhatt, 2010)

To achieve the goal of economic empowerment, SEWA has set itself two central targets: (a) full employment with greater work security, income security and access to social security (health care, childcare, insurance and shelter); and (b) self-reliance through asset creation, leadership development, self-sustainability, and individual and collective decision-making.

SEWA adopts an integrated approach to its members. By stressing the importance of creating employment opportunities through entrepreneurial activities, SEWA transcends the notion of these workers as simply victims. Importantly, SEWA's activities deal with workers holistically, not simply as producers, by creating childcare facilities, credit facilities (including the SEWAbank) and a range of social security benefits. Our interview (2010) with Mirai Chatterjei, head of social security in SEWA, made clear the key role of social security for members: "The need for social security emerged organically. First was child care, then health care, followed by water, sanitation and housing, then social insurance and finally pensions. Work and social security are two sides of the same coin."

By successfully organizing the self-employed in India, Ela Bhatt and SEWA transformed the way we think both about trade unions and about the household. The home is not, for these women, simply a site of reproduction; it is also a site of production, a workplace and a source of income. It was Ela Bhatt and SEWA that helped pioneer the ILO Home Work Convention, 1996 (No. 177), a crucial feminist advance for working-class women in the devel-oping world (Webster 2011).

But it would be quite wrong to see SEWA as a case of Indian exceptionalism. Throughout the developing world, informal workers are beginning to find a voice, sometimes joining existing unions, sometimes founding their own or forming coalitions with existing informal organizations (Lindell 2010). Not for the first time in the history of labour, the practice of workers' struggles and innovative organizational forms is ahead of current theories of labour (Thompson 1963).

Part 3: Reducing the decent work deficit

How can the decent work deficit be reduced? This can only be done, I argue, by each country developing a long-term goal that integrates decent work into its growth path. In other words, the goal of decent work should be seen as an objective to be progressively realized. Quite simply, this involves accepting that decent work is not an immediately achievable goal. Each country will have to take into account its specific social and economic context and set itself a series of immediate, medium-term and long-term goals.

South Africa is an interesting example of a country attempting to overcome the decent work deficit. The New Growth Path (NGP) adopted by the South African Government in 2010 is an example of an attempt to reduce unemployment, i.e. to overcome the employment gap. The NGP proposes three phases in the progressive realization of decent work. In the very short term the state can accelerate employment creation through direct employment schemes. In the short to medium term it can support labour-absorbing activities, especially in the agricultural value chain, light manufacturing and services, to generate large-scale employment. In the longer term the State must, the NGP suggests, increasingly support knowledge- and capital-intensive sectors in order to remain competitive (Department of Economic Development 2010: 7).

Table 1.1 is an attempt to integrate the different phases of the NGP with job creation and decent work indicators over the next two decades. It was commissioned by the Department of Economic Development of the Gauteng province of South Africa. The next step will be to identify a global template of qualitative and quantitative indicators through which progress can be measured (Webster et al. 2009).

A key process in the implementation of the NGP will be building con - sensus with the social partners – labour, employers, the community and government departments – around the idea of a social or developmental pact. The institutional preconditions for successful social dialogue already exist in South Africa in the structures of the National Economic Development and Labour Council (NEDLAC), a top-level social dialogue institution (Webster and Sikwebu 2010). The challenge will be managing the trade-offs between the social partners. This will require that "the state (a) facilitate national and workplace productivity accords, (b) support community organization, including through the Community Work Programme and other delivery

Table 1.1   Realizing decent work in South Africa through the NGP, 2011–30

Phase	Job creation/retention and skill development strategies, with targeted sectors	Decent work indicators
Very short term (2011): Direct job creation through the concept of government as the employer of last resort and the encouragement of self-employment	• Direct job creation through Expanded Public Work Programme (Phase 2) and CWP of 200,000 new job opportunities per annum in Gauteng – that is, one million by 2014 • Training of retrenched workers • Household security – e.g. vegetable gardening • Local procurement • Industrial Development Corporation (IDC) lending conditions • Self-employment, including the informal economy in such sectors as sports tourism	Employment opportunities Adequate earnings through enforcement of the minimum wage Social protection
Medium term (2011–16): Support for labour-absorbing sectors and development of an instrument to measure progress and develop realistic job creation strategies	• Support for labour-intensive manufacturing in consumer goods – e.g. textiles, furniture, design and clothing manufacturing • Steel-related industries • Beer and malt • Infrastructure expansion and investment • Agriculture (agro-processing and bio-tech, horticulture) • Business processing (e.g. call centres) • White goods • Solar energy technology	Social dialogue Employment stability at work Balancing work and family Equal opportunities Labour productivity Safe work environment Decent hours
Long term (2011–30): Gradual shift to higher productivity sectors; Gauteng Advanced Manufacturing Sector Key Action Plan (GAMSKAP); Industrial Development Zone at the O.R. Tambo International Airport; new non-resource-based economic activities	**Smart Industries** (Blue IQ Investment Holdings) aims to deliver strategic economic infrastructure: • ICT • Automotive parts and components • Business tourism • Sports tourism • Property asset management • Logistics • Energy • High-value-added manufacturing • Electric cars **Other sectors:** • Solar energy technology • Pharmaceuticals • Research and development • Engineering • Trade and services (including finance and film)	All indicators realized: Employment opportunities Adequate earnings Decent hours Security at work Balancing work and family Equal opportunity Safe work environment Social protection Social dialogue

Source: Adapted from DBSA, *Long term-planning and development* (2009).

mechanisms that build community and collective action, and (c) strengthen existing institutions for social dialogue, including NEDLAC, sectoral and local forums" (Department of Economic Development 2010: 30).

How have the social partners responded to the NGP? The initial response of the Congress of South African Trade Unions (COSATU), the largest trade union federation, was that the NGP "fell far short of the comprehensive and overarching development strategy . . . that will fundamentally transform our economy and adequately address the triple challenges of extraordinary high levels of unemployment, poverty and deepening inequality".[3] These criticisms continue to be articulated by COSATU in the structures of the ruling African National Congress (ANC) and are part of the process of political exchange. At the January 2011 ANC *lekgotla* (annual planning workshop) COSATU argued that the NGP monetary policy framework places emphasis only on inflation targeting, does not give enough attention to the unemployment rate, and is not addressing the "over-valued" currency (Ndlangisa and Mboyisa 2011: 5).

Labour may see the public employment schemes proposed in the NGP as a dilution of the labour standards to which the unions are committed. This misunderstands the aim of public employment schemes, namely to alleviate poverty and offer first-time jobseekers an opportunity to gain work experience and training, while contributing to the community. The fact that the jobs created accept the minimum wage in the respective sectors removes the threat to existing jobs from this form of employment. Indeed, in October 2010 a ministerial determination establishing conditions of employment for employees in public employment schemes came into effect.[4]

This attempt at imagining an alternative development path is not some wild revolutionary adventure, an exercise in "tilting at windmills", as it were. On the contrary, it is swimming very much with the current by grounding political innovations in successful social policy initiatives, as has also been done in countries such as Brazil and India. The Bolsa Família programme in Brazil is thought to be the biggest social transfer scheme in the world, currently covering some 46 million people at a cost of about 0.4 per cent of GDP (Cichon, Behrendt and Wodsak 2011: 15). The Mahatma Gandhi National Rural Employment Guarantee Scheme (MGNREGS) in India entitles every rural household to 100 days of work per year; the budget for this imaginative guarantee of employment in 2006/07 was 0.33 per cent of GDP (Chakraborty 2007).

These emerging welfare regimes are different from the European welfare state, which was based on three equal pillars: permanent full-time employment, a strong professional public service and the nuclear family (Herman and Mahnkopf 2010). By contrast, the emerging welfare regimes of the South – what Ian Gough calls informal security regimes – are grounded in informal work as well as a variety of livelihood strategies such as street trading, the extended family, and the villages and communities within which workers and their families are embedded (Gough 2004). As Sarah Mosoetsa describes in her pioneering book *Eating from one pot*, these households and community networks provide a form of social protection, but it is a fragile stability (Mosoetsa 2011; see also Bahre 2007).

Crucially, the social floor provided by these social security measures is an investment: it generates growth by increasing aggregate demand, and in times of economic crisis it maintains aggregate demand through providing temporary short-term employment. It is thus an automatic stabilizer (ILO 2008). To suggest that this social floor will provide a disincentive to work, as neo-liberals do, is disingenuous, for:

- it targets the non-active population;

- it is self-selecting;

- 30–40 per cent of the unemployed in the developing world are long-term unemployed. (Hoffer 2010)

But a social floor is only the first step in a metaphorical staircase through which decent work could be progressively realized (Cichon, Behrendt and Wodsak 2011). In the medium term, governments will need to develop economic strategies that prioritize meeting domestic and regional markets, rather than the export of manufactured goods to fuel over-consumption in the North. These strategies should focus on labour-intensive manufacturing, green jobs and agro-processing, as well as economic activities that improve core physical and social infrastructure (Cock 2009). The aim should be to reduce the cost of living for working people through providing cheaper food, public transport and public health care. Resources should be mobilized domestically to fund priority investments, not short-run inflows of capital through the stock and bond markets. This endeavour will also require a more strategic engagement of labour in the decision-making process, and a greater willingness of employers and government to engage in genuine social dialogue. Militancy without a long-term vision of how productivity can be raised hardens employers and governments' attitudes and entrenches the low trust dynamic that exists in most developing society industrial relations systems.

Significant progress is being made in South Africa in reducing the decent work deficit, with initiatives under all four of the headings set out below:

- Bridging the employment gap through the adoption and implementation of an NGP that foregrounds employment;

- Bridging the social protection gap with progress towards a national employment guarantee through the introduction of the Expanded Public Works Programme and now the Community Work Programme;

Figure 1.2   Reducing the decent work deficit

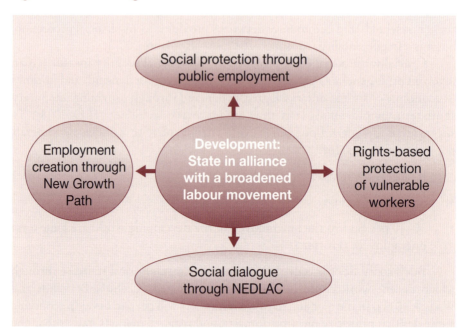

- Bridging the rights gap through the concept of regulated flexibility, giving workers rights but allowing for a degree of flexibility in the implementation of regulations, thereby ensuring that labour market institutions play a more active role in preventing the abuse of vulnerable workers through, for example, labour brokers (temporary agency work);

- Bridging the social dialogue gap through NEDLAC, an established top-level social dialogue institution. (Webster and Sikwebu 2010)

  These developments are summarized diagrammatically in figure 1.2.

Conclusion

In this chapter I have identified a decent work deficit logic within the global economy that is undermining the struggle for decent work. I have suggested that the labour movement, in alliance with democratic governments in the global South, is beginning to respond proactively to the disruption consequent on unregulated market-led growth by developing a new paradigm that integrates decent work into an alternative developmental path. I have further suggested that tentative steps are being made to reduce the decent work deficit through constructing a developmental state.

But, as Evans has shown, "the idea of a developmental state puts robust, competent public institutions at the centre of the development matrix" (Evans 2010: 37). This requires, he insists, two conditions: bureaucratic capacity and "embeddedness". The first condition requires that States approximate the ideal-typical Weberian bureaucracy:

> Meritocratic recruitment to public service careers offering long-term rewards commensurate with those obtainable in the private sector were institutional cornerstones of the East Asian economic miracle. Meritocratic recruitment was important, not only to promote competence but to give state employees a sense of esprit de corps and belief in the worthiness of their profession. Long-term career rewards based on performance kept competent individuals from deserting the public service. (Evans 2010: 45)

The second condition, embeddedness, requires that the State be in a position to orchestrate a concrete national project of development by drawing on "a dense set of concrete impersonal ties that enable specific agencies and enterprises to construct joint projects at the sectoral level" (Evans 2010: 46–47). Being able to avoid capture by capital and being able to discipline entrepreneurial elites are, Evans concludes, defining features of the "embedded autonomy" of East Asian development States, distinguishing them from less successful States in Asia and Africa (Evans 2010: 47).

I would add to Evans's second condition the need for an alliance with a broadened and autonomous labour movement. Whether such a relationship can be constructed by mobilizing workers as citizens with constitutional rights rather than as members of a political party is a key question facing this emerging Southern labour paradigm (Agarwala 2006).

Notes

[1] The ILO stresses that labour standards should not be used for protectionist trade purposes and that nothing in the ILO Declaration on Fundamental Principles and Rights at Work and its Follow-up, 1998, should be invoked or otherwise used for protective purposes; in addition, the comparative advantage of any country should in no way be called into question by this Declaration and its follow-up (ILO 1998). See also the WTO 1996 Singapore Ministerial Declaration (WTO 1996).

[2] I use the term "work" because it is wider than "employment" or "job". It includes wage employment, self-employment and home working. It also includes the range of activities in the informal economy and the care economy. It is therefore a comprehensive notion which corresponds to the idea that decent work is a universal aspiration.

[3] Recent years have seen a re-emergence of a much stronger anti-capitalist tendency, with a deep suspicion of the ANC and the State, in some of the COSATU affiliates, such as the National Union of Metalworkers of South Africa (NUMSA).

[4] Basic Conditions of Employment Act, 1997, Ministerial Determination 4; E.

Resources

Agarwala, R. 2006. "From work to welfare: A new class movement in India", in *Contemporary Asian Studies*, Vol. 38, No. 4, pp. 419–41.

Bahre, E. 2007. "Reluctant solidarity: Death, urban poverty and neighbourly assistance in South Africa", in *Ethnography*, Vol. 8, No. 1, pp. 35–59.

Bhagwati, J. 2008. *In defense of globalization* (New Delhi, Oxford Indian Paperbacks).

Bhatt, E. 2010. "Citizenship of marginals", seminar, 25 January, Ambedabad.

Bowles, P. 2010. "Globalization's problematic for labour: Three paradigms", in *Global Labour Journal*, Vol. 1, No. 1, pp. 12–31.

Chakraborty, P. 2007. *Implementation of the National Rural Employment Guarantee Act in India: Spatial dimensions and fiscal implications*, Working Paper No. 505. Levy Economics Institute of Bard College (New York, Bard College).

Chang, H-J. 2002. *Kicking away the ladder: Development strategy in historical perspective* (London, Anthem Press).

Cichon, M.; Behrendt, C.; Wodsak, V. 2011. *The UN Social Protection Floor Initiative: Turning the tide at the ILO Conference 2011* (Berlin, Friedrich Ebert Stiftung).

Cock, J. 2009. *Green jobs and women workers: Employment, equity and equality* (Madrid, International Labour Foundation for Sustainable Development).

Department of Economic Development, Gauteng province, 2010. *New Growth Path* (Johannesburg).

Development Bank of South Africa (DBSA). 2009. *Long-term planning and development* (Halfway House).

Evans, P. 2010. "Constructing the 21st century developmental state: Potentialities and pitfalls", in O. Edigheji (ed.): *Constructing a democratic state in South Africa* (Cape Town, HSRC Press).

Ganguly, P.K. 1996. "Labour rights and national interests", in J. John and A. Chenoy (eds): *Labour, environment and globalisation* (New Delhi, Centre for Education and Communication), pp. 43–46.

Ghai, D. 2003. "Decent work: Concepts and indicators", in *International Labour Review*, Vol. 142, No. 2, pp. 113–45.

Gough, I. 2004. "Welfare regimes in developing contexts: A global and regional analysis", in I. Gough and G. Wood (eds): *Insecurity and welfare regimes in Asia, Africa, and Latin America: Social policy in development contexts* (Cambridge, Cambridge University Press).

Hart, G. 2002. *Disabling globalisation: Places of power in post-apartheid South Africa* (Berkeley, University of California Press).

Hart, K. 1973. "Informal income opportunities and urban employment in Ghana", in *The Journal of Modern African Studies*, Vol. 11, No. 1, pp. 61–89.

Herman, C.; B. Mahnkopf, 2010. "Still a future for the European social model?", in *Global Labour Journal*, Vol. 1, No. 3, pp. 314–30.

Hoffer, F. 2010. *Social security in the 21st century: An ILO perspective*, paper presented at the first workshop on "Work, Livelihoods and Economic Security in the 21st Century, India and South Africa", International Center for Development and Decent Work, Kassel University, 7–8 April.

ILO. 1972. *Employment, incomes and inequality* (Geneva).

—. 1998. *Declaration on Fundamental Principles and Rights at Work and its Follow-up* (Geneva).

—. 2001. *Reducing the decent work deficit: A global challenge*, Report of the Director-General, International Labour Conference, 89th Session, Geneva.

—. 2008. *Can low income countries afford basic social security?* Social Security Policy Briefing Paper No. 3 (Geneva).

Jhabvala, R. 2010. "Financial crises, the informal economy and workers' unions", in N. Pons-Vignon (ed.): *Don't waste the crisis: Critical perspectives for a new economic model* (Geneva, ILO).

Lindell, I. (ed.). 2010. *Africa's informal workers: Collective agency, alliances and transnational organizing in urban Africa* (London and New York, Zed Books).

Mahendra, B. 1996. "Labour rights and globalization", in J. John and A. Chenoy (eds) *Labour, environment and globalization* (New Delhi, Centre for Education and Communication), pp. 43–46.

Moghadam, V. 2005. *Globalizing women* (Baltimore and London, The Johns Hopkins University Press).

Mosoetsa, S. 2011. *Eating from one pot: The dynamics of survival in poor South African households* (Johannesburg, Wits University Press).

Munck, R. 2010. "Globalization, labour and development: A view from the South", in *Transformation*, Vol. 72–73, pp. 205–24.

Ndlangisa, S.; Mboyisa, C. 2011. "Allies outgun Vavi at NEC", *Sunday Times*, 16 January.

Sanyal, K.; Bhattacharyya, R. 2009. "Beyond the factory: Globalisation, informalisation of production and the new locations of power", in *Economic and Political Weekly*, Vol. 44, No. 22, pp. 30–45.

Somavia, J. 2004. "The ILO Decent Work Agenda as the aspirations of people: The insertion of values and ethics in the global economy", in P. Dominique (ed.): *Philosophical and spiritual perspectives on decent work* (Geneva, ILO).

Standing, G. 1989. "Global feminization through flexible labour: A theme revisited", in *World Development*, Vol. 27, No. 3, pp. 582–602.

—. 2008. "The ILO: Agency of globalisation", in *Development and Change*, Vol. 39, No. 3, pp. 355–84.

—. 2009. *Work after globalisation: Building occupational citizenship* (Cheltenham, Edward Elgar).

—. 2011. *The precariat: The new dangerous class* (London, Bloomsbury Academic).

Theron, J. 2010. "Informalization for above, informalization from below: The options for organisation", in *African Studies Quarterly*, Vol. 11, No. 2/3.

Thompson, E.P. 1963. *The making of the English working class* (Harmondsworth, Penguin).

Webster, E. 2011. *Work and economic security in the 21st century: What can we learn from Ela Bhatt?*, Working Paper No. 1 (Kassel, International Center for Development and Decent Work, Kassel University).

—; Lambert, R.; Bezuidenhout, A. 2008. *Grounding globalization: Labour in the age of insecurity* (Oxford, Blackwell).

—; Phoskoko, D.; Machaka, J.; Bischoff, C.; Chinguno, C.; Guliwe, T.; Metcalfe, A. 2009. *A policy framework for the progressive realisation of the goal of decent work in Gauteng* (Johannesburg, Society, Work and Development Institute, assisted by the Department of Economic Development, Gauteng).

—; Sikwebu, D. 2010. "Tripartism and economic reforms in South Africa and Zimbabwe", in L. Fraile (ed.): *Blunting neoliberalism: Tripartism and economic reforms in the developing world* (Basingstoke and Geneva, Palgrave Macmillan and ILO).

World Trade Organization (WTO). 1996. *Singapore Ministerial Declaration*, WT/MIN(96)/DEC, adopted 18 December.

Interviews

Interview with Ela Bhatt, Ambedabad, 5 Dec. 2010.

Interview with Pratibha Pandya, Ambedabad, 6 Dec. 2010.

Interview with Mirai Chatterjei, Ambedabad, 7 Dec. 2010.

BEYOND THE CAPITALIST LOGIC: THEORETICAL DEBATES AND SOCIAL EXPERIENCES[1]

2

Melisa Serrano and Edlira Xhafa

The financial crisis of 2007–08 revealed starkly the systemic nature of the crisis within capitalism. The so-called structural crises in the modern era of capitalism – the long "first great depression" of the last quarter of the nineteenth century, the more concentrated "Great Depression" of the 1930s, the decade-long "stagflation" of the 1970s and the current crisis (Panitch and Gindin 2011) – have arguably been only the major ones in a system inherently prone to crisis.

According to Harvey (2010: 11), "financial crises serve to rationalize the irrationalities of capitalism" as "they typically lead to reconfigurations, new models of development, new spheres of investment and new forms of class power". Sure enough, profits of big banks and other financial institutions are back to their pre-crisis record highs, thanks to the massive state bail-outs. But once again it is the people who are paying the cost of the crisis – through state-enforced austerity measures, cuts on wages and social benefits, and suppression of forms of dissent and people's rights.

At the same time as people in both North and South have been resisting and fighting back against an intensifying regime of austerity, there has also been in recent years a growing momentum towards revising, rethinking and renewing old discourses on alternatives to neoliberalism and capitalism. To date, the Left has not come up with a fully worked-out, convincing project for an alternative to capitalism (Harnecker 2007). People's struggles have been sweeping the countries of Latin America and other regions, providing the space to imagine and construct possible alternatives despite the dominant mantra of "there is no alternative"; however, theoretical work to systematize and lend coherence to these diverse experiences so that they may possibly be replicated (not necessarily duplicated) in other contexts has been lacking.

This chapter aims to contribute to the discourse on alternatives to capitalism by establishing a "dialogue" between theoretical debates on the subject and existing social experiments and initiatives on meso and micro scales. Through this dialogue, we attempt to address the apparent disconnect between macro-level theoretical discourses and people's actual micro-level practices and struggles. In doing so, we aim to bring these theoretical debates into the perspective of those engaged in these practices and struggles in such a way as to develop their consciousness and capacities to become subjects of transformation, and at the same time to give more visibility to the emancipatory and transformative elements of meso- and micro-level initiatives. Finally, by identifying common elements in various struggles and experiments in diverse places, we attempt to connect these struggles and in so doing contribute to the construction of a coherent and inspiring alternative discourse to capitalism.

Problematizing the concept of "alternative"

What constitutes an alternative to capitalism has always been a contentious and divisive issue among the Left. Harnecker emphasizes that the distinction between reformists and revolutionaries is not always clear. For one thing, revolution is not necessarily linked to the use of violence. Citing Luxemburg, she stresses that "the problem is not saying yes or no to reform, but examining *when* it makes sense to fight for reform and *how* revolutionary fruit can be plucked from it" (Harnecker 2007: 50–51). Similarly, De Sousa Santos and Rodriguez-Garavito argue that even some initiatives that arise within the capitalist system "facilitate the acceptance of and lend greater credibility to alternative forms of economic organisation and labour solidarity" (2006: xxii–xxiii).

For Harnecker, an alternative involves "making possible tomorrow that which appears impossible today". This means identifying what is progressive in the present reality and strengthening it; and this in turn requires that the popular movement organize, grow and transform itself into a decisive pressure group to move the process forward, fighting against errors and deviations that arise along the way (Harnecker 2007: 70). This is what Marx (1845) referred to as "self-change": "the coincidence of the changing of circumstances and of human activity". Marx stressed that "it is only through the process of experimentation undertaken by the masses that the move is made from the economic to the political through circumstances and people themselves being changed simultaneously".

Echoing Marx, Lebowitz (2003: 180) stresses that "even though the needs they [social experiments and initiatives] attempt to satisfy do not in themselves go beyond capital, the very process of struggle is one of producing new people, of transforming them into people with a new conception of themselves – as subjects capable of altering their world". Here, Lebowitz emphasizes the central importance of developing people's capacity to engage in a transformational project.

In the light of these analyses, we conceptualize an alternative to capitalism as an ongoing process of people's economic and political struggle, whether at macro, meso or micro level, to transcend the capitalist logic in changing their circumstances and simultaneously transforming themselves in the process. The pursuit of full development of human potential, based on equality, solidarity and sustainability and through democratic participatory processes, is at the core of such an alternative. Of course, any alternative of this kind involves a long, slow, difficult and cumulative process of collective learning and struggle, during which people develop new capacities, capabilities and self-confidence that they can be subjects of a transformation to a new social formation.

Perspectives and debates on alternatives to capitalism: An overview[2]

It is evident that contemporary discourses on alternatives to neoliberalism in particular and capitalism as a whole provide an array of alternatives, from the developmental state model of capitalism to the revitalization of social democracy under capitalism (Keynesian approaches, more market regulation), the co-existence of capitalist and non-capitalist systems (mixed economy, solidarity economy, diverse economy, market socialism), a gradualist approach to a socialist agenda and a dramatic break from capitalism.

These alternatives to contemporary neoliberal capitalism, though by no means exhaustive, may be classified into two major groupings: varieties of capitalism outside the Anglo-American model; and socialist-oriented visions and models. Brief descriptions of each of these models and perspectives are provided here.

The first group, consisting of varieties of capitalism outside the Anglo-American model, which incorporate many elements of the coordinated market economy model, may in turn be divided into two distinct models:

- The *developmental state model*, which envisages a strong role for the State in the economy. For example, the East Asian developmental state growth model is anchored on five major elements, namely high household savings (mostly held in bank deposits), a high corporate debt-to-equity ratio (ratio of total liabilities to shareholders' equity), collaboration between banks, firms and the State, a national industrial strategy, and investment incentives to enhance international competitiveness (Wade and Veneroso 1998; Jomo 2001). Ha-Joon Chang and Giovanni Arrighi are among the advocates of the developmental state model.

- The *global social democracy* discourse promoted, albeit with different nuances, by Gordon Brown, Jeffrey Sachs, George Soros, Kofi Annan, Joseph Stiglitz and David Held. Proponents of this model see global-ization as an irreversible process that can be beneficial to all and propose (among other things) linking growth with equality, promoting socially and environmentally sound trade, promoting multilateralism, linking global market integration with global social integration, and cancelling or radically reducing the global debt of developing countries (Bello 2009a).

The other major group of alternatives advocate either a gradual or a dramatic break from capitalist social and economic relations. This group includes the following:

- *Deglobalization*, a term attributed to Bello, focuses on a domestic-oriented development model which is anchored on social solidarity, that is, "subordinating the operations of the market to the values of equity, justice, and community by enlarging the sphere of democratic decision making" (Bello 2009b).

- *Socialist globalization*, propounded by Sklair (2002), gives central place to domestic-oriented production and community control of the economy (i.e. self-governing communities of producer–consumer cooperatives). The globalization of human rights is at the heart of Sklair's socialist globalization paradigm.

- *Market socialism*, which according to David Miller (1989) rests on two main pillars – the market economy and the State. The market economy produces most goods and services, but within a distributive framework established and enforced by the State. The second pillar, the State, is composed of government agencies directly involved in the provision at least of public goods, such as transport systems and environmental protection, and in guaranteeing rights to welfare.

- The *solidarity economy* is a motley blend of diverse, locally rooted, grass-roots economic projects and initiatives, such as household economies, worker and consumer cooperatives, barter economies, community currencies, fair trade organizations, mutual aid collectives and self-help organizations, that are "small in scale, low in resources, and sparsely networked" and "are building the foundation for what many people are calling new cultures and economies of solidarity" (E. Miller 2009: 16).

- The *diverse economy* model calls for the generation of an alternative discourse of economy by cultivating a *language of economic difference*, within which alternative economic projects can be conceived, and through which alternative economic subjects can be validated and come to self-recognition (Community Economies Collective 2001: 97). Gibson-Graham (2006) argues that identifying non-capitalist activities and seeing them as prevalent and sustaining may provide more possibilities of participation in their creation.

- The *socialist project*, whose motivating vision incorporates the utopian sensibility with a concern with capacity building (Panitch and Gindin 2000: 22–24). This vision encompasses ten dimensions: overcoming alienation, attenuating the division of labour, transforming consumption, alternative ways of living, socializing markets, planning ecologically, internationalizing equality, communicating democratically, realizing democracy, *omnia sunt communia* (all things are in common).

- *Socialist economic policy* is a transitional strategy oriented towards market disengagement and market control, and democratic planning and coordination. It recognizes various ways of organizing economic and ecological relations and redefines full employment "in relation to the maximization of voluntary participation of the adult population in a socially-useful paid work at full-time hours for solidaristic wages" (Albo 2004: 134–35). Among the key principles of this policy are a "politics of time" which involves the re-allocation of work time and free time; the requalification of work, which would allow training for long-term, broad skills and skills that extend worker autonomy over the labour process; work-time reduction, allowing administrative time for workplace democracy; and decentralized popular planning in self-managed enterprises.

- *Participatory economics* rules out markets and central planning and instead focuses on participatory planning through self-managed worker and consumer councils (Albert and Hahnel 1991). Private property is removed and thus private ownership of the means of production disappears.

- *Socialism for the twenty-first century*, as outlined by Lebowitz (2006), accords primacy to human needs and human development. Lebowitz argues that the Bolivarian Republic of Venezuela under Hugo Chavez has been gradually moving to implement a humanist socialist vision of a social economy based on solidarity. This vision is anchored on "the elementary triangle of socialism": social ownership of the means of production, social production organized by workers, and production for social needs and purposes (Lebowitz 2010).

There are points of convergence and divergence between these two major groups. In general, both agree on the following: (1) the destructive effects of neoliberalism (self-regulating markets), leading to the need for market control and regulation; (2) an enhanced regulatory role for the State; (3) promotion of (full) employment; and (4) except for the participatory economy alternative, a recognition of the role of markets (qualified in the case of the socialist-oriented models by a shift of that role from capital accumulation to a mechanism of equitable redistribution).

The main points on which the two major groups diverge are: (1) the first group's belief in the irreversibility of globalization as against the second group's espousal of re-embedding "financial capital and production relations from global to national and local economic spaces" (Albo 1996; cited in Panitch and Gindin 2000: 23); (2) the former's focus on export orientation as against the latter's emphasis on inward- or domestic-oriented production and social relations; (3) the former's maintenance of the capitalist mode of production and division of labour as against the latter's advocacy of social ownership of the modes of production and egalitarian social relations; and (4) the former's espousal of the capitalist doctrine of production for capital accumulation as against the latter's emphasis on production for social needs and total development of human potentials.

Among the second, socialist-oriented, group there are convergences and divergences as well. All focus on: (1) principles and values of cooperation, solidarity, democracy, egalitarianism, mutuality, diversity and respect; (2) inward-looking or domestically oriented and ecologically sustainable production; (3) the development of human potentials; (4) social or collective control of the means of production (with workers' cooperatives or councils as the preferred institutional mode); (5) democratic and inclusive participation in political and economic decision-making at various if not all levels; (6) protection and social ownership of the commons; (7) the redistributive role of the State; and (8) internationalizing equality through global interconnectedness.

The major divergences in ideas and propositions within this group are: (1) recognition of the role of the market as a redistributive mechanism as against the total abolition of markets; (2) the mixed economy or diverse economy as against the abolition of private property (full collective or social ownership of production); and (3) co-management in enterprises as against workers' self-management. All are rooted in the choice between a gradualist, pragmatic approach to seeking an alternative to capitalism and a radical break from capitalism. But, as De Sousa Santos and Rodriguez-Garavito point out, "the success or failure of economic alternatives and transnational labor solidarity should be judged using gradualist and inclusive criteria" (2006: lv); and "projects should not be dismissed because they do not immediately present a radical break from capitalism" (Novelli 2008: 172).

Local experiments and struggles: Lessons and insights from case studies

How do various forms of people's solidarity economies and worker-/people-centred production systems become spaces or provide spaces for the development of counter-consciousness and at the same time build capacities for the development of projects, initiatives and economies beyond the capitalist logic and/or envisaged as alternatives to capitalism?

In order to address these questions, 13 case studies written by various authors were selected and reviewed.[3] The next section of the chapter elaborates on several generalized lessons and insights drawn from an analysis of the case studies using the analytical framework set out in figure 2.1.

The schemes, enterprises and programmes covered by the case studies can be grouped together into four categories as follows:

- *Worker-run factories*: Alcasa, an aluminium-manufacturing enterprise (Azzellini 2009); Invepal, a paper-manufacturing enterprise (Azzellini 2009); Inveval, a valve maintenance and repair factory for the oil industry (Azzellini 2009); Brukman, a clothing factory (Ranis 2006; Isitan 2008; Mosby 2008); Zanon, a ceramic tile factory (Ranis 2006); and Alcond, a wire machinery cooperative that produces wires for cranes and other hauling equipment in India (Bhowmik 2006).

- *Agricultural and informal workers' cooperatives and micro-lending programmes*: Maputo General Union of Agro-Pastoral Cooperatives (Maputo-UGC), a federation of agricultural and livestock cooperatives in Mozambique (Cruz e Silva 2006); two SEWA waste-pickers' cooperatives in Ahmedabad City, India (Bhowmik 2006); the 30 or so São Paulo recycling cooperatives and their micro-credit programme in Brazil (Gutberlet 2009); and the PATAMABA Region 6 micro-lending programme among home-based workers and other informal economy workers in Western Visayas in the Philippines (Nebla 2009).

- *State-initiated and state-supported democratic and participatory schemes*: participatory budgeting (Orçamento Participativo) in Porto Alegre (Bhatnagar et al. n.d.; Harvard University n.d.; Souza 2001) and the Chantier de l'économie sociale in Quebec, Canada (Neamtan 2002).

- *Community partnering for community and economic development*: a pilot project implemented between 1999 and 2000 that aimed at developing an alternative approach to community and economic development in the context of the Latrobe Valley, Victoria, Australia (Cameron and Gibson 2005).

Figure 2.1   The analytical framework

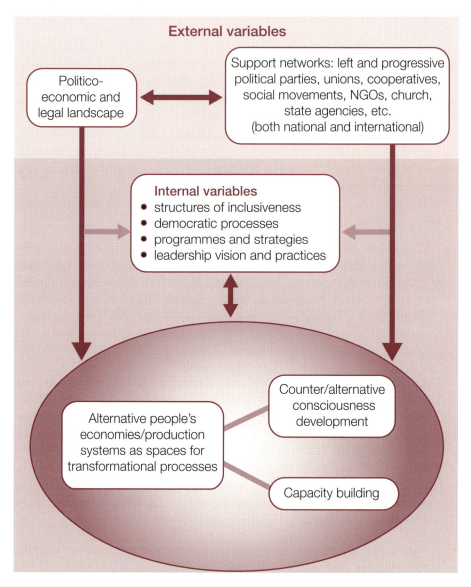

Generalized lessons and insights from the case studies

Nine general lessons and insights were drawn from the analyses of these various case studies.

(1)   Workers' cooperatives (particularly those fully owned, controlled and run by workers themselves), solidarity-based micro-economies and state-

initiated democratic/popular participatory schemes can provide organizational means and self-education processes for workers to gradually take over, manage and consequently change the modes of production within their workplaces and shift governance at the local government level towards a more democratic, egalitarian and human-development-centred approach. They have the potential to become spaces and means to build and develop greater confidence among workers, who become aware that they could transform prevailing socio-economic relations.

(2) Depending on a multiplicity of factors, these forms of economic solidarity and state-initiated openings for democratic citizen participation have a strong potential to develop several emancipatory elements that are critical to the development of a transformative consciousness. They can:

(a) increase self-organization among workers and the poor;

(b) sustain political activism on the part of workers and the poor;

(c) enhance direct participation and decision-making among workers and the poor;

(d) reduce alienation among workers;

(e) enhance the exercise of "citizenship" at the workplace and in the community; and

(f) develop a new form of relationship between cooperatives, unions, popular organizations, state apparatuses and the community based on cooperation, mutuality and democracy.

(3) The case studies involving mostly women in particular highlighted the potential for cooperatives and other forms of alternative economic organization to become spaces where women can recognize their role as subjects in a transformation and assume the role of protagonist at home, in the workplace and in the community.

(4) A process of political consciousness-raising can occur in and through these solidaristic and democratic forms. It involves empowering workers and the poor to become aware of existing inequalities and injustices as a precursor to their changing their present circumstances, existing modes of production or production systems in their workplace, and the State's system of governance (at least at the local level) through collective action (counter-consciousness) and participation.

(5) These initiatives and projects are multidimensional in nature. Though initially they have overt economic objectives, they eventually acquire

political as well as social dimensions. The development of a political dimension (transformative consciousness) counters the tendency for complacency to set in when material gains have been met, helping to prevent any reversion to "capitalist common sense" with cessation of the struggle for social transformation.

(6) The case studies indicate that there is no single model or logic for an alternative, but rather offer a collection of experiences with different features. These initiatives and projects are experiments in progress, involving trial and error and requiring patience, as attempts are made to create new social relations in production and in the community. Multiple factors are likely to be responsible for particular emancipatory outcomes in a given place, even among similar forms of economic solidarity, for example worker-run factories/cooperatives; similarly, multiple factors may constrain the economic, political and social outcomes of these initiatives. The more significant of these factors include the role of the State and the existence of political opportunities for the development of alternative economic organizations; the multidimensionality of an initiative and its breadth of inclusiveness; the existence or absence of mutual support networks (local, national and international); and the degree to which participatory democracy is exercised. Thus, in judging the sustainability and replicability of these "alternatives", note must be taken of the multiplicity of factors affecting the outcome in the original context.

(7) The visibility (social recognition) of perceived alternatives, as conceptualized by Gibson-Graham (2006), may have a domino effect to the extent that existing initiatives, projects and schemes motivate the pursuit of similar undertakings.

(8) Care should be taken not to romanticize the more successful initiatives, projects and schemes; it is more useful to assess critically how the factors and forces that contribute to more successful and sustainable outcomes can be maximized, and how constraints and obstacles can be minimized.

(9) Unions can play a critical role in the development of spaces that nurture counter-consciousness and transformative consciousness. In the worker-run factories, the local unions were involved in organizing workers' councils (Alcasa and Inveval); organizing internal schools for political education (Alcasa); organizing a referendum on the recall of a corrupt factory president (Alcasa); confronting a repressive factory administration and creating a democratically run factory with

impressive outreach to the community (Zanon); and taking the lead role in transforming the enterprise into a worker-run factory (Alcond). SEWA's initiative of organizing waste-pickers, among others, highlights what a union – and in this case a union composed mostly of women – can do beyond the formal workplace.

Establishing dialogue between theoretical perspectives and local experiments and initiatives

Many of the core concepts, principles, practices and programmes offered by the various alternative proposals cited earlier in this chapter are reflected to various degrees in the case studies. First, various forms of solidarity economy are articulated in the case studies. Their emergence, persistence and resilience prove that other economies are possible within capitalism – supporting the "diverse economy" discourse. As Gibson-Graham (2006) notes in stressing the power of visibility or social recognition, recognizing the actuality of non-capitalist activities in particular locations and seeing them as prevalent and sustaining encourages others to undertake similar activities. Indeed, it is through the diverse economy discourse that we could locate forms of solidarity economy as what Ethan Miller aptly calls "islands of alternatives in a capitalist sea" (E. Miller 2009: 16). Although, with the exception of Brazil's participatory budgeting and to some extent Quebec's social economy initiative, these cooperatives, labour enterprises and community-based initiatives are small in scale, low in resources and sparsely networked, they are building the foundation for "new cultures and economies of solidarity" (E. Miller 2009: 16). The collective struggles of each of these solidarity-based micro-economies are founded on common values and principles: direct democracy, unity in diversity, shared power, autonomy, communication, cooperation and mutual aid, local roots and global interconnection. These are the same values and principles advocated in Bello's deglobalization paradigm (Bello 2009b) and Sklair's socialist globalization (Sklair 2002).

In these diverse, locally rooted, grass-roots economic projects and initiatives are found some of the basic tenets of market socialism – collective ownership of the means of production, self-management, and citizenship in and beyond the workplace (D. Miller 1989). In many of these solidarity economies, the market is seen as a distributive mechanism rather than a tool for private accumulation. Market socialism's emphasis on the role of the State in ensuring a participatory form of politics finds expression in the case of participatory budgeting in Brazil.

The initiatives and projects adopted in the case studies show how people develop new capacities and capabilities through their activity and their struggles

– a concept central to Marx's thought. As micro processes of transformation, they facilitate the move beyond capitalism from within. This is the very essence of the concept of "concrete utopia" put forward by Bloch (1986; cited in Panitch and Gindin 2000) – "possibility as capacity" – which Panitch and Gindin (2000) have articulated in their "motivating vision" of a socialist project. All the dimensions of this motivating vision are, to varying degrees, present in the outcomes or achievements of the initiatives and projects undertaken in the case studies, at least within their organizations and communities; and at the same time the critical factors thereby developed contribute to the development of counter-consciousness and transformative consciousness.

Similarly, some of the key principles of Albo's (2004) socialist economic policy can be observed in the case studies, particularly in the worker-run factories. These are the "politics of time"; the requalification of work; work-time reduction; and decentralized popular planning in self-managed enterprises. Decentralized popular planning is also one of the tenets of participatory budgeting in Brazil.

Some of the elements of participatory economics as advocated by Albert and Hahnel (1991) are also visible in a number of the case studies, particularly those relating to worker-run factories/cooperatives. Self-management has been implemented in Inveval, Brukman, Zanon and Alcond, and in the Inveval case study a workers' council was established. In all these factories, private ownership of the means of production had been abolished, a new division of labour had emerged and participatory planning was being pursued, albeit to varying degrees. In the Inveval case, the goal of adopting a socialist factory model and the workers' proposal of a new distribution model (whereby their products would be given away free to state- and social-owned enterprises in exchange for a certain amount of money paid by the State according to their own needs and the needs of the local community) is akin to the alternative consumption principle advocated by participatory economics.

Finally, the case studies on worker-run factories and on participatory budgeting, and to a lesser extent all the other case studies as well, reflect some of the features of Lebowitz's humanist, democratic, participatory socialism. For Lebowitz, the goal is the full development of human potential, and the path that leads to this goal is socialism.

In all the case studies, the role of the State has been critical; and yet it is widely observed that the State plays a contradictory role – even in Venezuela, where worker-run factories under co-management have seen that some state mechanisms and government officials have agendas that contrast with Hugo Chavez's policies. In Argentina, while expropriation and bankruptcy laws provide opportunities for workers to take over production in bankrupt enterprises, they do not provide security and stability or any guarantee that these enterprises will continue to be run by workers' cooperatives. In the Alcond cooperative in India, the local government, controlled by the left party, initially supported the workers' bid to acquire the factory but withdrew its support later on. These experiences, particularly in the case of Venezuela, lend weight to Poulantzas' (2000) argument: that taking state power should be accompanied by the transformation of state apparatuses.

Conclusion

Many of the grass-roots and community-oriented social experiments under way across the world are infused with values (solidarity, cooperation, mutuality, participatory democracy, etc.) and offer socio-economic arrangements that are not within the capitalist canon. Though they do not represent dramatic breaks from capitalism, they "embody forms of production and sociability beyond the capitalist values and institutions" (De Sousa Santos and Rodriguez-Garavito 2006: xxi). Thus they open up spaces for further transformation of capitalist values and socio-economic arrangements.

It is difficult to see these initiatives, most of them on the micro level – worker-run cooperatives, various forms of solidarity economy and labour solidarity, and other grass-roots and community-rooted social experiments – as alternatives to capitalism. De Sousa Santos and Rodriguez-Garavito argue that "because of their anti-systemic nature, these proposals and experiments are fragile and incipient"; and such initiatives are often dismissed as marginal or merely reformist. However, it would be regrettable to deny the significance of such initiatives for people's lives or by classifying them as "contaminated by the dominant system" or just not radical enough. Such an approach could be very detrimental to the strengthening of an alternative framework as "it can close doors to proposals that might gradually bring changes that create pockets of solidarity within the heart of capitalism" (De Sousa Santos and Rodriguez-Garavito 2006: xxii–xxiii).

These endeavours surely draw inspiration from people's struggles to survive and work with dignity, and carry within them the potential for social transformation on a larger scale. They reflect the specificities of historical consciousness of people in different parts of the world. At the same time, these endeavours carry with them an original language of struggle that is the product of the specific historical moment and social relations.

Despite limitations in their scope and achievements, such initiatives provide the essential building blocks of knowledge and practice to inform any project of working out a strong and coherent alternative framework and programme beyond or outside capitalism. Indeed, as De Sousa Santos and Rodriguez-Garavito (2006: xxii) suggest, the role of critical thought and practice is to broaden the spectrum of possibilities, through experimentation in and reflection on alternatives for building a more just society. By suggesting possibilities beyond what actually exists, these forms of thought and practice question the separation between reality and utopia and formulate alternatives that are utopian enough to challenge the status quo and real enough to avoid being easily discarded as unviable.

At the same time, the identification of common strands or elements in people's struggles that have emancipatory or transformative potential, and their connection with theoretical discourses, contribute to a process of connecting the struggles of people across the globe in the common pursuit of a coherent and inspiring alternative to capitalism.

Notes

[1] This chapter is based on a research report by the authors, entitled *Beyond the capitalist logic: Visions, constructs and capacities* (Serrano and Xhafa n.d.). A follow-up research project is under way, supported by the GLU and the International Labour Office.

[2] For further discussion of these perspectives and debates, see Serrano and Xhafa (n.d.).

[3] For details of the case studies, see http://www.global-labour-university.org/fileadmin/GLU_research_projects/ alternatives_to_capitalism/Annexes_A-G_Summary_of_Case_Studies_on_Alternatives.pdf (accessed 16 June 2011).

Resources

Albert, M.; Hahnel, R. 1991. *Looking forward: Participatory economics for the twenty-first century* (Cambridge, MA, South End Press).

Albo, G. 1996. "The world economy, market imperatives and alternatives", in *Monthly Review*, Vol. 48, No. 7, p. 19; cited in Panitch and Gindin 2000.

—. 2004. "A world market of opportunities? Capitalist obstacles and left economic policy", in L. Panitch, C. Leys, A. Zuege, M. Konings et al. (eds): *The globalization decade: A critical reader* (London, Merlin Press), pp. 111–52.

Azzellini, D. 2009. "Venezuela's solidarity economy: Collective ownership, expropriation and workers' self-management", in *Working USA: The Journal of Labor and Society*, Vol. 12, No. 2 (June), pp. 171–91.

Bello, W. 2009a. "Capitalism's crisis and our response", speech delivered at the "Conference on the Global Crisis" sponsored by Die Linke Party and Rosa Luxemburg Foundation, Berlin, 20–21 March, http://www.tni.org/detail_page.phtml?act_id=19430&print_format =Y (accessed 16 June 2011).

—. 2009b. "The virtues of deglobalization", in *Foreign Policy in Focus*, 3 Sep., http://www.tni.org/article/virtues-deglobalisation (accessed 16 June 2011).

Bhatnagar, D.; Rathore, A.; Moreno Torres, M.; Kanungo, P. n.d. "Participatory budgeting in Brazil", unpublished paper, http://siteresources.worldbank.org/INTEMPOWERMENT/ Resources/14657_Partic-Budg-Brazil-web.pdf (accessed 16 June 2011).

Bhowmik, S. 2006. "Cooperatives and the emancipation of the marginalized: Case studies from two cities in India", in B. De Sousa Santos (ed.), pp. 70–94.

Bloch, E. 1986. *The principle of hope*, trans. N. Plaice, S. Plaice and P. Knight (Cambridge, MA, MIT Press).

Cameron, J.; Gibson, K. 2005. "Alternative pathways to community and economic development: The Latrobe Valley Community Partnering Project", in *Geographical Research*, Vol. 43, No. 3 (Sep.), pp. 274–85.

Community Economies Collective. 2001. "Imagining and enacting noncapitalist futures", in *Socialist Review*, Vol. 28, Nos. 3–4, pp. 93–135.

Cruz e Silva, T. 2006. "The General Union of Cooperatives of Maputo: An alternative production system?", in B. De Sousa Santos (ed.), pp. 95–120.

De Sousa Santos, B. (ed.). 2006. *Another production is possible: Beyond the capitalist canon* (London, Verso).

De Sousa Santos, B.; Rodriguez-Garavito, C. 2006. "Introduction: Expanding the economic canon and searching for alternatives to neoliberal globalization", in B. De Sousa Santos (ed.), pp. xvii–lx.

Gibson-Graham, J-K. 2006. *The end of capitalism (as we knew it)* (Minneapolis, University of Minnesota Press).

Gutberlet, J. 2009. "Solidarity economy and recycling co-ops in Sao Paolo: Micro-credit to alleviate poverty", in *Development in Practice*, Vol. 19, No. 6 (Aug.), pp. 737–50.

Harnecker, M. 2007. *Rebuilding the left*, trans. Janet Ducksworth (London, Zed Books).

Harvard University Center for Urban Development Studies Graduate School of Design and Inter-American Development Bank. n.d. "Assessment of participatory budgeting in Brazil", unpublished research report, http://www.sasanet.org/documents/Curriculum/Budget,%20 Literacy%20&%20SAC%20tools/Budgets/ParticipatoryBudget.pdf (accessed 16 June 2011).

Harvey, D. 2010. *The enigma of capital and the crisis of capitalism* (New York, Oxford University Press).

Isitan, I. 2008. *The women of Brukman*, 90-minute documentary film.

Jomo, K.S. 2001. *Growth after the Asian crisis: What remains of the East Asian model?*, G24 Discussion Paper Series, March (New York, UNCTAD).

Lebowitz, M. 2003. *Beyond capital*, 2nd edn (New York, Palgrave Macmillan).

—. 2006. *Build it now: Socialism for the 21st century* (New York, Monthly Review Press).

—. 2010. "Socialism: The goal, the paths and the compass", in *The Bullet*, E-Bulletin No. 315 (20 Feb.), http://www.socialistproject.ca/bullet/315.pdf (accessed 16 June 2011).

Marx, K. 1845. "Theses on Feuerbach", cited at http://www.marxists.org/archive/marx/works/1845/theses/original.htm (accessed 16 June 2011). Also in R. Tucker (ed.): *The Marx–Engels* reader (New York, W.W. Norton, 1978), pp. 143–45.

Miller, D. 1989. *Market, state and community: Theoretical foundations of market socialism* (Oxford: Clarendon Press).

Miller, E. 2009. "Other economies are possible: Building a solidarity economy", in E. Miller and M. Albert (eds): *Post-capitalist alternatives: New perspectives on economic democracy* (London, Ont., Socialist Renewal Publishing Project), pp. 16–22.

Mosby, J. 2008. *The women of Brukman: Revolutionary spirit in the wake of Argentina's economic meltdown*, http://www.thewip.net/contributors/2008/03/the_women_of_brukman_abandoned.html (accessed 16 June 2011).

Neamtan, N. 2002. "The social and solidarity economy: Towards an 'alternative' globalisation" Exploring Participation and Democracy in a Global Context, Carold Institute for the Advancement of Citizenship in Social Change, Langara College, Vancouver, 14–16 June (originally in French), http://www.unesco.ca/en/commission/resources/documents/social_and_solidarity_economy.pdf (accessed 16 June 2011).

Nebla, M. 2009. *Infusing new ways into time-tested practices: An integrated approach to microfinance. PATAMABA-Region 6 experience*, http://www.homenetseasia.org/timetest.html (accessed 16 June 2011).

Novelli, M. 2008. "Reinventing social emancipation: *Towards new manifestos* volumes I, II & III of five volumes – A review", in *Capital and Class*, No. 95 (Summer), pp. 166–77.

Panitch, L.; Gindin, S. 2000. "Transcending pessimism: Rekindling socialist imagination", in L. Panitch and C. Leys (eds): *Socialist Register 2000: Necessary and unnecessary utopias*, Vol. 36, pp. 1–29.

—. 2011. "Capitalist crises and the crisis this time", in L. Panitch, G. Albo and V. Chibber (eds): *Socialist Register 2011: The crisis this time*, Vol. 47, pp. 1–20.

Poulantzas, N. 2000. *State, power, socialism* (London, Verso Classics).

Ranis, P. 2006. "Factories without bosses: Argentina's experience with worker-run factories", in *Labor: Studies in Working-Class History of the Americas*, Vol. 3, No. 1, pp. 11–23.

Serrano, M.; Xhafa, E. n.d. *Beyond the capitalist logic: Visions, constructs and capacities*, forthcoming in Global Labour University Working Paper Series (Berlin).

Sklair, L. 2002. *Globalization: Capitalism and its alternatives* (Oxford, Blackwell).

Souza, C. 2001. "Participatory budgeting in Brazilian cities: Limits and possibilities in building democratic institutions", in *Environment and Urbanization*, Vol. 13, No. 1, pp. 159–84.

Wade, R.; Veneroso, F. 1998. "The Asian crisis: The high debt model versus the Wall Street–Treasury–IMF complex", in *New Left Review*, I/228 (Mar./Apr.), pp. 3–22.

ECONOMY, ECOLOGY AND THE NATURAL LIMITS TO GROWTH: THE GLOBAL "POLYCRISIS" AND SOUTH AFRICAN RESPONSES

3

Devan Pillay

Introduction

The global economic crisis cannot be understood separately from the global ecological crisis, even if the two have different historical origins and at times different rhythms. Industrial capitalism is characterized by accumulation for the sake of accumulation, along with the creation of an unending sequence of wants to drive increasing consumerism. As such it rests on the intensified exploitation not only of labour but also of nature – the latter through incessant consumption of finite, non-renewable fossil energy sources and the expansion of pollution and waste. A continuous succession of economic crises arises out of an inexorably declining rate of profit – due to over-production, class struggle and interfirm competition – met by temporary "fixes" that necessitate ever-increasing exploitation of labour and nature and include the financialization of capital, through the creation of fictitious commodities, to temporarily drive up profitability.

In South Africa, capitalism arose out of a minerals–energy–financial complex which formed the basis of the apartheid State. Post-apartheid South Africa's failure to free itself from the stranglehold of this complex has resulted in de-industrialization, rising inequality, increasing unemployment, persistent poverty and extensive environmental problems. Efforts to move out of this strait-jacket have been half-hearted, despite mounting pressure from below, including from the labour movement led by COSATU. It is a far cry from the "green new deal" that is necessary to ameliorate the worst aspects of the crisis, let alone more radical eco-socialist alternatives that seek to tackle the roots of the problem.

The global "polycrisis"

From an ecological perspective, the natural world or global ecosystem (including all living creatures) has been in various stages of crisis throughout the process of industrial development, with non-human animals crowded out of their natural habitats, forced into fenced-off parks and zoos, and hunted and sought for trophies; more recently, the destruction of forests, pollution and dangerous emissions threaten the very existence of the planet as we know it. The latter threat has become a concern for the privileged and powerful only since it has endangered their own system of production and consumption – and then acknowledged only grudgingly and partially. Many, indeed, are still in denial. However, when there is a crisis of profitability, such that the wealth of the rich and powerful is directly threatened, then – and only then – a "crisis" is proclaimed. And it is proclaimed with especial force when the rich and powerful at the centre of global capitalism – in North America and Western Europe – are affected, as has been the case since 2007.

The financial crisis that began in that year has had a direct impact on the real economy, with low consumer demand leading to a crisis in manufacturing and millions of job losses throughout the world. This crisis rapidly displaced the ecological crisis that had gripped the world's attention a few months previously (particularly when oil prices began to approach US$200 a barrel). The run-up to, and aftermath of, the December 2009 Copenhagen conference on climate change temporarily put the natural limits to growth back on the global agenda; however, with oil prices relatively low (around US$70 a barrel), the minds of the world's governments were insufficiently focused to produce a binding commitment to lowering carbon emissions and moving decisively towards a non-nuclear, renewable energy regime. Expectations of further progress in the December 2011 climate change conference in Durban, South Africa, are low – notwithstanding the rise in oil prices back above US$100 a barrel after the North African/Middle East uprisings in early 2011.

High oil prices and diminishing supplies of the fossil fuels (particularly oil) on which modern economies rely, and a whole range of ecological disasters – including oil spills, the destruction of rainforest, the displacement of millions of rural dwellers for the building of dams to supply industry, the rapid decline of biodiversity, burgeoning carbon emissions, rampant pollution such as acid rain and acid mine drainage (which endanger the health of both humans and the ecosystem) and natural disasters caused by climate change – all of these are rarely or weakly linked to the economic/financial crisis, and the socio-political consequences of the two strands of crisis are seldom drawn together.

And yet, when we speak of a "global crisis", it is necessary to concep-tualize the interconnected economic, ecological and socio-political crises, as well as the looming food crisis that arises out of them (Roberts 2008). Indeed, as Foster (1999: 195) observes, the word "ecology", coined by Ernst Haeckel in 1866, has the same Greek root *oikos* (household) which gave us the word "economy". Neoclassical economics, as Karl Polanyi (1944) argued, has sought to disembed economics from society, as well as nature, to produce what the political economist Ben Fine has called economics imperialism[1] – the subordination of the social and ecological sciences to a narrow, mathematized and dismal pseudo-science. The "polycrisis" points to the necessity to re-embed the economy in society and nature – and indeed to subordinate it to them.

These crises are rooted in a centuries-long process of what David Harvey (2005), following Rosa Luxemburg, calls "accumulation by dispossession" – the dispossession of people's land and livelihoods, of the commons, of the natural environment. We are witnessing, in South Africa and globally, the commodification of all that is valued, where wealth is measured not in terms of the intrinsic value of things and relationships, or what Karl Marx called their "use-value", but in terms of their exchange value, that is, what they can be bought and sold for – money.

Capitalism, in other words, is not characterized solely by the marvels of innovation, entrepreneurship, modernization, higher standards of living and increasing consumer choice. Indeed, for most world citizens the promise of "modernization" – of expanded growth that will eventually bring "development" to all the world's population – has proven to be more myth than reality. Instead, poverty and inequality between and within nations has increased significantly (Bieler, Lindberg and Pillay 2008).

The most recent capitalist crisis has evoked a variety of responses. These range from the very narrow, one-dimensional approaches (free market and Keynesian-lite) which see the crisis purely as a financial one, through broader Marxist (and Keynesian–Marxist) approaches which conceptualize the crisis as economic, rooted in the stagnation of the real economy (particularly the falling rate of profit in manufacturing), to the very broad, multidimensional eco-Marxist approaches which see the crisis as a complex interaction between economic, ecological and social crises that have their roots in a pattern of industrialization that relies on the exploitation of fossil fuels – what Altvater (2006) calls "fossil capitalism".

As Brenner (2009) argues, the financialization of capitalism is not the cause of the capitalist crisis, but was itself a *response* to the stagflation of the 1970s, which was the result of repeated crises of profitability and over-production (see also Arrighi 2007).[2] This response is what Beverly Silver (2004) calls the financial fix, which accompanies other "fixes" such as the spatial fix (relocation of production to cheaper locales), the technology fix (to reduce labour costs through innovation) and the product fix (shifting from one product to another in the search for profitability). Inherently crisis-ridden, the financial "fix" has spawned a number of short-term crises in different parts of the world over the past two decades.

Foster and Magdoff (2009), in an extension of the Baran and Sweezy (1968) analysis, characterize the new stage of capitalism as monopoly-finance capitalism. It is based on ever-increasing concentrations of capital, under the rule of mega-financial institutions that straddle the globe, within which manufacturing firms are intermeshed with financial firms and investments. Despite the anger against these institutions for "causing" the financial crisis, governments in the United States and Europe are reluctant to take decisive action against them, regarding them as "too big to fail". Indeed, executives of these institutions continue to pay themselves enormous salaries and bonuses, in the face of opposition that amounts to much talk but little action. This is unsurprising, given the fact that core government elites are themselves part of what David Rothkopf (2009) calls the "superclass" – 6,000 people in a planet of 6 billion who, in addition to controlling powerful governments and international financial institutions, also run trans-national corporations and global media houses.

Fossil capitalism is a system of accumulation based on mass consumerism, which itself relies on the creation of constantly renewed wants. When rising global inequality and stagnant or declining real wages mean that new wants cannot be satisfied, as potential consumers do not have the means to purchase the commodities produced, the only way out is increased indebtedness. In the United States, household debt increased from 62 per cent of GDP in 1997 to 92 per cent of GDP in 2005 (Foster and Magdoff 2009: 47), while consumer debt as a percentage of disposable income increased from 62 per cent in 1975 to 127 per cent in 2005 (Foster and Magdoff 2009: 29). This mirrors the increased indebtedness of the US economy as a whole, as the country borrows on the financial markets to maintain its dominant global position by sustaining its large defence budget (a form of military Keynesianism), preserving its social and internal security spending, continuing to provide subsidies to threatened industries (particularly agriculture) and, of course, bailing out the banking system.

The end result of over two centuries of "accumulation by dispossession" is a system of uneven development, with rising inequality both at the national level, in general, and at the global level. According to the noted African econ - omist Samir Amin (2008), the proportion of "precarious and pauperized" members of the working classes (broadly defined to include formal and informal workers and the unemployed) has over the past 50 years risen from less than one-quarter to more than one-half of the global urban population.

The ecological limits to growth

Economic globalization has, since the 1980s, simultaneously enlarged the periphery within the core countries, with increased informalization of work and unemployment and a declining social wage, and the core within the periphery (and particularly within the semi-periphery – countries such as Brazil, India, South Africa, and, increasingly, China), as capital moves around globally. However, with a few exceptions such as the Republic of Korea, the overall global picture of uneven, enclave development remains intact, at least for the foreseeable future. This is despite ostentatious claims by national elites in (to take a notable example) India, that their country will be "fully developed" within the next 30–50 years – conveniently ignoring the fact that 95 per cent of its workforce is informal labour (Bieler, Lindberg and Pillay 2008). In the rural areas "development" has deepened immiseration, causing a massive increase in farmer suicides and leading to the rapid rise of Maoist groups championing the cause of the rural poor (Perry 2010).

The islands of privilege in these countries are, of course, modelled on Western patterns of consumption – particularly that of the United States. Thomas Friedman (2008) warns about "too many Americans" in the world today – meaning too many hyper-consumers, influenced over the past decades by American mass media (particularly films, advertising, television shows and magazines) that celebrate the "American Dream" of unsustainable consumption based on the creation of incessant wants, as opposed to real needs. Friedman, a short while ago a celebrant of economic globalization based on spreading growth everywhere (Friedman 1999, 2005), now warns against "America's affluenza", "*an unsustainable addiction to growth*" (2008: 54, emphasis added).

Developing country elites understandably object to being asked to slow down their industrial development because of the damage caused by the rich countries. They demand their "carbon space", as Mike Muller, a former government official in South Africa, argues (Muller 2011). The solution, Friedman counters, is partly for the rest of the world to leapfrog unsustainable technologies and develop on a green basis (which China is beginning to do, albeit inconsistently, given its rising addiction to private cars and carbon-intensive power plants).

Green capitalism or eco-socialism?

The above analysis resonates to some extent with the emerging eco-Marxist or eco-socialist school of thought (Albo 2006; Altvater 2006; Burkett 2006; Foster 2009; Kovel 2002, Lowy 2006;). If the socio-economic and ecological crises have a common origin – industrial capitalism – can a solution to these crises be found *within* capitalism, or does the very nature of capitalism need to be *transcended* in order that solutions may be found for all of humanity, in harmony with the natural environment?

Friedman (2008) argues for a "green revolution" within the logic of regulated capitalism. However, he is critical of the tepid greenwashing that passes for sustainable development, promoted by global institutions and transnational corporations. Instead, he makes a strong case for a fundamental re-orientation of our economies, in the course of which *state regulation* and *standards* need to be imposed in order to spur on innovation towards green solutions to our energy problems.

Foster (2009) directly engages with Friedman, criticizing his devotion to nuclear power and unproven "clean coal" technology, which are also elements of US President Obama's (now stalled) green strategy. Instead, he asserts the value of "the more radical ecological solution that seeks an immediate closing down of coal-fired plants and their replacement by solar, wind, and other forms of renewable power – coupled with alterations on the demand-side through the transformation of social priorities" while at the same time acknowledging that this "is viewed by vested interests as completely undesirable" (Foster 2009: 21).

A "transformation of social priorities" that addresses enclave development and ecological destruction at the national and global levels would have to take on those vested interests – implying a class struggle between the power elite at the top of the pyramid and the subordinate classes at the bottom. There is, however, a difference between traditional twentieth-century Marxist-Leninist (or social democratic) socialist struggles and a new form of twenty-first-century "eco-socialist" struggle. While the former is state-centric, and facilitated by a hierarchical (whether vanguardist or mass-based) political party, the latter is society-centric, and facilitated by mass participatory democracy. The form of struggle has a direct bearing on the outcome, following the Gandhian principle "be the change you want to see". This is a long-term battle that is already taking shape in discussions and activism, for example at the World Social Forum, as well as in places where the subordinate classes have actually taken power, as in the Plurinational State of Bolivia and the Indian state of Kerala.

In the wake of the global crisis that has delegitimized the certainties of neoliberal economics, there is a growing literature on what is entailed by shifting social priorities (e.g. Eisler 2009; Korten 2009; Patel 2009; Ransom and Baird 2009). According to Bolivian president Evo Morales (2009: 168), "It is nothing new to live well. It is simply a matter of recovering the life of our forbears and putting an end to the kind of thinking that encourages individualistic egoism and the thirst for luxury. Living well is not living better at the expense of others. We need to build a communitarian socialism in harmony with Mother Earth."

For eco-socialists, what this actually means in practice is a work in progress, a feeling-around for policies and practices that build social solidarity in harmony with nature. It includes, at minimum, the extension of the commons, so that public social goods, including basic services such as water, electricity, education, health, communication and transportation, are acknowledged as human rights, not commodities to be bought and sold (Morales 2009). It means using renewable forms of energy that preserve the earth for future generations, based on the principle of "sufficiency" (Kovel 2002) and not on endless growth fuelled by and reliant on endless wants.

Eco-socialists tend to place emphasis on local and regional economies to, among other things, maximize democratic participation and minimize carbon footprints caused by long-distance trade, particularly in fresh produce (what some term "food miles"). For example, Cuba (notwithstanding the limitations of its one-party system) has achieved universally recognized success in getting local communities to produce organic fruit and vegetables in urban food gardens, for consumption by local communities (Barclay 2003). The Bolivarian Alliance for the Americas (ALBA), which brings together a range of Latin American countries, including Bolivia, Cuba, Ecuador, Nicaragua and Venezuela, offers a radical reconceptualization of trade relations based on fair trade, social solidarity and meeting human needs, as opposed to the cut-throat competition embedded in "free" trade (Hattingh 2008).

In the longer term, an eco-socialist vision means shorter working time. This, it is argued, can substantially address the problem of unemployment, provided that it rests on a substantial social wage in the form of free or heavily subsidized public services, funded by, for example, global taxation. It also means more "leisure" time to pursue creative and socially useful activities (Bullard 2009).

Whether one adopts a "green new deal" perspective or a more radical eco-socialist perspective,[3] both pose fundamental challenges to capitalism's growth-at-all-costs tendencies.

The South African minerals–energy–financial complex

Despite the fact that South Africa's financial sector was much better regulated than those at the centre of the global system, the financial crisis has deepened an already severe socio-economic crisis. It accelerated declining manufacturing output with the de-industrialization of the economy (Mohamed 2010), partly because of a decline in global demand and partly because of the rand's rise against the British pound and US dollar. Most severely, up to 1 million jobs were lost in 2009 (Makgetla 2010), in a context of massive unemployment (unofficially close to 40 per cent of economically active citizens), rising social inequality and persistent poverty (Marais 2011).

In South Africa, racial capitalism emerged historically on the basis of a minerals–energy complex (Fine and Rustomjee 1996) – a synergy between the mining industry and fossil energy systems that sustain it. Augmented by the financial sector that it generated, it became the minerals–energy–financial complex that remains central to South African capitalism, subordinating all other economic activities, including manufacturing. It rests on the exploitation of fossil fuels and the maintenance of risky mining operations that have seen the death of tens of thousands of people over the last century. A slowly deracial-izing minority experiences the only tangible benefits, while the (mainly black) majority lives in conditions of underdevelopment in the predominantly rural former homelands, or in polluted slums and townships in the urban areas.

Efforts to move out of this dependence have been half-hearted – a combination of limited redistribution (mainly poverty alleviation through grants), an incoherent land redistribution programme, short-term public works programmes, repeated attempts at an industrial policy and a gradually visible but hitherto lame effort at "sustainable development".

Labour's response to the crisis

The labour movement in South Africa, like labour movements elsewhere, has until recently been ambivalent about the minerals–energy complex. It understandably fears that massive job losses might result from a sudden shift to renewable energy sources, especially given that costs in the renewable sector are currently still higher than those of non-renewable sources (Lloyd 2011). The environmental lobby is slowly gaining ground, following global trends, but has yet to convince policy-makers that a radical shift to a green economy will be cost-effective and provide sufficient decent jobs to replace those lost in mining and polluting manufacturing sectors.

Another key issue is that the biggest labour formation, COSATU, is enmeshed in an alliance with the ruling party, the ANC. Critics claim that this has limited its ability to formulate creative policy alternatives that challenge the roots of the minerals–energy–financial complex. COSATU claims that its presence in the alliance has limited the destructive potential of the "predatory elite" and resulted in some shifts in policy, albeit not enough. With its ally the SACP, COSATU was pivotal in bringing Jacob Zuma to power, first as ANC president in 2007, and then as the country's president in April 2009. The hope was that under his leadership the ruling party would return to its "working class bias" (Pillay 2008). However, COSATU has been severely disappointed in the Zuma Government's subsequent performance and the continued rise of a "predatory elite". It has pointed out that black economic empowerment, instead of tackling the roots of class power and social inequality, mainly facilitates the entry of black elites into the world of white economic power and hyper-consumption. It has increasingly posed critical questions related to the continued adherence to an orthodox macroeconomic trajectory, rising social inequality, growth priorities and the ecological limits to growth. There were for a moment signs of such shifts in thinking within the SACP (Bond 2009; Cronin 2009) but, since senior party officials became part of the Government, the party's voice has become muted.

Union pressure has played a significant role in strengthening countervailing tendencies in government. COSATU achieved a major victory in getting one of its brightest leaders, Ebrahim Patel, appointed to the new position of Minister of Economic Development in April 2009. In May 2010 the Government convened the Green Economy Summit, attended by a range of ministries and the presidency, and driven in large part by Patel. It seems that much was achieved to address criticisms that government efforts up to that point had been ad hoc, piecemeal and incoherent.

The Summit was followed in November 2010 by the launch of Patel's New Growth Path (NGP), which attempts to shift the emphasis in economic development towards a green industrial growth path. COSATU, however, complains that, despite its bold intentions, this programme is still mired in a conservative framework that does not address the structural foundations of jobless growth. This criticism provoked an unprecedented public attack by SACP deputy general secretary Jeremy Cronin, who accused COSATU of "entirely missing the bigger picture" and having a "redistributionist approach to transformation" which, he implied, did not ask "what is right and wrong about our productive economy". This "paradigm shift", he asserted, was implicit in the NGP's emphasis on job creation (Cronin 2011).

In his attack on COSATU, however, Cronin completely ignored its own substantial policy document on a new growth path, issued in September 2010. Far from being narrowly "redistributionist", it is a far-reaching call for decisive intervention in the economy to steer it away from the minerals–energy–financial complex. Moreover, COSATU did register its appreciation of the fact that the Government's plan did contain progressive proposals around job creation, and that Patel's department seemed to have won the battle to become the lead department in economic policy development – a potentially significant breakthrough. However, COSATU is clearly of the view that the NGP has not shifted the Government away from a neoliberal paradigm, which contradicts the developmental goals set out in the NGP.

COSATU general secretary Zwelinzima Vavi, in an address to Barometer SA in March 2011,[4] indicated that COSATU was engaging with the Government and the ANC on the need for a "radically different macroeconomic strategy, based, among others, on lower interest rates, a weaker rand, and more tariff protection for vulnerable industries identified by IPAP2[5] and NGP as potential job drivers". He also underlined the need for a "much bigger role [for] the state in directing investment into the sectors where jobs can be created", including using state-owned enterprises to create jobs (Vavi 2011).

COSATU has set up a task team to make inputs into the Government's consultative process around the Green Paper on climate change. Like the Government's Integrated Resource Plan for Electricity, which was promulgated by the Department of Energy on 6 May 2011, the Green Paper is caught between wanting to address the ecological limits to growth and satisfying powerful interests in the minerals–energy complex. The task team is composed of leading environmentalists in the country, and is a strong indication of COSATU's increasing recognition of the need to link job growth to the ecological question. It also underscores COSATU's increased willingness to work with groups outside the ruling alliance. Indeed, the labour federation ignited great concern within the ANC and SACP when it held a civil society conference in November 2010 and did not invite its alliance partners (Pillay 2011).

Outside the ANC–SACP–COSATU alliance, there are embryonic moves to build an alternative pole of attraction through the newly formed Democratic Left Front (DLF), which has explicitly raised the possibility of a grass-roots democratic, eco-socialist, feminist political programme (CDL 2009; DLF 2011) as an alternative to the crisis of fossil capitalism. The DLF is a broad coalition of left formations representing small groups of community activists and intellectuals from around the country (including former SACP leaders). It includes a wide range of left opinion in the country, similar to the range of groups found at the World Social Forum – namely, anarchists, Marxist-Leninists of various stripes, social democrats and Gramscian Marxists. While the leadership of this new formation is keen to emphasize its open, non-dogmatic character, and to hold out an olive branch to COSATU and activists within the SACP and the ANC, it remains to be seen whether it can hold together such a wide range of disparate forces. The hope is that, eventually, COSATU will realize that the ANC is a dead end, offering only false promises, and will break away to help build a counter-hegemonic alternative that places an ecologically informed socialism firmly on the agenda. Given the powerful gravitational pull of the African continent's oldest liberation movement, "eventually" might be a long time off.

Whether COSATU's membership will continue to offer support to the ANC-led alliance in the future depends partly on the signals from the union leadership, but mainly on whether it continues to see benefits accruing from an ANC Government – mainly to itself as a body of organized, employed workers in permanent jobs, but also to the larger working communities within which it lives. Recent public sector strikes and rising community unrest are beginning to stretch the bonds, and breaking point may not be far off.

Conclusion

This chapter has argued, following Brenner (2009) and Arrighi (2007), that the current financial and economic crisis cannot be separated from a broader crisis of capitalist growth that is itself rooted in a manufacturing crisis of profitability, from the enduring social crisis experienced by the majority of the world's (and

South Africa's) population, and from an ecological crisis of multiple dimensions (including resource depletion, pollution of various kinds and climate change) that threatens the very existence of the earth as we know it (Foster 2009).

South Africa is in many ways a microcosm of the world crisis, given its history of plunder, exploitation and enclave (or bifurcated) development. The wealth of the few is dialectically interlinked with the poverty of the many – a notion that sits uncomfortably with those who now dominate the ideological discourse in the country and the world. Instead of the dominant view that separates the "alleviation of poverty" of the majority from the "accumulation of wealth" of the few, or the "economic" from the "social" and "ecological", it is necessary to take a more holistic view of the "polycrisis" at the global level in order to understand its impact at the national or local levels. In this sense, the *alleviation of wealth* becomes a central precondition for the *eradication of poverty* (Sachs 2001).

Ecological issues, as integral to the social and economic spheres, are increasingly being placed on the world's policy agenda, particularly in parts of Latin America. The financial and ecological crisis has raised awareness about the need for fundamental alternatives among activists in social movements and trade unions around the world (Angus 2009; Ransom and Baird 2009).

In South Africa the latest attempt to address these problems, the New Growth Path, is a far cry from the ambitious "green new deal" that is necessary to ameliorate the worst aspects of the crisis, let alone more radical eco-socialist alternatives that seek to tackle the roots of the problem.

Notes

[1] In remarks made at a Global Labour University workshop in Johannesburg, October 2009.

[2] The thesis of the falling rate of profit derives from Marx, and has been elaborated by Brenner in his classic work *The boom and the bubble* (Brenner 2003). See also Murphy (2009).

[3] Ransom and Baird's *People first economics* (2009) contains alternative perspectives that straddle the "green new deal" and eco-socialist spectrum.

[4] Barometer SA is a series of events hosted by Citadel and *Business Times*.

[5] Industrial Policy Action Plan 2 – the second version of an ongoing industrial policy initiative.

Resources

Albo, G. 2006. "The limits of eco-localism: Scale, strategy, socialism", in L. Panitch and C. Leys (eds), pp. 337–63.

Altvater, A. 2006. "The social and natural environment of fossil capitalism", in L. Panitch and C. Leys (eds), pp. 50–71.

Amin, S. 2008. "Preface", in A. Bieler, I. Lindberg and D. Pillay (eds), pp. i–x.

Angus, I. (ed.). 2009. *The global fight for climate justice: Anticapitalist responses to global warming and environmental destruction* (London, Resistance Books).

Arrighi, G. 2007. *Adam Smith in Beijing* (London, Verso).

Baran, P.; Sweezy, P. 1968. *Monopoly capitalism* (Harmondsworth, Penguin).

Barclay, E. 2003. "Cuba's security in fresh produce", in *Food First*, 12 Sep., http://www.foodfirst.org/node/1208 (accessed 16 June 2011).

Bieler, A.; Lindberg, I.; Pillay, D. (eds). 2008. *Labour and the challenges of globalisation: What prospects for transnational solidarity?* (London, Pluto).

Bond, P. 2009. "Comments on 'The current financial crisis and possibilities for the left' by Jeremy Cronin", Joe Slovo Memorial Lecture (Chris Hani Institute), Johannesburg, 28 Jan., http://www.ukzn.ac.za/ccs/default.asp?2,68,3,1681 (accessed 16 June 2011).

Brenner, R. 2003. *The boom and the bubble: The US in the world economy* (London, Verso).

—. 2009. "Overproduction not financial collapse is the heart of the crisis: The US, East Asia, and the world", interview with Jeong Seong-jin, in *Asia–Pacific Journal*, Vol. 6, No. 1 (7 Feb.), http://www.japanfocus/-S_J-Jeong/3043 (accessed 16 August 2011).

Bullard, N. 2009. "To live well", in D. Ransom and V. Baird (eds), pp. 153–64.

Burkett, P. 2006. *Marxism and ecological economics* (Leiden, Brill).

Conference of the Democratic Left (CDL). 2009. *Unite to make another South Africa and world possible!*, pamphlet issued by the National Convening Committee, Yeoville, Johannesburg.

Cronin, J. 2009. "The current financial crisis and possibilities for the left", Joe Slovo Memorial Lecture (Chris Hani Institute), Johannesburg, 28 Jan., http://www.ukzn.ac.za/ccs/default.asp?2,68,3,1681 (accessed 16 June 2011).

—. 2011. "Let's consolidate support for the new growth path", in *Umsebenzi Online*, Vol. 10, No. 2, 19 Jan.

Daniel, J.; Naidoo, P.; Pillay, D.; Southall, R. (eds). 2010. *New South African Review*, 1: *Development or decline?* (Johannesburg, Wits University Press).

Democratic Left Front (DLF). 2011. "DLF calls for sustained mobilisation for 1 million climate jobs and against unemployment, starvation wages, poor service delivery and pro-capitalist policies of the South African government", statement issued 21 Feb., http://democraticleft.za.net/index.php?option=com_content&view=article&id=84:dlf-calls-for-sustained-mobilisation-for-1-million-climate-jobs-and-against-unemployment&catid=34:articles&Itemid=59 (accessed 16 June 2011).

Eisler, R. 2009. *The real wealth of nations: Creating a caring economics* (San Francisco, Berrett-Koehler).

Fine, B.; Rustomjee, Z. 1996. *The political economy of South Africa: From minerals–energy complex to industrialisation* (Boulder, CO, Westview Press).

Foster, J.B. 1999. *Marx's ecology* (New York, Monthly Review Press).

—. 2009. *The environmental revolution* (New York, Monthly Review Press).

—; Magdoff, F. 2009. *The great financial crisis* (New York, Monthly Review Press).

Friedman, T. 1999. *The lexus and the olive tree* (London, Allen Lane).

—. 2005. *The world is flat* (London, Allen Lane).

—. 2008. *Hot, flat and crowded* (London, Allen Lane).

Harvey, D. 2005. *The new imperialism* (Oxford, Oxford University Press).

Hattingh, S. 2008. "ALBA: Creating a regional alternative to neo-liberalism?", http://mrzine.monthlyreview.org/2008/hattingh070208.html (accessed 16 June 2011).

Korten, D.C. 2009. *Agenda for a new economy: From phantom wealth to real wealth* (San Francisco, Berrett-Koehler).

Kovel, J. 2002. *The enemy of nature: The end of capitalism or the end of the world?* (London, Zed Books).

Lloyd, P. 2011. "Expensive energy is about to become department's policy", in *Business Day*, 1 Mar., p. 15.

Lowy, M. 2006. "Eco-socialism and democratic planning", in L. Panitch and C. Leys (eds), pp. 294–309.

Makgetla, N. 2010. "The international economic crisis and employment in South Africa", in J. Daniel, P. Naidoo, D. Pillay and R. Southall (eds), pp. 65–86.

Marais, H. 2011. *South Africa pushed to the limit: The political economy of change* (Cape Town, UCT Press).

Mohamed, S. 2010. "The state of the South African economy", in J. Daniel, P. Naidoo, D. Pillay and R. Southall (eds), pp. 39–64.

Morales, E. 2009. "How to save the world, life and humanity", in D. Ransom and V. Baird (eds), pp. 165–68.

Muller, M. 2011. "Demand our fair share of carbon space", in *Business Day*, 28 Feb.

Murphy, T. 2009. "In the eye of the storm: Updating the economics of global turbulence, an introduction to Robert Brenner's update", in *Asia–Pacific Journal*, Vol. 49, No. 1, 7 Dec., http://www.japanfocus.org/-R_Taggart-Murphy/3265 (accessed 16 June 2011).

Panitch, L.; Leys, C. (eds). 2007. *Socialist Register 2007: Coming to terms with nature* (New Delhi, Leftword Books).

Patel, R. 2009. *The value of nothing: How to reshape market society and redefine democracy* (London, Portobello Books).

Perry, A. 2010. *Falling off the edge: Globalization, world peace and other lies*, 2nd edn (London: Pan).

Pillay, D. 2008. "Cosatu, the SACP and the ANC post-Polokwane: Looking left but does it feel right?", in *Labour, Capital and Society*, Vol. 41, No. 2, pp. 5–37.

—. 2011. "The tripartite alliance and its discontents: Contesting the 'national democratic revolution' in the Zuma era", in J. Daniel, P. Naidoo, D. Pillay and R. Southall (eds), *New South African Review*, 2: *New paths, old (com)promises* (Johannesburg, Wits University Press; forthcoming Sep.).

Polanyi, K. 1944. *The great transformation* (Boston, Beacon Press).

Ransom, D.; Baird, V. (eds). 2009. *People first economics* (Oxford, New Internationalist Publications).

Roberts, P. 2008. *The end of food: The coming crisis in the world food industry* (London: Bloomsbury).

Rothkopf, D. 2009. *Superclass: How the rich ruined our world* (London: Abacus).

Sachs, W. (ed.). 2001. *The Jo'burg-memo: Memorandum for the World Summit on Sustainable Development* (Johannesburg, Heinrich Böll Foundation).

Silver, B. 2004. *Forces of labour* (Cambridge, Cambridge University Press).

Vavi, Z. 2011. *A growth plan or empty promise?*, input to the Barometer SA debate on the New Growth Path, Johannesburg, 9 Mar., http://www.polity.org.za/article/cosatu-vavi-address-by-the-general-secretary-on-the-growth-path-at-the-barometer-sa-debate-johannesburg-09032011-2011-03-09 (accessed 16 June 2011).

UNDERSTANDING THE PAST TO CHANGE THE PRESENT: THE SOCIAL COMPROMISE, THE CORPORATE THEORY OF SOCIETY AND THE FUTURE SHAPE OF INDUSTRIAL RELATIONS

4

Conor Cradden

Introduction

Most analyses of the difficulties experienced by labour movements in the face of the neoliberal challenge to worker self-organization focus on economic and institutional factors rather than on ideas. In the literature, detailed treatment of changes in the law and the economy are rather more common than attempts to understand the political and ideological aspects of change in government and employer policy and trade union responses to these. Yet change in industrial relations regimes cannot be understood in isolation from an understanding of change in the ideas and conceptualizations that underpin policy. This essay will show how the turn away from generalized support for collective industrial relations has been justified on the basis of an underlying theory of society very different from that which supported the older policy consensus, in which worker self-organization and collective bargaining were encouraged rather than resisted. It will argue that restarting progress towards more democratic and equitable workplace relations demands an engagement with the new "corporate theory of society" and a radical reformulation of the aims and goals of trade unionism.

Private enterprise and the public interest

In the context of the market economy, the public interest has historically been understood in terms of maximizing the *material* benefits of private enterprise while simultaneously ensuring that market forces do not have an undue *normative* impact. As the US economist Sumner Slichter put it in the 1930s, "the kernel of the problem of industrial control" is "how to prevent industry from unduly molding our opinions, how to prevent our ideals, our scales of values, from being too much affected by the standards of the market-place" (Slichter 1931, cited in Kaufman 2004: 109). In the next decade, the ILO came at the issue from the other side, defining those norms that in its view had to take precedence over "the standards of the market place". In the Declaration of Philadelphia, it affirmed that "all national and international policies and measures, in particular those of an economic and financial character" should be evaluated in the light of the degree to which they promote the conditions under which "all human beings, irrespective of race, creed or sex, have the right to pursue both their material well-being and their spiritual development in conditions of freedom and dignity, of economic security and equal opportunity" (ILO 1944).

Unequal distribution of access to material resources means that the vast majority of citizens are obliged by material necessity to work for a living. The legal prerogatives of employers mean that, in order to stay in work, citizens are obliged to comply with their employers' commands. Thus economic necessity means that most citizens are obliged to accept subordination to employers, regardless of whether in so doing they put themselves in opposition to their own well-being or that of their families and communities. The public interest would therefore seem to demand a resolution of the apparent conflict between employer authority and the individual and collective liberty of employees.

The background consensus on industrial relations policy that dominated policy thinking in the post-war period was one such resolution. Crouch has called this policy position the "post-war social compromise" (Crouch 1999).

The theory of the social compromise

Two basic assumptions underpin the theory of the social compromise. First, it is assumed that conflict between the values and interests of workers and those of the owners of capital and their agents in management is inevitable because the "demands of the market" are value-laden rather than politically neutral or disinterested. Second, these two sets of values and interests are held to be equally legitimate in themselves and their pursuit equally important to society as a whole. Investment, competitiveness and growth are important aspects of the public interest, but so are fairness and security for employees. Neither set of values and interests, in itself, can be deemed to be representative of the general good.

Given these assumptions, the only rational way to proceed is for each of the parties to participate in the negotiation of a modus vivendi based on a realistic appreciation of the social, political and economic weight of the other. There are both pragmatic and normative reasons for this. Pragmatically speaking, neither party can have *everything* it wants, because getting everything it wants would mean sacrificing the cooperation of the other side, without which it cannot have *anything* it wants. From the perspective of the functionalist sociology that informed this "pluralist" position (Fox 1966; Kerr 1964), this meant that the idea that the situation could be optimal from the perspective of either workers or employers was illusory. Instead, the maximization of organizational effectiveness in practice depended on finding a joint optimization of decision-making along both an economic/technical dimension and the socio-political dimension of workers' interests. From the normative perspective, on the basis of the most fundamental principles of natural justice and democratic self-determination, it was clear that workers were entitled to at least equal participation in the making of decisions that had an impact on their values and interests. Collective bargaining, whatever its precise institutional form, was therefore understood both as a technical process by which the optimal mode of the organization of production was determined, and as a political process in which the conflicting values of labour and capital were reconciled.

The theory of the social compromise allows the decision to participate in an employment relationship to be conceived as freely made so long as the parameters of that relationship are subject to the agreement of workers acting collectively. Enterprise action and management authority are acceptable to the extent that instructions to employees are consistent with the collective contracts that are the outcome of bargaining. In short, employer authority and worker compliance can be conceived as normatively legitimate – and hence in the public interest – if the employment relationship is governed by regulation arising from free collective bargaining.

Questioning the social compromise

The questioning of the social compromise was prompted essentially by the pursuit of material interests. Although collective bargaining was supposed to give rise to the most effective forms of industrial organization that were possible in practice, by the mid- to late 1960s the seemingly effortless economic progress that had characterized the years after the Second World War was stalling. Throughout the 1970s, policy interventions intended to revive the economy proceeded principally on the basis that the fundamental theoretical approach that under-pinned the social compromise was sound, and that what was required was simply a rebalancing or recalibration. Depending on how serious the situation was thought to be, interventions ranged from modest reform of the institutions of industrial relations to the introduction of radical forms of industrial democracy and economic planning. However, the persistence of economic crisis and industrial conflict despite these interventions handed the political initiative to the neoliberal critics of the trade union movement. These critics argued that it was precisely the economic policies and structures of workplace governance characteristic of the post-war consensus that were to blame for the malaise, and that as a consequence trying to fix the existing system was pointless.

While the critics were clear that the solution involved reducing the scope of collective bargaining and limiting the capacity of the unions to resist employer plans and strategies, there was a need to find some way to justify this reassertion of managerial prerogative in a political context in which the democratic right to self-determination was firmly associated with unionized industrial relations. The critics of the social compromise had to provide a means of showing how employer authority could be legitimate even where it was not derived from collective contracts freely negotiated and agreed by organized workers.

The corporate theory of society

What is called here the "corporate theory of society" aims to demonstrate that corporate power is both procedurally and substantively legitimate: that the logic of decision-making is pragmatically and normatively sound, and that the exercise of the managerial right to decide is consistent with valid political and ethical principles. The theory as outlined here has not been explicitly proposed by any corporation or political party. Rather, it is an interpretation and reconstruction of the principles that appear to underpin neoliberal policy argumentation, academic arguments and corporate public relations (see Cradden 2004, 2005, 2010).

The normlessness of the market

Perhaps the most fundamental assumption of the corporate theory of society is that markets are autonomous social structures that come into being as a consequence of the freedom of individuals to enter or not to enter contracts. Markets are presumed to be both unavoidable and beyond conscious human control; hence it is thought to be rational to treat them as a fixed element of the environment for action. The market is assumed to operate according to a set of rules that can in principle be scientifically investigated and understood *but not changed*.

From this perspective, the structuring effect that markets have on society reflects not the partial interests of the capital-owning classes but merely certain objective features of the economic landscape that are the case regardless of how much we may wish them to be otherwise. These assumptions can easily be discerned in neoliberal political argument. The British Conservative Party under the leadership of Margaret Thatcher, for example, repeatedly accused the trade unions of wilfully ignoring the inability of corporations to concede just anything: "Those who negotiate around the table must understand and be aware of the constraints within which they are operating, and must have a responsible attitude to those realities" (Howe et al. 1977: 7). This obviously implies that the range of settlements which maintain a corporation's conformity with market requirements is not set by what employers are prepared to accept, but exists independently of any agreement that may be reached.

Depoliticized management

The argument that managers hold their posts by virtue of possessing some kind of expertise rather than because of a direct or indirect property relationship with the corporation is not a new one. In the 1930s, for example, the founding editor of the *Harvard Business Review* envisaged the creation of "a body of [business] knowledge comparable to those that existed in older professions like medicine and law" (Stone 1997). In fact, from the end of the nineteenth century, a steady stream of research and argument linked successful management with one or other predominant field of technical knowledge directly related to the production process (Pugh and Hickson 1989; Rose 1978). Some of the principal candidates were rational bureaucratic administration (Max Weber, Henri Fayol), "scientific" job design (Frederick Taylor), sociological interpretation of the dynamics of the work group (Elton Mayo), and the relationship between organization structure and different types of production technology (Joan Woodward).

According to the corporate theory of society, the strategic and operational choices that managers make on behalf of their corporations are based exclusively on a technical assessment of the objective functional characteristics of the relevant market. It may be the case that society has to accept certain forms of organization and certain forms of relationship that otherwise might not have been chosen, but this is a consequence of the market environment, not of the choices made by managers. Hence the corporate theory of society justifies employer authority and worker compliance on the basis that managerial plans and strategies are an expert response to the objective demands of the environment for action in the context of the overarching shared goal of economic success. The question of how to achieve a balance between economic and non-economic values is dismissed.

Questioning the corporate theory of society

The corporate theory of society is deeply flawed and its claims and pretensions have been repeatedly attacked. Most of the criticism has centred on the claim that markets are neutral and objective, but objections have also been raised to the characterization of management as a technical process.

Can market imperatives really be normless?

There are two major reasons why the claim that the market is inherently neutral or normless is problematic. The first is that detaching the normative in this way obliges us to accept that the efficiency of material reproduction comes first, and that only once its demands have been satisfied can we sit down to consider what can be salvaged from the remains of our social and political priorities. There is no way to include norms and values *within* decisions about how to organize the achievement of our material goals. At the same time as this kind of economic rationality can appear cruel and inhumane, it is also dangerously seductive since, as Polanyi argued, it allows us to "delude ourselves that destitution and suffering [are] nobody's fault" (Fevre 2003: 13).

The second problem is that to assume that norms and values play no role in economic behaviour is quite simply wrong. It is straightforwardly untrue that normative factors are incidental or marginal to the functioning of the economy, and the predictions of any theory that excludes them are likely to be inaccurate. Kaufman argues that

> it is impossible to separate ethics and economics even on purely "positive" grounds of prediction and understanding. With incomplete contracts, self-interest can quickly turn dysfunctional and anti-social. Because of bounded rationality, imperfect information and lock-in from fixed costs, economic agents have an incentive to cheat, lie, misrepresent, renege and extort both in the ex ante process of making a contract and the ex post process of contract implementation. This corruption of the economic exchange process can cause markets to self-destruct ... Neoclassical economics [also] neglects justice on the grounds that it is a metaphysical concept or non-scientific value judgement. Real people, however, judge economic transactions by not only price but also fairness, and transactions that are deemed unfair lead to predictable negative consequences, such as quitting, holding back work effort, striking and forming a union. (Kaufman 2004: 108)

In a paper discussing the possibilities for a theory of innovation, William Lazonick (2003) argues that markets are an outcome rather than a cause of economic development. It is organizations rather than markets that allocate resources to those innovative production processes that generate economic development. Whereas the conventional theory of the market economy would have it that "participants in the economy have no possibility of strategically changing the technological and market conditions that they face ...[,] the strategic transformation of technological and market conditions is what innovation is all about" (Lazonick 2003: 24).

Morris Altman's argument is that market criteria do not permit a socially rational choice to be made between high- and low-yield work cultures. Having assessed the available empirical research, he argues that there is "rapidly amassing evidence that a certain set of work practices yield relatively large permanent increases in labour productivity, yet these work practices are simply not adopted and more often than not resisted by management" (Altman 2002: 274). These practices include employee participation, cooperative employment relationships associated with a minimally hierarchical management system, a relationship between wages and productivity, and employment security. Altman argues that since it is not employees but managers who determine what the work culture will be, the costs of adopting and developing the new culture, mistrust between workers and managers, and an institutional investment environment that privileges short-run returns are likely to combine such that "members of the firm hierarchy may find it utility maximizing to maintain their firm's competitive position within the framework of the traditional work culture, even if this involves reducing the level of their employees' pecuniary and non-pecuniary benefits or keeping them below what they otherwise might be" (Altman 2002: 283).

Contesting the political neutrality of management

The 80 years that have passed since the editor of the *Harvard Business Review* predicted the establishment of a secure body of business knowledge comparable to that established in the field of medicine have seen remarkably little progress towards that end. The absence of agreement on management techniques is hardly surprising, however, since once it has been recognized that market imperatives embody contestable norms, it can be seen that politically neutral technical management expertise is impossible by definition. There are those who argue that the sole legitimate yardstick for corporate success is "shareholder value", while others point to innovation or brand recognition or even socially oriented measures of performance. Nor is much of the research that underpins management properly scientific. Even though it is hardly controversial to argue that the formal organizational structure of an enterprise does not begin to give a full picture of the social relationships which exist within it, researchers continue to focus on management interventions alone, correlating effects – in the sense of what enterprises actually do – with only a very small part of the spectrum of possible causes. In a review of the development of organization theory, for example, Lounsbury and Ventresca argue that "as organizational theory emerged as a management subfield, conceptualizations of both social structure and organizations became increasingly instrumental, driven by functional imperatives, and animated by the prominence of narrow exchange approaches to behavior" (Lounsbury and Ventresca 2003: 462).

What criticisms of the social compromise model should we accept?

One of the principal difficulties of the social compromise model is that its core institutional structure, collective bargaining, gives rise to systems of normative regulation that inspire minimal compliance rather than commitment and enthusiasm. Bargained rule systems are adhered to not because the rules are valid in themselves but because if they are not adhered to participants will not get what they want and/or need from the relationships that those rules regulate. There is an incentive for participants to do the minimum required to stay in the game, which focuses the attention of both sides not on what the enterprise is actually doing and whether or not that is a good idea, but on whether or not the other side is cheating. Significant organizational resources on both sides are devoted to running monitoring and control systems rather than getting on with the task in hand, whatever that may be. There is a good deal of evidence that moving away from these compliance-oriented rule systems towards more cooperative working relationships has tangible advantages for all involved, workers and employers alike (for a review, see Martin and Cradden 2006).

Perhaps an even greater weakness of the social compromise model is that it assumes that when conflict about the normative choices made by enterprises does arise it cannot be resolved by reference to shared interests. It assumes that the values and interests of workers and employers are permanently and incorrigibly conflicting. Any resolution, therefore, can only be achieved via bargaining. This in turn means that each "side" is left to establish its own priorities in isolation from any consideration either of the values and interests of the other side or of those of wider society. The result is a compromise that reflects the balance of power between the two sides involved at the point in time at which the negotiations are conducted, together with the skill with which the negotiators play their respective cards. If the outcomes of bargaining are in the public interest, this is no more than a happy coincidence.

This essay contends that a just and sustainable market economy is perfectly possible, but also that it would not closely resemble what we currently have. In this respect, Michael Aglietta draws a crucial distinction between the capitalism that we currently have and the (theoretical) market economy: "A market economy and capitalism are linked but not identical. The market paradigm is one of exchange among equals; it can be formalized as competitive equilibrium. Capitalism is a force of accumulation. It is not self-regulating and does not converge to any ideal model. Inequality is its essence" (Aglietta 2008: 62). Elsewhere, I have argued that there is no reason why the market economy need necessarily have socially negative effects so long as certain conditions are fulfilled (Cradden 2005). Perhaps the most important of these is that the basic goals of the business organization are such that the pursuit of profit remains a means rather than an end. Organizations might therefore aim to:

- make a good quality product or deliver a decent service at a reasonable price;

- organize production or service delivery effectively, in a way that makes best use of the available technology and the talents of those involved;

- avoid causing environmental or other social problems;

- distribute profits among the organization's members in a way that fairly reflects their contribution to production.

These goals may seem banal, but they frame the basic aims of the organization in a way that makes it clear that its activities are primarily intended to maintain or improve the general level of social well-being rather than, for example, simply enriching a certain category of organization member (the owners of its capital).

Corporate legitimacy

A "world image" that could take the place of both the social compromise model and the corporate theory of society would provide an alternative means of resolving the contradiction between democracy and liberty on the one hand and the economic dependence of workers on employers on the other. The discussion above suggests that a new world image would contain at least one essential element from each of the existing approaches.

From the social compromise model we must retain the belief that economic and organizational choices are normative – that they involve moral, political and ethical judgements. This being the case, then management cannot reasonably be conceived of as a technical function. Rather, it is a political function. As such, the most basic principles of natural justice and human rights demand that it be subject to democratic oversight and accountability.

From the corporate theory of society we must keep the idea that legit - imate corporate action is possible; that the context of production for profit and the competitive market does not in itself mean that economic activity involves choices that are at best arbitrary from the perspective of society as a whole. In effect, to use the terminology of academic industrial relations (Fox 1966), we need to adopt a "unitarist" approach to industrial relations, which is to say to assume that the employment relationship can in principle be based on wholehearted agreement between employers and employees about the goals and underlying values of organizational action.

The combination of these ideas suggests that the apparent contradiction between economic dependence and liberty is resolved when the employment relationship as a whole is normatively legitimate – both externally, in terms of the corporate action to which the relationship contributes, and internally, in terms of social relationships within the organization. To hazard a more precise definition, employment relationships will be legitimate when the actions of the employing organization contribute to rather than damage the communities and wider societies within which they exist; and when the tasks and working relationships of individual employees reflect a reasonable balance between the social or general interest, the collective interest of all of the organization's stakeholders and the individual interests of the employee.

Crucially, however, our new perspective suggests that there is absolutely no reason why just one set of stakeholders – the owners of capital – should possess the right unilaterally to define these legitimacy conditions, to have the final say on whether or not they have been fulfilled, and to demand that management consistently privilege their interests above those of other groups in decision-making. This in turn suggests that there needs to be fundamental change in the nature and processes of organizational decision-making.

Against hierarchy

The point of any kind of organization is to do things that individuals cannot manage on their own. Organizations *organize* groups of people so that by working together they can achieve something that would be more difficult or impossible if each of them were working alone. So the actions of people working in organizations are "coordinated" – the job that each person does is one element in a bigger picture.

According to Habermas (1984, 1987), every human being has an innate capacity for social action coordination. In essence, this is the capacity to persuade people that you are right about something – plans of action, the allocation of tasks, the nature of the environment for action – using only the force of the better argument; without having the power to force agreement by threatening to sack someone, for example. Habermas argues that this kind of unforced communication is how we come to know everything that we know – not only what is true about the physical world, but also what is the right way for people to interact and behave towards each other.

Formal hierarchies such as are typically found in employing organi-zations are designed precisely to circumvent this mode of coordination. Hierarchical social structures effectively predetermine the weight that will be given to the beliefs and opinions of certain individuals and groups, giving them the power to impose their assessment of the situation, regardless of what the majority within the group think and believe. This has two important consequences. The first is that, within hierarchically organized social structures, criteria other than what can be shown to be true and right can count in the search for what is true and right. Hierarchy allows action which is rational from everyone's perspective to be set aside. Instead, action can be designed to suit the purposes of smaller groups, or can be based on a world-view which is not widely shared.

Democratizing decision-making procedures within organizations ought therefore to be about the dismantling of hierarchy. It should be about opening up decision-making processes to any reason for action that any member of the organization wants to put on the table, and about preventing rational discussion from being arbitrarily closed down. It may be that a specialist coordinating function remains necessary within organizations, particularly those that are large and complex; but in order to clear an appropriate space for democracy, those who perform this function should not be permitted to *require* compliance by threatening the application of sanctions. In practice this means two things. First of all, the enforcement of worker discipline and decisions about career progression must be separate from any coordinating function, based on open and transparent procedures and (of course) compatible with the principles of natural justice. Second, both levels of pay and the distribution of profits or surpluses between those who contribute capital and those who contribute labour must be determined on the basis of open and transparent procedures, and agreed by all stakeholders.

Conclusions: A new agenda for union action

Unions have always sought to promote the interests of their members by using the bargaining power that arises as a result of worker self-organization to demand an input into corporate decision-making processes with a view to increasing the justice and fairness of their outcomes. We are certainly not proposing that this should change. Traditionally, however, the principal point of intervention has been in the definition of the contractual rights and duties of employees (pay, conditions, working practices and so on). Unions typically seek to ensure that managerial definitions of the needs of the employing organization are not in themselves acceptable grounds for change to these rights and duties. Collective bargaining is the process by which rights and duties are defined and changed, subject to the agreement of employing organizations and worker representatives. The implication of our new "corporate legitimacy" world image, however, is that the needs of the employing organization *are* in fact acceptable and sufficient grounds for change to the rights and duties of employees. If certain actions or modes of organization are the right thing for an organization to do, it follows that members of the organization owe it to their colleagues to act coherently with those objectives. Crucially, however, the new model also implies that the needs of the organization and what these needs imply for employees cannot be defined unilaterally by shareholders or managers. Rather, they should be defined via a democratic decision-making process involving all stakeholders.

From the corporate legitimacy perspective, then, the principal focus of union intervention backed by bargaining power needs to shift from defining contractual rights and duties to defining spaces within which unreserved cooperation and participation are rational for employees because their union has negotiated appropriate guarantees with respect to the process and outcomes of that participation. Rather than protecting workers by placing limits on the duties they owe to the organization, unions should protect workers by allowing them to take ownership of the organization via their voice in the definition of "the right thing" for the organization to do – in the broad sense outlined above, which includes not only basic goals and values but also working practices, procedures and relationships.

Collective bargaining can be understood as one means of defining the right thing to do with respect to a limited but important range of organizational practices and procedures. Particularly where workers' rights are under-specified or poorly respected, it is likely to remain of great value to the labour movement. However, our discussion strongly suggests that unions should recognize its limitations and that they should not see it as the final goal of unionized industrial relations. On this basis, we want to suggest the following agenda for union action. Unions should:

- openly accept and promote the idea that normatively legitimate corporate action – doing the right thing – is possible and that defining, implementing and maintaining that legitimacy is the right and duty of *all* stakeholders in an organization;

- openly accept and promote the idea that where corporate action is legitimate – where corporations consistently "do the right thing" – the employment relationship should and will be characterized by willing cooperation rather than minimal compliance;

- actively seek employee participation in all aspects of organizational decision-making while using their bargaining power to demand that employee input is not merely consultative but *determinative*; that organi -zational decision-making proceeds not only on the basis of employee involvement but also on the basis of employee consent;

- actively seek participative processes based on open-ended discussion and debate in which decision-making has a direct relationship with action;

- actively seek to remove organizational hierarchies, and in particular to break the relationship between the technical coordination of action and decisions about career progression, discipline and pay.

Resources

Aglietta, M. 2008. "Into a new growth regime", in *New Left Review*, No. 54 (Nov.–Dec.), pp. 61–74.

Altman, M. 2002. "Economic theory and the challenge of innovative work practices", in *Economic and Industrial Democracy*, Vol. 23, No. 2, pp. 271–90.

Cradden, C. 2004. *Beyond pluralism: Reconciling the British industrial relations tradition and Habermas' theory of communicative action* (Fiesole, European University Institute).

—. 2005. *Repoliticizing management: A theory of corporate legitimacy* (Farnham, Ashgate).

—. 2010. "The place of ideas in the 'reform' of British industrial relations: Did the unions simply lose the argument?", paper presented to Cardiff Employment Research Unit Annual Conference, Cardiff, 13–14 Sep.

Crouch, C. 1999. *Social change in Western Europe* (Oxford, Oxford University Press).

Fevre, R. 2003. "Economy and morality: The end of economic sociology", in *Proceedings of the European Sociological Association Conference*, Murcia, 23–26 Sep., http://www.um.es/ESA/papers/Rn6_3a2.pdf (accessed 16 June 2011).

Fox, A. 1966. *Industrial sociology and industrial relations* (London, HMSO).

Habermas, J. 1984. *The theory of communicative action*, Vol. 1: *Reason and the rationalization of society* (Cambridge, Polity Press).

—. 1987. *The theory of communicative action*, Vol. 2: *Lifeworld and system: A critique of functionalist reason* (Cambridge, Polity Press).

Howe, G. et al. 1977. *The right approach to the economy: Outline of an economic strategy for the next Conservative government* (London, Conservative Party).

International Labour Organization (ILO). 1944. Declaration Concerning the Aims and Purposes of the International Labour Organisation (Declaration of Philadelphia), Annex to the ILO Constitution (Geneva).

Kaufman, B.E. 2004. *The global evolution of industrial relations: Events, ideas and the IIRA* (Geneva, International Labour Office).

Kerr, C. 1964. *Labor and management in industrial society* (Garden City, NY, Doubleday).

Lazonick, W. 2003. "The theory of the market economy and the social foundations of innovative enterprise", in *Economic and Industrial Democracy*, Vol. 24, No. 1, pp. 9–44.

Lounsbury, M.; Ventresca, M. 2003. "The new structuralism in organization theory", in *Organization*, Vol. 10, No. 3, pp. 457–80.

Martin, B.; Cradden, C. 2006. *Partnership and productivity in the public sector: A review of the literature* (Wellington, New Zealand Partnership Resource Centre).

Pugh, D.S.; Hickson, D.J. 1989. *Writers on organizations* (London: Sage).

Rose, M. 1978. *Industrial behaviour: Theoretical development since Taylor* (London, Penguin).

Stone, N. 1997. "The practical value of ideas", in *Harvard Business Review*, Vol. 75, No. 5, p. 14.

THE NEW ECONOMY AND LABOUR'S DECLINE: QUESTIONING THEIR ASSOCIATION 5

Bill Dunn

Introduction

The labour movement in rich countries has been in decline for 30 or 40 years. The same period has witnessed substantial economic restructuring. Not unreasonably, the two processes are often associated.

Both spatial changes ("globalization") and social reorganizations (described by terms like "post-Fordism" and the "new economy") are typically held responsible for labour's misfortune. Some accounts go further, seeing economic transformation as rendering notions of class and exploitation redundant or at least precluding the possibility of any effective action by or for workers (Lash and Urry 1987; Beck 1992; Castells 2000). Supporters of labour are typically more cautious, but perceptions that economic change has profoundly weakened its organization and potential have become pervasive. This question, of course, has serious implications for how, and indeed if, overtly pro-labour responses to the post-2007 crisis can be developed. This essay considers evidence from the preceding period, but the interpretation of this directly influences an understanding of present practices.

Relations between structures and agents are, and always were, complex and contested. Against more extravagant flights of post-modernism, it is surely reasonable to expect people's economic situation to influence their willingness and capacity to organize. As is obvious from a moment's reflection, this does not imply a straightforward, simply determined relationship. Union densities vary within and between countries, even ostensibly similar ones. They vary within industries and even within particular firms. Nevertheless, people might reasonably be expected to be influenced by economic structures. Workers in local government, the construction industry, shoe factories and banks face different pressures. Even some authors making strong claims of economic transformation envisage some groups of workers benefiting. For example, in the account of Piore and Sabel (1984), the new economy creates a privileged "neo-artisanate". According to Strange (1996), transport workers such as truck drivers might gain power from globalization. It is not obvious that everyone should be sinking, let alone going down at the same speed. Such variability creates possibilities of a systematic evaluation of claims of restructuring and its effects.

This chapter presents evidence which questions the attribution of labour's misfortunes to economic change. The focus is on key claims of the "new economy" literature. The term encompasses a variety of supposed transformations, among other things building on ideas of a post-industrial, knowledge-based society where consumer-led economies of scope replace advantages of size and in which, finally, high-tech innovation and productivity gains become ubiquitous (Atkinson 2006; see also e.g. Bell 1974; Lash and Urry 1987; Castells 2000). There are many claims why these changes should weaken labour, but two seem crucial. First, it is often suggested that there has been a transformation of industrial structure, with networks replacing giant corporations. This means smaller workplaces with less hierarchy, which makes workforces harder to organize. Second, with a shift from relatively basic manufacturing to more knowledge-intensive production and service work, there has been a transformation of the labour process. The suggestion is that, at least in rich countries, high-skill and, by assumption, high-wage sectors grow quickly while others lose ground (Wood 1994; Acemoglu 2003). This trend sees a reduction in the number of semi-skilled workers who once provided the backbone of labour organization. On the one hand, increasing numbers of highly skilled workers thrive as individuals with little need of organization. At the other end of the spectrum, the flexibility is all on capital's side, with casualization and more temporary and part-time work. This trend has a strongly gendered and racialized element (MacEwan and Tabb 1989). Historically, casualized workers have been hard to organize. Such changes have profound strategic consequences. At the very least, the working class has become more heterogeneous and polarized, so that any future for unions requires "new strategic imagination" (Hyman 1999).

The mechanisms by which restructuring is believed to undermine labour are not always clear and can therefore be hard to test systematically. However, it is possible to offer some evidence to address questions of workplace size and sectoral change and their consequences for pay and organization. The emphasis in this essay is on the United States. This reflects both constraints of space and the fragmentary nature of the data, but seems legitimate as it is in that country that the "new economy" is widely perceived to have advanced furthest. Of course, evidence from one country cannot be simply extrapolated to others; but it is hoped that the qualifications identified here might strengthen the case for a more general careful and critical scrutiny of evidence before accepting what have been rather strongly anti-labour discourses.

At least in the United States, arguments of declining average workplace size seem misplaced. Brief examinations of the data on aggregate and gender inequality also highlight that these are outcomes of institutional and political action rather than simply inscribed by capitalism's structure or restructuring. More cautiously, it is possible to question claims relating to the impact of technological and skill change. Evidence for this from data on sectoral wage shares in the United States is not convincing. Nor is some more rudimentary evidence from a few other countries. A broader cross-country and cross-sectoral comparison of levels of industrial action again fails to find clear evidence of correspondence between economic structures and labour's experiences.

This investigation touches on but does not directly address issues of globalization. Many accounts have linked the ideas of a new economy and labour's social dispersal with processes of spatial transformation. The emphasis on the former here is not intended to downplay the significance of the latter. However, the globalization literature has already attracted a substantial "sceptical" response which, often by implication but sometimes explicitly, qualifies many of the claims of labour's spatial weakening (see Walker 1999; Dunn 2004, 2009).

The conclusions offered here temper claims that economic transformation is the basis of labour's weakness. This provides grounds for optimism. However, in some senses it also has troubling implications for labour's own institutions. If our problems can be blamed on a deeply and increasingly hostile environment, we can at least be reassured that the faults lie elsewhere. We are doing our best in difficult circumstances. If not, some more uncomfortable introspection may be in order.

Labour organization and workplace size

Claims around changing workplace size can be dealt with quite briefly. To summarize the argument rather crudely, the giant factories of "Fordism", epitomized by Ford's own River Rouge plant near Detroit, disappear – at least from rich countries. The decline of large-scale industry then contributes to, if it does not directly cause, the decline of labour's organization. Smaller workplaces mean less hierarchy, a decentralization of authority (Lash and Urry 1994) and, in the extreme, with management reduced to intermediary between workers and clients, "the blurring of the distinction of the opposition between manager and worker and consequently, the elimination of the opposition between capital and labour" (Vilrokx 1999: 72). More prosaically, it seems reasonable to believe that small workplaces are hard to organize.

Table 5.1   Enterprise size and union density by industry, United States, 2006–09

	Percentage working in enterprises employing 500 or more	Average enterprise size	Log of average size	Union density (%)
Agriculture, forestry, fishing & hunting	0	7	0.86	2.0
Mining	56	27	1.43	8.5
Utilities	82	94	1.97	28.8
Construction	15	9	0.97	16.0
Manufacturing	56	48	1.68	11.1
Wholesale trade	39	18	1.26	5.0
Retail trade	60	22	1.34	5.3
Transportation & warehousing	62	25	1.40	29.4
Information	74	45	1.66	10.2
Finance & insurance	67	25	1.40	2.3
Real estate & rental & leasing	31	7	0.86	3.8
Professional, scientific & technical services	38	10	1.02	1.6
Management of companies & enterprises	88	109	2.04	5.1
Administrative/support waste management/ remediation services	63	31	1.49	12.9
Educational services	55	40	1.61	33.9
Health care and social assistance	52	27	1.43	9.6
Arts, entertainment & recreation	n.a.	17	1.23	7.8
Accommodation & food services	40	24	1.39	2.3
Other services (except public administration)	15	8	0.91	3.0
Correlation with union density	**0.35**	**0.35**	**0.44***	

* designates statistically significant at the 90% confidence level.
n.a. = not available.

Sources: Census (2010); Hirsch and Macpherson (2010).

However, historical and industrial studies suggest that workplace size provides at best a "rule of thumb" in respect of the likelihood of unionization (Ackers, Smith and Smith 1996). One more recent British survey of union membership reports that "workplace size and qualifications were never statistically significant" (Bryson and Gomez 2005: 183). Large-scale industry is neither a sufficient nor a necessary condition for effective organization. Unionization preceded the large-scale factory system. Plants like River Rouge, when they finally became established, remained exceptional. It might also be recalled that many large factories, including those at Ford, remained unorganized long after their establishment. Before Ford finally conceded unionization, the strikes of the 1930s, as de Angelis points out, also involved "hospital workers, trash collectors, gravediggers, blind workers, engineers, prisoners, tenants, students and baseball players" (2000: 52). Nevertheless, contemporary evidence from the United States does suggest some association between workplace size and labour organization. Table 5.1 shows figures for different industries. Correlations between average enterprise size and union density are in the "right" direction, albeit at best marginally statistically significant.

Even a weak correlation allows that a systematic shrinking of enterprise size could contribute to labour's weakening. The remarkable thing here is the lack of evidence of substantial change. Granovetter (1984), arguing against then prevailing assumptions of increasing workplace size, demonstrated that in the United States there had been almost no change in the 60 years since 1923. Table 5.2 presents more recent data. Any change is marginal. Granovetter's study also provides data for establishment size by industry in 1977. In many cases he uses broader categories than those used in table 5.1, but some comparisons are possible. The average establishment size in manufacturing shrank from 60 to 48 employees and in mining from 30 to 27. There was a marginal rise in construction (from 8 to 9) and substantial ones in wholesale (from 12 to 18) and retail (from 11 to 22). Similar phenomena can be observed within industries. So, for example, as auto manufacturers increased their subcontracting during the 1990s and 2000s their direct employment fell but a smaller number of suppliers increased in size (Dicken 2007). This brings out what is perhaps the crucial point: that workplaces in some formerly well-organized sectors contracted while others grew.

Similarly, at an international level the decline of manufacturing (and possibly of workplace size) may describe the situation in developed economies. Some poorer countries are also de-industrializing. However, over the same period large-scale industry has become established in many parts of the world where it did not hitherto exist. In only some of these has it coincided with the rise of organized labour. Once more, the association between factory size and effective organization is weak.

Table 5.2 The shrinking workplace? Percentage of employees by establishment size, United States, 1980–2007

No. of employees in workplace	1980	1990	2000	2007
Under 20	26	26	24	25
20–99	28	29	29	30
100–499	24	25	25	25
500–999	8	7	7	7
1,000 and over	14	13	13	13

Source: Census (2010).

Moreover, while the workplace is probably the most appropriate unit of analysis for evaluating labour's potential, it is worth noting that labour's power can be exercised in more specific (departmental or sectional) locations and at more general (firm or industry) levels. Increasingly integrated production systems may allow employers to sidestep insubordinate workers but can also be sensitive to disruption and vulnerable to labour action in relatively small workplaces. Workers can win improved bargains, at least temporarily. Herod's account of the impact of a strike at a single General Motors components plant (Herod 2000) is exemplary here. There are at least some other empirical examples of this power being used by workers and recognized by employers.

Income inequalities and skill differences

Depictions of changing work typically involve claims of increasing intra-class polarization. On the one hand, technological innovation means that a core of highly skilled workers succeed in the new economy on the basis of their individual attributes rather than their collective strength, to which they therefore have little recourse (see e.g. Piore and Sabel 1984; Atkinson 1985; Collins 1998). Meanwhile, an unskilled periphery is casualized and hard to organize (Harrod 1987; Hyman 1999). There is less semi-skilled middle, long an important basis of labour organization. Such arguments have considerable intuitive plausibility – as new technologies were introduced, income inequalities increased in many countries and labour organization declined.

Again, there are both conceptual and empirical difficulties, which suggest labour supporters should be cautious. First, and particularly problematically, one influential approach, following neo-classical economics, simply accepts that income is fair reward for skill and reads back from widening differentials in pay to increasing skill polarization. For Wood (1994) and Reich (1991), education and the lack of it become the key to understanding increased income inequality in the new economy. Empirically, in almost every country, there is a positive association between levels of education and income (Babones 2010).

However, evidence from the United States suggests that rising inequality is attributable to "extravagant gains by the already rich" (Galbraith and Hale 2009: 27), rather than increasing intra-class polarization. Table 5.3 shows the differences in relative incomes across different deciles of the US population between 1973 and 2005. It shows that wages at the bottom fell marginally compared with those in the middle, while those at the top rose dramatically. What is perhaps even more interesting in this context is what happened at the 70th percentile. Roughly 30 per cent of working-age Americans now hold at least a bachelor's degree, but the 70th percentile experienced only a marginal rise against the median. Even against the 10th percentile its relative pay

Table 5.3 Wage inequality in the United States: Wages as a percentage of the median, 1973–2005

Year	10th percentile	Median	70th percentile	90th percentile
1973	52.3	100	133.3	191.5
1989	48.2	100	138.8	258.8
2000	51.5	100	140.3	284.2
2005	50.4	100	139.0	291.8

Source: calculated from Mishel, Bernstein and Allegretto (2007).

increased only from 255 to 276 per cent. By contrast, against the 90th percentile the 70th percentile lost substantial ground, its relative pay falling from 69.6 to 47.6 per cent. This appears to contradict the models that equate education with skill and anticipate its being rewarded accordingly. Wood (1998) acknowledges that many graduates in the United States did not experience the expected boon from their studies, while observing that those without such education have done even worse. It is probably reasonable to assume that technological change tends to require more skills, and that greater skills and (which is not always the same thing) greater educational achievement put workers in a stronger labour market position. However, this has long been the case, so cannot without addition explain recent increases in inequality (Mishel, Bernstein and Allegretto 2007). Nor is it obvious why, despite the application of similar technologies, trends were very different across countries (see e.g. ILO 2008; OECD 2010).

Problems with the equation of income and skill become particularly clear in relation to women and non-white workers, whose pay and levels of organization remain lower than those of white men. So, for example, gender gaps in pay narrowed only slowly in most rich countries (OECD 2008). By contrast, gaps in education between men and women shrank substantially. Indeed, in the United States they were reversed, so that every year since 1982 more women than men were awarded bachelor's degrees and by 2008 the proportions of men and women aged over 25 with degrees had almost reached equality at 30.1 and 28.9 per cent respectively (Census 2010). Similarities in education and skill were not fully reflected in income, emphasizing the insti-tutional "lumpiness" and frequently discriminatory nature of labour markets. Similar points could be made about ethnicity, where again pay differentials are inadequately explained by differences in abilities. Undoubtedly labour is heterogeneous, and in important respects this heterogeneity has increased. There are more women in paid employment, and many workforces more mixed in terms of ethnicity, than was the case even a few decades ago. Many social and institutional obstacles remain to building solidarity across gender and ethnic divisions. However, with statistics (see e.g. Census 2010) suggesting that women and non-white workers gain most when they are organized, these need not be insuperable. It is deeply problematic to imply something inherently "peripheral" about women and ethnic minority workers, and in practice they often appear more sympathetic towards, and more likely to join, unions than white men (Chen and Wong 1998).

Sectoral change and its consequences for skill and income

If aggregate national data are unconvincing, one potentially useful approach is to investigate sectoral change and its impact on pay and organization. Changes to the labour process are attributed to what has been called skill-biased technical change (Acemoglu 2003). Sometimes linked to globalization and increasing trade specialization (Wood 1994, 1998), this involves a sectoral shift within national economies, which accounts for much of the increase in inequality. An important and immediate qualification here is that trade-based arguments suggest that the situation in many poorer countries will be reversed. However, in developed economies, sectors requiring higher-skilled workers who attract higher pay are expected to expand, and those requiring low skills to shrink. The experiences of the skilled and unskilled (typically associated with more or less education) should accordingly diverge.

The work of Galbraith and Hale (2009) seems particularly useful in this respect. They quantify inequality using "Theil's T". According to this, total inequality across sectors is given by:

$$T_{\text{sectors}} = \Sigma P_i/p \times y_i/\mu \times \ln(y_i/\mu).$$

That is, T is the sum across all the sectors of the number of jobs in each sector (p_i), divided by the total number of jobs (p), multiplied by the average wage in each sector (y_i), as a share of all jobs (μ), multiplied by the natural logarithm of this same function. The natural log of 1 is 0, so sectors with the average wage contribute nothing towards inequality. If wages in a sector are below the average, y_i/μ is less than 1 and $\ln(y_i/\mu)$ is negative. But for any sector to have below average wages, another must have higher than average wages and this will contribute positively to inequality. The logarithmic function is set up to produce positive results – and the more strongly positive the result, the greater the inequality.[1]

Galbraith and Hale (2009) also investigate regional inequalities but find them much smaller than those between sectors. They also confirm that, although the differentiation increases as one breaks sectors down into detailed subsectors, intra-industry inequalities are relatively small and tend to vary less than those between sectors, "partly for institutional reasons, such as the stability of intrafirm pay hierarchies" (Galbraith and Hale 2009: 3). They therefore attribute the majority of US inequality to the differences between 21 major industries. Between 1990 and 2007 Theil's T for between-sector pay inequality rose from about 0.07 to around 0.11. Among other things, manufacturing pay rose but, because the sector shrank, it contributed less towards inequality. The relative income share and contribution to inequality rose significantly in some "new economy" sectors. These included industry information, finance and insurance, and professional and technical services. However, the same variables rose even more quickly in mining and utilities. The sectors in which income fell included construction, education, retail, and arts, entertainment and recreation. Notably, there was a different pattern in the years leading up to the dot.com boom and in those that followed in the 2000s, with different sectoral winners and losers. So "students who studied information technology in the mid-1990s were lucky; those completing similar degrees in 2000 faced unemployment" (Galbraith and Hale 2009: 16). Conversely, construction workers did very well in the recent boom. Of course, many construction workers are highly skilled but, for the most part, in rather more traditional trades than those conjured up in most presentations of the "new economy". Indeed, one useful study has argued that in this sector, rather than increasing polarization, technological change compressed skills towards the centre – reducing the demand both for highly skilled craft work and for manual lift-and-carry tasks (Thieblot 2002). As will be discussed below, this trend provided little succour to union organization. Moreover, the subsequent crisis put many building workers out of work. Galbraith and Hale suggest that "education and training have become a kind of lottery, whose winners and losers are determined, *ex post*, by the behaviour of the economy" (2009: 16).

There are insufficient data to make comprehensive international comparisons. However, table 5.4 applies the same measure of intersectoral inequality to several other countries. It also indicates for each country those sectors whose contributions to overall inequality increased and decreased most significantly. The series are taken, for as many sectors as possible, for as long a time span as possible between 1991 and 2008. The evidence is clearly fragmentary, with reasonable time-series data for both the size and average pay of different sectors available for only a few countries. It is also based on industrial classifications available from the ILO which are broader than those used above, reducing the numerical values. However, it does indicate some interesting results. First, these data, which include only employees' pay, produce substantially lower values for T than those for the United States, which include employers' remuneration. Second, with reference to the anticipated polarization, there is little evidence of increased intersectoral inequality in the established rich countries. Conversely, contrary to the trade-based theories in particular, inequality rose significantly in some poorer ones. Third, and perhaps most pertinent to the discussion in this section, there is a great

Table 5.4   Changes in intersectoral inequality (measured as Theil's T), selected countries, 1991–2008 (various periods)

	Period	T_1*	T_2*	Sectors increasing inequality	Sectors decreasing inequality
Canada	1991–2008	0.0463	0.0369	Education; manufacturing	Financial intermediation; real estate, renting and business
Chile	1996–2005	0.0373	0.0615	Construction; wholesale and retail trade	Community, social and personal services; financial services
Egypt	1997–2007	0.0442	0.0658	Real estate, renting and business; education	Construction; utilities
Israel	1995–2008	0.0354	0.0516	Transport, storage and communications; health and social work	Manufacturing; real estate, renting and business
Mexico	1995–2008	0.0748	0.0206	Wholesale and retail trade; financial intermediation	Agriculture; public administration
Netherlands	1995–2005	0.0090	0.0088	Education	Health and social work; financial intermediation
Poland	1994–2007	0.0252	0.0203	Mining and quarrying; manufacturing	Agriculture; financial intermediation
Sweden	1997–2007	0.0021	0.0029	Real estate, renting and business	Construction

* T_1 = Theil's T at the beginning of the period specified; T_2 = Theil's T at the end of the period.
Source: calculated from ILO (2010); Heston, Summers and Aten (2009).

variety in the sectors whose contribution to inequality rose and fell. Rather than there being a clear rise in "new economy" sectors, like finance and perhaps education, and transport and communications, and a fall in "old economy" sectors like mining, construction and manufacturing, there is a highly mixed picture.

Sectoral change and labour's action

It is also possible, albeit provisionally, to investigate whether sectoral change had an impact on labour organization. Table 5.5 summarizes the results of a comparison across 20 developed and 31 developing countries of rates of industrial action in manufacturing, construction, and transport and communications. Historically, in many countries, these sectors were reasonably well organized. However, they might be expected to fare differently in the new economy. Manufacturing has been the paradigm case of union decline, seen as a victim of

Table 5.5   Cross-country trends in levels of industrial action, 1980–2008

	Strikes				Strikers				Strike days			
	Total	M	Con	T&C	Total	M	Con	T&C	Total	M	Con	T&C
Developed countries												
No. in sample	15	15	15	15	17	17	17	17	20	20	20	20
Average	−0.06	−0.08	−0.08	−0.03	−0.05	−0.09	−0.05	−0.04	−0.05	−0.09	−0.06	−0.02
Standard deviation	0.04	0.05	0.06	0.05	0.06	0.05	0.08	0.06	0.06	0.05	0.10	0.08
Developing countries												
No. in sample	25	25	25	25	27	27	27	27	27	27	27	27
Average	−0.06	−0.07	−0.09	−0.06	−0.04	−0.07	−0.06	−0.05	−0.04	−0.06	−0.02	−0.03
Standard deviation	0.05	0.06	0.09	0.08	0.06	0.07	0.11	0.09	0.07	0.07	0.15	0.10
Overall average	−0.06	−0.07	−0.09	−0.05	−0.05	−0.08	−0.06	−0.05	−0.04	−0.07	−0.04	−0.03
Standard deviation	0.05	0.05	0.08	0.07	0.06	0.06	0.10	0.08	0.07	0.07	0.13	0.10

M = Manufacturing, Con = Construction, T&C = Transport, Storage and Communications
Source: calculated from ILO (2010).

workplace polarization and, although this is not discussed in detail here, of globalization. As noted above, in construction, skill requirements were typically compressed rather than polarized. For obvious reasons, this sector is also relatively protected from globalization and threats of relocation. Finally, transport and communications workers have been seen, at least in some influential accounts, as something of an exception to the general weakening, occupying an important strategic location within the global economy (Strange 1996; Castells 2000). Many transport and communications workers, perhaps particularly the latter, seem likely to work with newer technologies and be towards the high-skilled end of the spectrum.

The table shows trends of industrial action according to the absolute number of strikes and lockouts, the number of people involved and the days "lost". Measures of standard deviation are also included, indicating the variety between countries. Strike data are, of course, an imperfect measure of union power, and the statistics are collected on very different bases in different countries, so that straightforward international comparisons are of little value. However, time series within countries allow the construction of trends which may then usefully, if cautiously, be compared.

The figures show considerable international variation, particularly among poorer countries, but very little evidence of any systematic difference between labour in rich and poor countries or between sectors. There is some suggestion that in rich countries transport and communications workers fared somewhat less badly than those in the broader labour movement, but they did not escape an overall downward trajectory. Trends of industrial action in manufacturing indeed fall sharply. However, the strike data are numerical rather than per capita values, and the decline in manufacturing employment in rich countries – and in several poorer ones – means they should be interpreted cautiously. Construction often occupies a middle position. The decline in the number of strikes here was even more precipitous than in manufacturing, while the number of strikers and strike days fell less sharply than in manufacturing but more steeply than in transport and communications. In short, evidence of different work in different sectors having different effects on labour organization seems rather weak.

Once again, it is worth emphasizing the negative character of this conclusion. It points only to the absence of a straightforward relationship between enterprise structure and labour's situation. More factors are involved. In some countries workers in the transport and communications and construction sectors have been among the groups most susceptible to a redefinition of industrial relations, with increasing self-employment, for example, encouraged by changing tax regulations (Harvey 2001). This can have serious implications for the prospects of labour organization, even where the recategorization may mask important continuities in power relations. The point is simply that such changes should be seen as social and political achievements, not simply economic and (still less) technological inevitabilities.

Conclusions

There are some elegant arguments why economic restructuring should be thought to weaken labour. However, there are many reasons for labour supporters to treat them with some scepticism. The relationship between workplace size and labour organization was never very strong, and while it seems plausible to argue that the re-emergence of really small-scale, cottage industry would undermine labour's potential, there is little evidence of this occurring. The relationships between technological change, skill, work and organization are also highly mediated and contingent. They are accordingly hard to assess. Nevertheless, it is far from clear that income polarization or poor labour organization should be attributed to skill differentiation. Again, there is a danger of reading back effect as cause. Flexibility and income polarization can *reflect* a lack of organization. Labour's weakness extends to sectors little affected by globalization and the new economy. It extends to sectors one might expect to see strengthened by economic change. It has affected the skilled and unskilled. It has occurred both in rich and powerful countries and in poor ones.

Many claims of labour's being undermined should therefore be qualified. This provides reasons for optimism. The material bases for organization and resistance have not been swept away. There is little reason to believe we need to radically rethink notions of class or strategies for social action. A further implication is that labour's problems are, at least partially, also a political achievement, and therefore potentially contestable (Walker 1999). From the 1970s, governments of various hues have pushed anti-labour policies. This trend has itself been read as a simple structural imperative (Castells 2000). However, Thatcher and Reagan went to work before most of what have been seen as the new economy transformations really took off. The continued attempts at labour market reform well into the twenty-first century also suggest that labour's opponents remain unconvinced that mere economic imperatives provide sufficient discipline.

This is not to discount the significance of restructuring. It was suggested above that well-organized economic sectors, as well as firms and particular workplaces, may have declined in number. The unorganized grew. But there is a vital institutional element to this development. The successful bargains of the 1950s and 1960s, at firm, industry and national level, may have left labour ill prepared and structurally ill adapted to deal with the more confrontational conditions that followed. For whatever reasons, unions and the broader Left failed to repel the attacks on their organizations. There were important struggles and some significant successes, at least in the negative sense of limiting the anti-labour thrust in many countries. Nevertheless, fewer political protections and more aggressive management practices became the norm.

The recent crisis foregrounds the political dimensions of the current situation. The crisis that began in 2007 was, of course, primarily an economic crisis, which nobody planned but of which workers around the world, in their millions, were the principal victims. However, two things quickly became clear. First, States were not reduced to mere bystanders and remained crucial to sustaining the global economy. They were capable of rescuing financial institutions and implementing stimulus measures. Second, rather than prompting a return to Keynes, the crisis quickly shifted the focus, particularly in Europe, to reducing budget deficits and pressing further attacks on labour. It was far from clear that this made sense in strictly economic terms; but at the time of writing the contest of political forces rather than strict economic logic seemed likely to determine our future.

Note

[1] To illustrate, imagine a two-class economy, with national wealth of 12 divided between the two equal-size classes either (i) in the ratio 2 to 10 or (ii) in the ratio 4 to 8. Then:

$$T_i = (0.5 \times 2/6 \times \ln2/6) + (0.5 \times 10/6 \times \ln10/6) = -0.183 + 0.426 = 0.243$$
$$T_{ii} = (0.5 \times 4/6 \times \ln4/6) + (0.5 \times 8/6 \times \ln8/6) = -0.135 + 0.192 = 0.057.$$

Resources

Acemoglu, D. 2003. "Patterns of skill premia", in *Review of Economic Studies*, Vol. 70, No. 2, pp. 199–230.

Ackers, P.; Smith, C.; Smith, P. (eds). 1996. *The new workplace and trade unionism* (London, Routledge).

Atkinson, J. 1985. "Flexibility: Planning for an uncertain future", in *Manpower, Policy and Practice*, Vol. 1, No. 1, pp. 26–29.

—. 2006. "Is the next economy taking shape?", in *Issues in Science and Technology*, Vol. 22, No. 2, pp. 62–68.

Babones, S.J. 2010. "Trade globalization, economic development and the importance of education-as-knowledge", in *Journal of Sociology*, Vol. 46, No. 1, pp. 45–61.

Beck, U. 1992. *Risk society: Towards a new modernity* (London, Sage).

Bell, D. 1974. *The coming of post-industrial society* (London, Heinemann Educational).

Bryson, A.; Gomez, R. 2005. "Why have workers stopped joining unions? The rise of never-membership in Britain", in *British Journal of Industrial Relations*, Vol. 43, No. 1, pp. 67–92.

Castells, M. 2000. *The information age: Economy, society and culture*, Vol. 1 (Oxford, Blackwell).

Census. 2010. *Statistical abstract of the United States*, http://www.census.gov/ (accessed 16 June 2011).

Chen, M.; Wong, K. 1998. "The challenge of diversity and inclusion in the AFL-CIO", in G. Mantsios (ed.): *A new labour movement for a new century* (New York, MRP).

Collins, H. 1998. "Flexibility and empowerment", in T. Wilthagen (ed.): *Advancing theory in labour law and industrial relations in a global context* (Amsterdam, North-Holland).

de Angelis, M. 2000. *Keynesianism, social conflict and political economy* (Basingstoke, Macmillan).

Dicken, P. 2007. *Global shift: Mapping the changing contours of the world economy* (London, Sage).

Dunn, B. 2004. *Global restructuring and the power of labour* (Basingstoke, Palgrave Macmillan).

—. 2009. "Myths of globalisation and the new economy", in *International Socialism*, Vol. 121 (Winter), pp. 75–97.

Galbraith, J.K.; Hale, J.T. 2009. *The evolution of economic inequality in the United States, 1969–2007*, UTIP Working Paper No. 57, 2 Feb. (Austin, University of Texas Inequality Project).

Granovetter, M. 1984. "Small is bountiful: Labor markets and establishment size", in *American Sociological Review*, Vol. 49, No. 3, pp. 323–34.

Harrod, J. 1987. *Power, production, and the unprotected worker* (New York, Columbia University Press).

Harvey, M. 2001. *Undermining construction: The corrosive effects of false self-employment* (London, Institute of Employment Rights).

Herod, A. 2000. "Implications of just-in-time production for union strategy: Lessons from the 1998 General Motors–United Auto Workers dispute", in *Annals of the Association of American Geographers*, Vol. 90, No. 3, pp. 521–47.

Heston, A.; Summers, R.; Aten, B. 2009. *Penn World Table*, Version 6.3 (Philadelphia: Center for International Comparisons of Production, Income and Prices at the University of Pennsylvania), Aug.

Hirsch, B.T.; Macpherson, D.A. 2010. *Union membership and coverage database*, http://www.unionstats.com (accessed 16 June 2011).

Hyman, R. 1999. "Imagined solidarities: Can trade unions resist globalization?", in P. Leisink (ed.): *Globalization and labour relations* (Cheltenham, Edward Elgar).

International Labour Office (ILO). 2008. *Global Wage Report 2008/09* (Geneva).

—. 2010. LABORSTA database, http://laborsta.ilo.org (accessed 16 June 2011), data extracted various dates June–Aug.

Lash, S.; Urry, J. 1987. *The end of organized capitalism* (Cambridge, Polity).

—; —. 1994. *Economies of signs and space* (London, Sage).

MacEwan, A.; Tabb, W.K. 1989. "Instability and change in the world economy", in A. MacEwan and W.K. Tabb (eds): *Instability and change in the world economy* (New York, New York University Press).

Mishel, L.; Bernstein, J.; Allegretto, S. 2007. *The state of working America, 2006/7* (Ithaca, ILR Press).

Organisation for Economic Co-operation and Development (OECD). 2008. *Employment Outlook* (Paris).

—. 2010. http://stats.oecd.org/ (accessed 16 June 2011), data extracted 21 June 2010.

Piore, M.; Sabel, C. 1984. *The second industrial divide: Possibilities for prosperity* (New York, Basic Books).

Reich, R.B. 1991. *The work of nations* (New York, Simon & Schuster).

Strange, S. 1996. *The retreat of the state: Diffusion of power in the world economy* (Cambridge, Cambridge University Press).

Thieblot, A.J. 2002. "Technology and labor relations in the construction industry", in *Journal of Labor Research*, Vol. 23, No. 4, pp. 559–73.

Vilrokx, J. 1999. "Towards the denaturing of class relations? The political economy of the firm in global capitalism", in P. Leisink (ed.): *Globalization and labour relations* (Cheltenham, Edward Elgar).

Walker, R.A. 1999. "Putting capital in its place: Globalization and the prospects for labor", in *Geoforum*, Vol. 30, No. 3, pp. 263–84.

Wood, A. 1994. *North–South trade, employment and inequality: Changing fortunes in a skill-driven world* (Oxford, Clarendon Press).

—. 1998. "Globalisation and the rise in labour market inequalities", in *Economic Journal*, Vol. 108, No. 450, pp. 1463–82.

PART II

RESPONSES TO THE CRISIS:
DEVELOPING INTERNATIONAL STRATEGIES

GLOBAL UNIONS, LOCAL LABOUR AND THE REGULATION OF INTERNATIONAL LABOUR STANDARDS: MAPPING ITF LABOUR RIGHTS STRATEGIES[1]

6

Mark P. Thomas

The crisis in global financial markets that began in 2007 sparked many debates regarding the impacts of neoliberal globalization in economies around the world. The consequences of the crisis have included widespread unemployment and growing economic polarization within the nations hardest hit, prompting many to raise the prospect of new regulatory strategies to temper the longer-term tendencies of neoliberalism and global capitalism, ranging from calls for neo-Keynesian solutions to more fundamental critiques of the capitalist system (Albo, Gindin and Panitch 2010; Teeple and McBride 2011). In this context, labour movements have sought to develop strategies designed to counter the heightened power of transnational capital. While the crisis exacerbated conditions of inequality and instability, these conditions may also create opportunities for organized labour to advance more progressive strategies for labour market reregulation (Hoffer 2010).

The challenges faced by labour movements in the contemporary global economy are profound and long-standing. As processes of neoliberal globalization have transformed the global economy, labour movements have struggled to counter the power of transnational corporations (Barton and Fairbrother 2009). Labour movements in transnational industries have increasingly sought to develop strategies that could both counter the "race to the bottom" in labour standards and create more just working conditions within the global economy. Some of these strategies have emerged through Global Union federations (GUFs) and have included efforts to improve and expand the standards of the ILO and develop forms of transnational collective bargaining through international framework agreements (IFAs) (Stevis and Boswell 2007; Thomas 2011b). However, while these initiatives are emerging at the international level, a profound disconnect between international norms and localized workplace practices in transnational industries – the "global" and the "local" – hampers the ability of international unions to counter the power of transnational capital.

This chapter is a case study of the global labour rights strategy developed by the International Transport Workers' Federation (ITF) for seafarers in the international shipping industry.[2] The ITF, a Global Union federation that represents workers in a wide range of transport industries, has developed a unique labour rights strategy for seafarers that integrates the core standards of the ILO with both a transnational collective bargaining agreement and a local-level worksite inspections process, thereby aiming to implement and enforce transnational standards (including ILO standards) at the level of the worksite. As a strategy for regulating labour standards in a transnational industry, the ITF approach raises key questions. How are the international labour rights norms that frame the ITF's inspection programme implemented and enforced? And to what extent does the ITF's approach offer potential to other Global Unions seeking to challenge downward pressure on labour standards in transnational industries?

To address these questions, in particular to think through relations between the "local" and the "global", the chapter adopts an approach that aims to understand the "multi-scalar" dimensions to labour organizing as developed through recent scholarship in labour geography (Bergene, Endresen and Knutsen 2010; Herod 2001; Tracey, Caspersz and Lambert 2009). Rather than studying isolated spaces or "levels" within the global economy, this approach places emphasis on understanding interconnections between local, national and international scales. No single scale is considered to be primary and/or determinant of what happens elsewhere. Seen from this perspective, labour organizing becomes a process that works through interdependent scales characterized by non-hierarchical "nested relationships", rather than as a stepladder that proceeds from one level to another.

The chapter begins with a review of scholarly literature examining themes of globalization, labour standards and labour market regulation. The ITF's global labour rights strategy is then presented as a model of labour rights regulation that aims to challenge corporate power by integrating international standards with local inspections and enforcement processes. The chapter concludes by drawing out the implications of a multi-scalar approach to labour market regulation.

Regulating transnational labour standards

Scholarly research on globalization and labour standards suggests that, as a result of growing corporate power, the geographical fragmentation of production and the predominance of neoliberal labour market policies, workers in the contemporary global economy are increasingly insecure. In globalization research, several prominent explanations have been advanced for the relationship between these processes and a downward pressure on labour standards. First, the combined patterns of intense labour exploitation in the South and the growth of insecurity in industrialized labour markets in the North have created the dynamics for a "race to the bottom" or a "harmonizing down" of labour standards, where the labour rights of workers in both the global South and the global North are undermined by capital mobility and corporate power (Ross 2004; Wells 2009). Second, traditional state-based methods of regulating labour standards, in particular national and subnational labour laws, are undermined by neoliberal approaches to public policy (Standing 1999). Third, the regulation of labour standards has been marginalized within the institutions that regulate trade within the global economy, as the neoliberal orientation of these institutions has produced weak and/or ineffective mechanisms for the purpose (Bair 2007; Bensusan 2002; Elliott and Freeman 2003).

Recent labour rights scholarship has directed attention towards a number of emerging approaches to transnational labour rights regulation that aim to counter these tendencies. Two prominent strategies involve the core labour standards of the ILO and corporate codes of conduct (Block, Ozeki and Roomkin 2001; French and Wintersteen 2009; Weil and Mallo 2007); and much of the research has been fairly critical of the capacity of either ILO Conventions and Recommendations or corporate codes to exercise a significant impact upon the regulation of labour standards, owing to a lack of enforceability of the principles enshrined therein (Gökhan Koçer and Fransen 2009; Reed and Yates 2004; Thomas 2011a; Wells 2007).

The lack of enforceability of ILO standards and the inherent weaknesses of corporate codes of conduct have prompted some GUFs to negotiate IFAs.[3] Like corporate codes, IFAs are designed to regulate labour standards across transnational supply chains and are built upon the core international labour standards of the ILO. Unlike the corporate codes, however, IFAs are designed to establish an ongoing process of consultation and dialogue between trans-national corporations (TNCs) and GUFs (Miller 2004; Riisgaard 2005; Stevis and Boswell 2007). Moreover, Global Unions that have pursued IFAs as a labour rights strategy see the agreements not only as a way to regulate labour standards "from above", but as a way to promote unionization across a supply chain by putting pressure on suppliers to respect freedom of association rights and by providing a framework through which local-level agreements may be negotiated (Hammer 2005). Currently, there are over 80 IFAs negotiated by seven GUFs.[4]

However, there remain key limitations to IFAs (Thomas 2011b). First, they are voluntary agreements: TNCs are under no legal obligation to negotiate or implement them.[5] While some Global Unions have been successful in their negotiations with TNCs, many of the existing IFAs are in sectors with tradition-ally high levels of unionization, indicating that sectoral union density and strength may be key elements in negotiating IFAs (Hammer 2005). Finally, even when an agreement is negotiated, there is no assurance of uniform application and enforcement across the supply chain (Riisgaard 2005). While IFAs establish processes for social dialogue between TNCs and Global Unions, their effective implementation must be accompanied by strong and localized workplace-based organizing and representation.[6]

Thus, among all three of these strategies for transnational labour rights regulation, a common problem of how to bridge the gap between international standards and local practices persists, despite the particularities of each approach. In outlining the case study of ITF labour rights strategies, this chapter highlights the need to explore the ways in which international institutions and norms may take on strategic importance in local contexts through the pursuit of multi-scalar strategies in the processes of labour rights regulation.

The ITF global labour rights strategy

The ITF is a Global Union federation of over 700 union affiliates representing approximately 4.6 million workers in 155 countries.[7] Founded in 1896 in London, to promote international solidarity among seafarers and dockers,[8] the ITF has expanded to include affiliates from a wide range of transport industries. The federation facilitates communication and information sharing among affiliates, promotes solidarity actions, engages in international campaigns to promote labour rights, provides representation within international institutions such as the ILO, conducts international-level bargaining with employers' associations, and coordinates a labour standards inspections system for seafarers.

The remainder of this chapter focuses on the work of the ITF to improve international labour standards for seafarers – those who work on ships that transport goods around the globe. There are approximately 1.5 million seafarers worldwide, and over 600,000 are represented by unions affiliated with the ITF. Seafarers often face extreme hardships with respect to working conditions on ships, owing to their isolation and a lack of effective labour rights legislation (ITF 2006).[9] The chapter focuses on the ways in which the ITF has built a multi-scalar labour rights strategy that incorporates the ILO Maritime Labour Convention, an IFA, ITF port inspectors and local dockworker solidarity.

ILO Maritime Labour Convention, 2006

The ILO's Maritime Labour Convention is a key component within the overall ITF strategy. Its aim is to establish a core set of labour standards for seafarers by consolidating over 60 ILO Conventions and Recommendations.[10] The Convention sets minimum standards including a minimum age of 16 for employ -

ment on a ship; regular pay periods; maximum work-hours of 14 hours per day; and overtime regulations. The Convention also includes the ILO's core labour standards of freedom of association, the elimination of forced labour and child labour, and protections against discrimination.

While the Maritime Labour Convention establishes key labour standards for seafarers, its ability to enforce those standards *on its own* is highly limited.[11] Like all ILO standards, unless the ILO Convention is ratified by a sufficient number of member States and subsequently introduced into national legislation, it does not apply (ILO 2009).[12] Moreover, for the Convention to apply in respect of a particular vessel it must be ratified by the country with which that ship is registered. In the global shipping industry, many ships are registered in countries with very weak national labour legislation to enable shipowners to escape regulation (this is known as using a "flag of convenience" or FOC) (discussed below), further complicating the application of the Convention.[13]

As a key proponent of the Convention, the ITF has engaged in a political campaign to promote its ratification and implementation.[14] It is also working with the ILO to educate governments and shipowners about the Convention and to promote compliance. More importantly, as adoption of the Convention is voluntary, the ITF has sought to ensure its implementation by integrating the Convention into a process of transnational collective bargaining through the International Bargaining Forum.

The International Bargaining Forum

As discussed above, IFAs have emerged to create a collective bargaining process between GUFs and TNCs. The ITF participates in such a process for the global shipping industry through the International Bargaining Forum (IBF), which was formed in 2003. The IBF's membership comprises the International Maritime Employers' Committee (IMEC), the Korea Shipowners' Association (KSA) and the International Seafarers Employers' Group (ISEG).[15]

The IBF serves as a forum to establish labour standards for seafarers through an IFA.[16] The 2008–09 IBF framework agreement included the following as basic standards: a nine-month period of employment; an eight-hour workday; overtime hours paid at 1.25 the normal rate of pay; a minimum of nine days' holiday per year; a minimum of ten hours of rest per day; and protection against workplace harassment as established in the Maritime Labour Convention. Moreover, while IFAs have been criticized for a lack of enforcement capacities, the ITF–IBF agreement is enforced through an inspections system, which is made up of ITF inspectors located at ports around the world.[17]

For the ITF, the IBF produces "a collective agreement applied at an international level".[18] Though the process is still in its infancy, ITF representatives consider the IBF as creating the potential to establish international benchmarks for labour standards for seafarers.[19] However, like the Maritime Labour Convention, the IBF agreement is insufficient on its own to create an enforceable system of labour rights. The agreement itself is implemented through a system of labour rights inspection carried out by ITF inspectors.

ITF ship inspections

The ship inspections process is a key component of the ITF global labour rights strategy. This process, through which ITF inspectors determine compliance with the IBF agreements, becomes a means to enforce the international standards that are present in the IBF agreements, making port sites a space where the global and the local meet. At present, there are 135 inspectors in 49 major port cities around the world, including in India, the Mediterranean, North America, northern Europe and the Philippines, (ITF 2011).[20] In 2010, 8,302 ships were inspected and over US$23.7 million in back wages and compensation was recovered for seafarer crews.

When ships dock, inspectors attempt to board and talk to crews about working conditions on the ship. They also review ship logs to determine compliance with standards on hours and wages: "You make sure of several things: that the negotiated collective agreements are being adhered to ... you go through the wage accounts ... you make sure that the time agreements are adhered to. As this is the big problem in these vessels, where the employer doesn't follow these agreements."[21]

These inspections often confirm that seafarers face frequent violations of labour standards: "The main grievances are no pay, back wages [are owed], no proper food, no proper accommodation, in cabin three seafarers are staying, [in some places] ... the cabins are not good."[22]

As complaints go through the ITF inspectors, the inspections process reduces the pressure on workers to deal individually with their employers. Further, conducting the complaints process through the ITF creates the capacity to develop a stronger enforcement mechanism, bringing the resources of the GUF to bear in support of the complaints: "The enforcement arm is the ITF inspectorate. If a shipowner doesn't comply we hammer him and make sure the crew gets wages."[23]

More specifically, if shipowners fail to address labour standards violations, the ITF has a variety of tactics at its disposal to gain compliance. The inspector may engage with local authorities to "arrest" the ship – that is, have it held in port until the violations are addressed. The actions of the inspectors are also supported by the potential for workplace action by ship crews if labour standards violations are not addressed: "A crew will take industrial action ... If they haven't received salary, they might hang a sheet over [the] side of the boat saying 'on strike' ... When push comes to shove, if we can't negotiate with [the] shipowner then the crew takes action."[24]

If the ship leaves port without a resolution, the ITF may also use its network of inspectors to track ships from port to port until they can be forced to address complaints.[25]

In addition to monitoring labour standards violations, the inspections process is also used to facilitate union organizing.[26] Specifically, as approximately only one-third of ships are covered by collective agreements, inspectors will attempt to "put pressure on shipowners that don't have bargaining agreements in place".[27] "The role of the ITF inspectors is to ensure first of all that ships coming into port have valid agreements ... If they don't ... then to try and ensure that they sign ITF approved agreements."[28]

While the inspections process creates the capacity for enforcing the international standards enshrined in the framework agreement, the process is far from smooth. ITF inspectors report frequent resistance from shipowners and captains to their attempts to gain access to ships and ship records.[29] Moreover, even once the inspectors are on board, crews may be unaware of whether or not there is a collective agreement in force,[30] and may be very reluctant to be open about their experiences through fear of a variety of forms of retribution: "Access to the crew is one very big problem ... It could be because of bad owners, bad captains and to be realistic it's also the fear amongst the seafarers ... The seafarers know that they are being exploited, and yet you know they need their job."[31] "Sometimes it is also the fear factor ... A seafarer is afraid that if he makes a complaint to an ITF inspector, when he goes back he might be subjected to violence. He might be subjected to denial of a job next time ... They blacklist the seafarers."[32]

Another problem relates to retribution once a vessel has left port: "After they sail out from the port, these owners and the captain try to get back the money that they have received after the campaign, after the ITF [got] these people paid in a proper manner. They try to snatch this money back again and make ... their salary to a lower level."[33]

Finally, the FOC system, whereby shipowners register with countries where labour standards are low as a means to avoid regulation, compounds the problems faced by ITF inspectors: "An owner always tries to register his company where there are no laws. Like there are about 32 FOC countries ... for example Panama, Liberia ... They will just register the ship and they are free to employ any seafarer from all over the world and with their own salary and all that. So no union will be involved and no law will be applied. That is known as FOC."[34]

Inspectors report that the FOC system adds urgency to the need to bring ships under the framework of IBF agreements.[35] "You'll never get rid of the FOC programme ... I want this guy here [on a FOC ship] to be as strong as the union dockers are. I want them to say ... 'My union says I don't have to do that. I have a union contract' ... if we can get that established then we have won the war."[36]

In order to apply pressure on shipowners to allow access to ships' crews and records, and to sign collective agreements where none exist, ITF inspectors use another element of the overall labour rights strategy: the potential for solidarity action by dockworkers to support the inspections process.

Labour solidarity on the docks

The inspections system, while creating the capacity for enforcement of inter - national labour standards for seafarers, cannot achieve this on its own. Another key component of the system of regulation is the potential for solidarity actions undertaken by dockworkers – specifically through refusals to offload ships – in support of seafarers who are experiencing labour standards abuses. Inspectors identify the potential for dockworker solidarity as a key dimension of the leverage they are able to exert on shipowners to gain access to ships and to ensure that labour standards violations are addressed: "I will first try to negotiate with the company to correct the problems, get the wage, without trying to get other people into it. But in many cases you have to involve outside help. Particularly if you could engage the dockers' union, it's a big help. So I try to keep them as informed as possible, because they are an affiliate of the ITF."[37] "[ITF] strength is good. But what gives us strength on the ground is locals like ILWU [the International Longshore and Warehouse Union]. They are well respected ... it is the situation of leverage over the companies: do you want cargo and do you want it in a timely fashion ... so that's the leverage."[38]

Promoting solidarity between affiliates is a primary aim of the ITF. The coordination of solidarity actions between seafarers and dockworkers is a concrete manifestation of this broader goal:

> What the ITF has done over the years is with inspectors. They go on ships and inspect. They issue a certificate to owners indicating their compliance with ITF conditions. In some cases we arrest ships and hold them in ports until the back pay is paid. The ability [to do that] depends on the dockworkers. They will refuse to unload ships. We have run an international solidarity campaign for 50 years.[39]

Through engagement in solidarity action between seafarers and dockworkers, the ITF links the inspections process (which is itself linked to both the IBF agreement and ILO standards) to an approach rooted in local labour organizing.

Inspectors did not report the frequency of actual work stoppages by dockworkers. Rather, the *threat* of work stoppage was articulated as a part of the overall inspections process, the *potential* result that could occur should shipowners fail to comply with the inspectors' stipulations. The willingness and capacities of dockworkers to engage in these kinds of actions varies considerably, and is highly dependent upon conditions within local dockworker unions.[40] Nonetheless, all inspectors reported that they regularly use the threat of dockworker solidarity as part of their repertoire of tactics to put pressure on employers.[41]

This practice is rooted in a long history of solidarity between dockworkers and seafarers (ITF n.d.d). An example of this solidarity can be seen in the annual ITF regional weeks of action where inspectors, ITF affiliates and dockworkers campaign to force FOC shipowners to sign ITF agreements and to settle outstanding seafarer wage claims. For example, in 2010 ITF inspectors boarded over 250 ships in ten countries in a Baltic Week of Action, securing over US$200,000 in back wages owed to seafarers (ITF 2011). In the 2009 Baltic Week of Action, German dockworkers in the port city of Hamburg refused to unload a ship that was found to have abrogated its ITF agreement (ITF 2010). The ship was German-owned, but operating under an Antiguan FOC. After the dockworkers' action, the shipowners agreed to sign a new ITF agreement not only for the ship in question but also for two other ships not hitherto covered by agreements. Similarly, during the 2008 Baltic Week of Action Danish owners of a ship operating under a Hong Kong FOC and with no ITF agreement faced a work stoppage by members of the Finnish Transport Workers' Union (ITF 2009). The boycott led to both the negotiation of an ITF agreement for the ship and payment of approximately US$100,000 in outstanding wages for the crew. These examples of the role of dockworkers in supporting ITF inspections highlight the significance of ports as a space where the global and local meet in the regulation of transnational labour standards.

Conclusion: Towards "multi-scalar" transnational labour rights regulation

This analysis of the ITF's global labour rights strategy illustrates a multi-scalar approach to labour rights regulation. The strategy implements transnational labour standards through an international framework agreement, a local labour standards inspection process, and local, workplace-based solidarity actions. In this framework, it becomes possible to see the connections between the "global" and the "local", and between different links in a network of actors and institutions where the relationships are mutually reinforcing rather than hierarchical. This multi-scalar approach is illustrated in table 6.1. The standards of the ILO, ratified at nation-state level, are implemented through the collective agreement negotiated through the IBF. The IBF agreement is enforced through

Table 6.1   Multi-scalar transnational labour rights regulation

Level or scale of regulation	Mechanism or standard of regulation
International standard	ILO Maritime Labour Convention (MLC)
International framework agreement	International Bargaining Forum
Nation-state regulation	Ratification of MLC
Worksite collective agreements	ITF ship collective bargaining agreements
Local labour standards inspection	ITF port inspectors
Local labour solidarity	Dockworker support for inspectors and seafarers

the inspections process carried out by ITF inspectors in port cities. The work of the ITF inspectors is supported through pressure created by the potential for solidarity actions on the part of dockworkers.

These interconnections illustrate the potential for multiple and interacting sites of labour standards regulation, involving both international and local institutions and actors, both workers and their organizations, in shaping the dynamics of global capital. By identifying the ways in which the ITF has integrated the Maritime Labour Convention into its labour rights strategy, specifically through the IBF framework agreement and the inspections process, the analysis challenges the assumption that international standards are "toothless". Instead, it illustrates the potential for such instruments to be used as strategic tools within a broader labour movement strategy. In identifying the ways in which the ITF has developed an inspections process to enforce the IBF agreements, this chapter provides an indication of how an IFA could be implemented at the level of a local worksite.

These insights also highlight the need for further study of the spatial dynamics of labour standards regulation and labour solidarity. In particular, the analysis raises questions regarding the ways in which the localized dynamics of labour standards regulation may create variation in the successes and challenges of implementing the broader ITF global strategy. Further research is needed to uncover the ways in which the dynamics of labour solidarity, the specifics of labour laws and the uniqueness of local labour markets condition the regulation of international norms and agreements.

Further research is also needed regarding the potential for multi-scalar strategies in other transnational industries, as the global transport industry is highly distinctive, indeed unique, in character, and has a long history of militancy in unions like the ILWU. These factors suggest that it would be difficult for other GUFs simply to follow the ITF model. Yet the ITF approach indicates that the gap between international standards and local enforcement is not insurmountable. Research should explore ways in which other transnational sectors that have IFAs could integrate transnational codes with local inspections processes. Research is also needed to identify means by which transnational standards can be implemented through multi-scalar strategies that move beyond the voluntaristic approaches, such as corporate codes of conduct, that are widely prevalent in transnational industries such as garment production. The particular logics of multi-scalar engagement will depend upon the specificities of a given sector in the global economy: different industries call for different industry-specific strategies. Nevertheless, the ITF model indicates that international instruments may be combined with local implementation and enforcement strategies. Such strategies should aim to integrate the local with the transnational; one perspective should not be abandoned at the expense of the other in the process of challenging the power of transnational capital.

Notes

1 The research for this chapter was funded through a grant from the Social Sciences and Humanities Research Council of Canada. Earlier versions of the chapter were presented at the International Sociological Association World Congress of Sociology in Gothenburg, Sweden, in July 2010, and at the Global Labour University conference in Berlin, Germany, in September 2010. The author would like to thank Nishant Upadhyay and Sarah Rogers for research assistance with the chapter.

2 The analysis for this chapter is based on documents collected from the ITF and ILO, and interviews conducted with ITF representatives (India, United Kingdom) and ITF inspectors (Canada, India, United States) between December 2007 and June 2010 (coded as ITF-#). Background interviews were also conducted during the same period with the following groups: (1) representatives from corporate social responsibility (CSR) departments in companies with transnational supply chains (coded as CSR-#); (2) representatives from non-governmental organizations (NGOs) engaged in labour rights advocacy (coded as NGO-#); and (iii) representatives from Global Union federations (coded as GUF-#).

3 Hellman (2007); interview, ITF-1, Dec. 2007.

4 See http://www.global-unions.org/framework-agreements.html (accessed 16 June 2011).

5 Interview, GUF-1, June 2007.

6 Interviews, GUF-1, June 2007; GUF-3, Dec. 2007.

7 http://www.itfglobal.org/about-us/moreabout.cfm (accessed 16 June 2011).

8 ITF (n.d.a). For a detailed history of the ITF, see ITF (1996).

9 Interview, ITF-1, Dec. 2007. For a brief discussion of working conditions of seafarers, see also ITF (n.d.b), pp. 41–43.

10 Somavia (2006). See also ITF (n.d.c).

11 Interviews, ITF-1, Dec. 2007; ITF-7, Aug. 2009.

12 The Maritime Labour Convention will come into effect 12 months after it has been ratified by at least 30 member States accounting for one-third of the world's shipping fleet (ILO 2006). When the Convention was adopted in 2006, the ILO proposed a five-year plan to ensure its implementation by 2011 (ILO 2007). As of July 2010, the Convention had been ratified by 13 ILO member States: Bahamas, Benin, Bosnia and Herzegovina, Bulgaria, Canada, Croatia, Liberia, Marshall Islands, Norway, Panama, Saint Vincent and the Grenadines, Spain and Switzerland; see http://www.ilo.org/ilolex/cgi-lex/ratifce.pl?C186 (accessed 16 June 2011).

13 Interviews, ITF-1, Dec. 2007; ITF-3, Aug. 2009.

14 Interview, ITF-4, Aug. 2009.

[15] The ISEG represents shipowners from Australia, Austria, Bahamas, Canada, Chile, Croatia, Cyprus, Denmark, France, Germany, Greece, Hong Kong (China), India, Islamic Republic of Iran, Isle of Man, Italy, Kuwait, Latvia, Lithuania, Luxembourg, Monaco, the Netherlands, Norway, Philippines, Poland, Republic of Korea, Romania, Russian Federation, Singapore, Slovenia, Spain, Sri Lanka, Sweden, Switzerland, Taiwan (China), Turkey, the United Arab Emirates, the United Kingdom and the United States.

[16] 2008–09 International Bargaining Forum Framework Total Crew Cost Agreement: see http://www.itfseafarers.org/files/seealsodocs/9008/IBF%20Framework%20TCC%20CBA%202008-2009%20-%20pdf%20version.pdf (accessed 16 June 2011).

[17] Interview, ITF-1, Dec. 2007.

[18] Interview, ITF-1, Dec. 2007.

[19] Interviews, ITF-3, ITF-4, ITF-5, Aug. 2009.

[20] Interview, ITF-2, Oct. 2008. Currently the ITF does not have inspectors in the China, the Maldives, Middle East or Myanmar.

[21] Interview, ITF-9, Nov. 2009.

[22] Interview, ITF-8, Aug. 2009.

[23] Interview, ITF-2, Oct. 2008.

[24] Interview, ITF-2, Oct. 2008.

[25] Interviews, ITF-1, Dec. 2007; ITF-3, Aug. 2009.

[26] Interview, ITF-8, Aug. 2009.

[27] Interview, ITF-2, Oct. 2008.

[28] Interview, ITF-3, Aug. 2009. This interviewee reported that there are around 20,000 FOC vessels sailing around the world, only 9,000 or so of which are covered by valid collective agreements.

[29] Interviews, ITF-3, Aug. 2009; ITF-9, Nov. 2009.

[30] Interview, ITF-9, Nov. 2009.

[31] Interview, ITF-3, Aug. 2009.

[32] Interview, ITF-4, Aug. 2009.

[33] Interview, ITF-6, Aug. 2009.

[34] Interview, ITF-8, Aug. 2009.

[35] Interview, ITF-3, Aug. 2009.

[36] Interview, ITF-10, June 2010.

[37] Interview, ITF-9, Nov. 2009.

[38] Interview, ITF-10, June 2010.

[39] Interview ITF-1, Dec. 2007.

[40] Interview, ITF-3, Aug. 2009.

[41] One inspector reported that, as a strategy to avoid these kinds of pressures, shipowners are starting to unload ships in locations where labour standards are low and then move goods on overland – for example, unloading in Mexico and then trucking goods into the United States, rather than unloading on the west coast of the United States. Interview, ITF-10, June 2010.

Resources

Albo, G.; Gindin, S.; Panitch, L. 2010. *In and out of crisis: The global financial meltdown and left alternatives* (Oakland, CA, PM Press).

Bair, J. 2007. "From the politics of development to the challenges of globalization", in *Globalizations*, Vol. 4, No. 4, pp. 486–99.

Barton, R.; Fairbrother, P. 2009. "The local is now global: Building a union coalition in the international transport and logistics sector", in *Industrial Relations*, Vol. 64, No. 4, pp. 685–703.

Bensusan, G. 2002. "NAFTA and labor: Impacts and outlooks", in E.J. Chambers and P.H. Smith (eds), pp. 243–64.

Bergene, A.C.; Endresen, S.B.; Knutsen, H.M. 2010. "Re-engaging with agency in labour geography", in Bergene, Endresen and Knutsen (eds), pp. 3–14.

—; —; — (eds). 2010. *Missing links in labour geography* (Farnham, Ashgate).

Block, R.N.; Ozeki, K.R.C.; Roomkin, M.K. 2001. "Models of international labor standards", in *Industrial Relations*, Vol. 40, No. 2, pp. 258–91.

Bronfenbrenner, K. (ed.). 2007. *Global unions: Challenging transnational capital through cross-border campaigns* (Ithaca, NY, ILR Press).

Chambers, E.J.; Smith, P.H. (eds). 2002. *NAFTA in the new millennium* (La Jolla, CA, Center for US–Mexican Studies).

Elliott, K.A.; Freeman, R.B. 2003. *Can labor standards improve under globalization?* (Washington, DC, Institute for International Economics).

French, J.D.; Wintersteen, K. 2009. "Crafting an international legal regime for worker rights: Assessing the literature since the 1999 Seattle WTO protests", in *International Labor and Working-Class History*, Vol. 75, No. 1, pp. 145–68.

Gökhan Koçer, R.; Fransen, L. 2009. "Codes of conduct and the promise of a change of climate in worker organization", in *European Journal of Industrial Relations*, Vol. 5, No. 3, pp. 237–56.

Hammer, N. 2005. "International framework agreements: Global industrial relations between rights and bargaining", in *Transfer*, Vol. 11, No. 4, pp. 511–30.

Hellmann, M. 2007 *Social partnership at the global level: BWI experiences with global company agreements* (Geneva, Building Woodworkers International)

Herod, A. 2001. *Labor geographies: Workers and the landscapes of capitalism* (New York, Guilford Press).

Hoffer, F. 2010. "The Great Recession: A turning point for labour?", in *International Journal of Labour Research*, Vol. 2, No. 1, pp. 99–117.

International Labour Organization (ILO). 2006. *Maritime Labour Convention, 2006: Frequently asked questions* (Geneva).

—. 2007. *Maritime Labour Convention, 2006: Action plan 2006–2011* (Geneva).

—. 2009. *Guidelines for flag State inspections under the Maritime Labour Convention, 2006* (Geneva).

International Transport Workers' Federation (ITF). 1996. *Solidarity: The first 100 years of the International Transport Workers' Federation* (London, Pluto Press).

—. 2006. *Out of sight, out of mind: Seafarers, fishers, and human rights* (London).

—. 2009. *Seafarers' Bulletin*, No. 23 (London).

—. 2010. *Seafarers' Bulletin*, No. 24 (London).

—. 2011. *Seafarers' Bulletin*, No. 25 (London).

—. n.d.a. *About the ITF*, http://www.itfglobal.org/files/extranet/-1/968/aboutitfleaflet.pdf (accessed 16 June 2010).

—. n.d.b. *Workers' rights are human rights: An ITF resource book for trade unionists in the transport sector* (London).

—. n.d.c. *A seafarers' bill of rights: An ITF guide for seafarers to the ILO Maritime Labour Convention, 2006* (London).

—. n.d.d. *Globalising solidarity: An ITF resource book for trade unionists in the transport sector* (London).

Irish, M. (ed.). 2004. *The auto pact: Investment, labour, and the WTO* (London, Kluwer Law International).

Miller, D. 2004. "Preparing for the long haul: Negotiating international framework agreements in the global textile, garment and footwear sector", in *Global Social Policy*, Vol. 4, No. 3, pp. 215–39.

Reed, A.; Yates, C. 2004. "The limitations to global labour standards: The ILO Declaration on Fundamental Principles and Rights at Work", in M. Irish (ed.), pp. 243–56.

Riisgaard, L. 2005. "International framework agreements: A new model for securing workers' rights?", in *Industrial Relations*, Vol. 44, No. 4, pp. 707–36.

Ross, R. 2004. *Slaves to fashion: Poverty and abuse in the new sweatshops* (Ann Arbor, University of Michigan Press).

Somavia, J. 2006. *A new "bill of rights" for the maritime sector: A model for fair globalization* (Geneva, ILO).

Standing, G. 1999. *Global labour flexibility: Seeking distributive justice* (London, Macmillan).

Stevis, D.; Boswell, T. 2007. "International framework agreements: Opportunities and challenges for global unionism", in K. Bronfenbrenner (ed.), pp. 174–94.

Teeple, G.; McBride, S. (eds). 2011. *Relations of global power: Neoliberal order and disorder* (Toronto, University of Toronto Press).

Thomas, M. 2011a. "Regulating labour standards in the global economy: Emerging forms of global governance", in G. Teeple and S. McBride (eds), pp. 95–117.

—. 2011b. "Global industrial relations? Framework agreements and the regulation of international labor standards", in *Labor Studies Journal*, Vol. 36, No. 2, pp. 269–87.

Tracey, W.; Caspersz, D.; Lambert, R. 2009. *Recovering an optimism of agency: Multi-scalar organizing in the Triton dispute*, paper presented at "The Future of Sociology", Australian Sociological Association 2009 annual conference, http://www.tasa.org.au/conferences/conferencepapers09/papers/Caspersz,%20Donella,%20Tracey,%20Will%20&%20Lambert,%20Rob.pdf (accessed 16 June 2011).

Weil, D.; Mallo, C. 2007. "Regulating labour standards via supply chains: Combining public/private interventions to improve workplace compliance", in *British Journal of Industrial Relations*, Vol. 45, No. 4, pp. 791–814.

Wells, D. 2007. "Too weak for the job: Corporate codes of conduct, non-governmental organizations and the regulation of international labour standards", in *Global Social Policy*, Vol. 7, No. 1, pp. 51–74.

—. 2009. "Local worker struggles in the global South: Reconsidering Northern impacts on international labour standards", in *Third World Quarterly*, Vol. 30, No. 3, pp. 567–79

PRIVATE EQUITY INVESTMENT AND LABOUR: FACELESS CAPITAL AND THE CHALLENGES TO TRADE UNIONS IN BRAZIL

7

José Ricardo Barbosa Gonçalves and Maria Alejandra Caporale Madi

The effect on workers of private equity is also clear: it is basically a business model that is antagonistic to labour. (ITUC 2007)

Introduction

The current global crisis offers an outstanding opportunity to observe the tensions within the changing relations among States, capital and labour. The redefinition of the role of the State has brought about a recomposition of the capitalist accumulation pattern.[1] Contemporary debates have emphasized that the combination of capital concentration with mobility, deterritorialization, market integration and labour flexibilization denotes new conditions for the dynamics of production, circulation and consumption.[2] A global market for capital followed the deterritorialization of wealth that resulted not only from the limitations of capital reproduction but also from the expectations of society. The market integration that supported the concentration of wealth required new guidelines at national level, having generated a situation that can be understood as a financialization of social relations. The axle of finan-cialization has been the determination of social activities through financial circuits that have been favoured by the generalization of systemic inter-ventions on social actions.

Capital without locus tends to create conditions that make possible a new form of reproduction.[3] The deregulation, as well as the global integra-tion, of the market fosters capital flows based on the creation of new financial instruments by individuals who articulated themselves as a social group that has coalesced around the task of managing wealth. Financial operators' decisions have increasingly involved risk and allocation management among debt, equity and real assets. In this environment the institutional investors charged with the management of "financial savings" diversified their portfolios in order to take advantage of profit opportunities as fast as possible.

At the same time, labour flexibilization in contemporary capitalism has brought about changes both in the practice of labour and, consequently, in its organizing principles. These changes have included the redefinition of categories of workers, tasks and control mechanisms; and, in the EU for example, genuine integration of national labour markets. In these conditions, new trends in collective demands and contractual relationships have become increasingly widespread, revealing profound transformations in the working classes' conditions of existence.[4]

In this setting, the expansion of financial capital by means of private equity funds (PEFs) has been a form of wealth reproduction. The fund managers have privileged short-term returns and "rationalization" strategies in which labour has borne the brunt of cost-saving measures. Their expectations of returns and their focus on exit strategies have posed increasing challenges to the protections negotiated by trade unions through collective bargaining. Many studies have reported in particular the effects of restructuring actions on efficiency, employment and investment in specific countries.[5] However, less attention has been given to the nexus between the financialization of the PEFs' management practices and labour (Jacoby 2008), despite the fact that these funds are now responsible for the employment conditions of tens of millions of workers. In response to this scenario, many GUFs have cooperated in joint efforts and activities to promote regulatory reforms to address the problems raised by these major "invisible" employers.[6]

The reconfiguration of markets has been punctuated by successive crises since the 1990s.[7] In the present global crisis, Brazil – by reason of its structural and conjunctural conditions – has proved highly attractive to global investors. In their search for financial returns, PEF managers have been looking to emerging markets where the specific forms of repro-duction favour their preferences for short-term profits and rationalization strategies, particularly in investments related to family business.[8] In these circumstances, the questions that have been discussed within the GUFs are relevant to an analysis from the perspective of organized labour. This essay aims to foster a greater understanding of the challenges to labour and trade unions arising as a result of the expansion of PEFs in Brazil. The first section considers the growth and strategies of PEFs. The second section analyses the impacts of PEFs on labour conditions. The third section identifies challenges to trade unions and their responses.

Fund managers, investment and labour

The global scenario

The contemporary global scenario has favoured the emergence of a new group of social actors: the money operators, the so-called fund managers. It might even be suggested that a new social configuration has emerged around the three pillars of owners of capital, managers and workers in modern society.

Written against the background of British decline and the ascendancy of American supremacy, the work of the nineteenth-century American economist and sociologist Thorstein Veblen represented an effort to understand social behaviour in a market economy. In his *Theory of the leisure class*, Veblen (1965) pointed to the incongruence between the interests of business managers on the one hand, and those of the community at large and the survival of the firm as an institution on the other, noting the spread of the pecuniary culture and of working opportunities related to the social expressions of that pecuniary culture. Nowadays, private equity investment firms tend to prioritize the pecuniary motive in the use of wealth, and their fund managers' chief objective is to select investments that will generate financial returns quickly.

The services performed by fund managers include raising investment funding, analysing financial statements, selecting companies for investment, implementing restructuring programmes and monitoring investments.[9] In essence, they centralize endowments from financial institutions, institutional investors – including pension funds – and wealthy individuals, among others, in order to assume a key role in acquisitions of high profit potential. The investors are attracted by fund managers who offer not only the incentive of high short-term profits but also the seductive detachment that relieves them of any responsibility towards the companies that make up their portfolio of acquisitions.

Thus, under the increasing influence of the PEFs, the movement of wealth takes on an impersonal, "faceless" character, revealing the abstract dimension of capital (see Marx 1978a; Foster 2010). The answers to the questions where and how capital reproduces itself and who benefits from that reproduction revolve around the actions of the fund managers who attract the owners of capital to specific businesses. The fund managers assume full responsibility for the business and thus have autonomy to implement any kind of restructuring strategy they choose. Capital reproduction turns out to benefit the investors, whose return on investment is extracted using whatever elements in the repertoire of alternatives at the disposal of the fund manager will maximize profits most rapidly. As a result, PEF investment in firms frequently leads to changes in working conditions that include, among other features, "increased outsourcing & casualization to cut costs, sell-offs & closures regardless of productivity & profitability; deteriorating working conditions; diminished employment security" (IUF 2007: 17).

This system is highly detrimental to workers already struggling to defend rights hard won over many decades. The challenges that have recently been mounted to employment conditions negotiated by trade unions through collective bargaining reveal the emergence of PEFs as major "invisible" employers.[10] As Rossman and Greenfield pointed out:

> If these private-equity funds were recognized as TNCs (given their extensive control over manufacturing and service companies globally) and included in UNCTAD's top 100 non-financial TNCs, they would easily displace the top 10 corporations. General Electric, ranked first in UNCTAD's list, controls less foreign assets and employs fewer workers overseas than either Blackstone, Carlyle Group or Texas Pacific Group. (2006: 6)

These features of the private equity business model have been particularly present in private equity leveraged buy-out deals.[11] The evidence from the United Kingdom and United States, for example, shows that after takeover many portfolio companies leave the stock market and accumulate high levels of debt to an extent that jeopardizes long-run productive investment and employment.

The PEFs' selection of companies for investment is influenced largely by expectations of short-term cashflow, mainly through anticipated dividends and fees. Investment decisions may also be conditioned by the present and potential capital structure of the company, the potential for operational change, the existence of management incentives and the available exit options. PEFs receive a return on their investment in companies through various means, ranging from an initial public offering (IPO) on the stock market to the sale of the company, often to another fund, a merger, or even dividends paid out by recapitalization. The real target, however, is to sell the company within ten years of the original acquisition.

After 2008, liquidity preference increased in the international environment, putting pressure on the private equity industry to consolidate its operations towards greater concentration at the global level. At the same time, the credit squeeze and the volatility of asset valuations in recession conditions made it difficult to guarantee the required levels of funding and debt provision for many transactions. As a result, following the downturn caused by the international financial crisis, private equity fundraising and investment fell in 2009, particularly sharply in the United States and Europe. Among the rising economies known as the BRICs (Brazil, Russian Federation, India, China), the participation of fund managers in Brazil grew steadily, in terms of both fundraising and capital invested, between 2000 and 2008 (table 7.1).[12] The sharp falls in funds raised in 2009 reflect the restrictions placed on fund managers by the global crisis.

Table 7.1 Private equity funds in the BRICs: Fundraising and investments, 2001–09 (US$ million)

Country	2001	2002	2003	2004	2005	2006	2007	2008	2009
Fundraising									
China	152	105	213	311	2 243	4 279	3 890	14 461	6 671
India	259	142	236	706	2 741	2 884	4 569	7 710	3 999
Brazil	**323**	**270**	**230**	**480**	**158**	**2 098**	**2 510**	**3 589**	**401**
Russia/CIS	375	100	175	200	1 254	222	1 790	890	456
Investment									
China	1 575	126	1 667	1 389	2 991	8 200	9 458	8 994	6 288
India	320	40	456	1 272	1 377	5 687	9 905	7 483	4 011
Brazil	**281**	**261**	**321**	**120**	**474**	**1 342**	**5 285**	**3 020**	**989**
Russia/CIS	77	127	113	240	240	402	805	2 647	217

Source: Emerging Markets Private Equity Association (EMPEA) (2010).

The scenario in Brazil

The comments above emphasize the significance of the PEF business model, particularly in buy-out deals. This kind of investment has been growing in Brazil across many sectors, including real estate, agribusiness, food and education.[13] The PEFs' selection of portfolio companies has been influenced by market share, potential market growth and profits, potential for restructuring, workers' profile and labour organization, among other factors, in a business environment characterized by market concentration.

The capital invested in the private equity industry in Brazil has been growing in the last decade, to a peak of 1.7 per cent of GDP in 2008 (figure 7.1), and the number of companies held in private equity portfolios increased from 306 in 2004 to 482 in June 2008. It is worth noting that foreign investors increased their participation between 2003 and 2006, when they were responsible for 66 per cent of the total capital invested; however, by June 2008 the proportion of foreign investors had fallen to 57 per cent (US$15.2 billion) in a context where private equity firms have been trying to attract more diverse investors (GVcepe 2008).[14] It is also relevant to note the increasing partic - ipation of pension funds in private equity investments since 2000.

In terms of the number of investments (table 7.2), information technology and electronics continued to be one of the main sectors in 2008, although its relative prominence has declined since 2004. The four sectors with the highest increase in number of investments between 2004 and 2008 were: civil construction, communication and media, energy, and education. Of the total number of investments made between January 2005 and June 2008, 3 per cent were related to buy-outs, 9 per cent to later-stage investment and 35 per cent to equity expansion.[15]

Figure 7.1   Private equity in Brazil: Capital invested in relation to GDP,
1999–2008

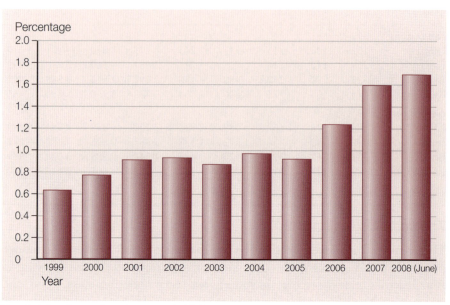

Note: Includes private equity and venture capital deals.

Source: ABDI (2011).

Once a controlling interest in a company has been acquired by a PEF, the implementation of the business model centred on "rationalization" has marked effects on social conditions. GUFs have reported that PEFs, especially in the case of buy-outs, have been threatening employment, working conditions and workers' rights in their acquisitions in pursuit of their financial strategies (IUF 2007). In the United States and many European countries, fund managers' actions have been based on profit targets, with the aim of increasing short-term cashflow, to the detriment of workers' jobs, pay and conditions.[16] Beyond the "rationalization" strategies, social conflicts and tensions are exacerbated as restructuring programmes reshape employment arrangements, fostering increased control and turnover of workers, outsourcing and casual work.

Under pressure from the fund managers to meet economic efficiency targets, the portfolio companies tend to experience a marked deterioration in labour conditions, with longer working hours, job losses, high turnover and increased outsourcing. Workforce displacement and erosion of workers' rights are also part of the repertoire of management options for reducing costs. Montgomerie (2008) gives striking examples of the changing working conditions in Germany and the United Kingdom, showing that labour has

Table 7.2   Private equity funds in Brazil: Investments by sector, 2005–08

Sector	% of total
Civil construction	18
Industrial products and services	16
Information technology; electronics	14
Energy	11
Communication and media	9
Agribusiness	8
Retail	5
Financial services	3
Food and beverages	3
Medicine and cosmetics	3
Transport and logistics	3
Education	3
Infrastructure	2
Biotechnology	1
Other	1
Total	100

Note: Data related to 394 private equity and venture capital investments.

Source: ABDI (2011).

borne the brunt of cost-saving measures, first through longer working hours, then with the abolition of holiday pay, and finally through reductions in the workforce and workers' geographical displacement.

From the 1990s onwards, Brazil implemented policies designed to attract international finance and to reposition itself competitively in the new international division of labour. It has also supported financial liberalization in the expectation that this would enhance investment flows, economic growth and employment. The operation of the economy was recalibrated according to the neoliberal agenda, with macroeconomic policies and regulation of markets directed according to new principles and implemented via new parameters and mechanisms. In order to accommodate national structures to the modernization process, economic, institutional and political reforms have been implemented in accordance with the international financial institutions' agenda, formulated to promote international integration. In the course of this adjustment, increased labour precariousness and flexibilization have been part of the process of eliminating restrictions in pursuit of a homogeneous workforce within the global order. Up to 2004, the economic environment of high real interest rates supported by low inflation targets restricted domestic demand and employment creation. In this context, the search for economic efficiency involved the adoption of cost-reducing strategies, including job reductions, outsourcing, and technological and organizational innovations. These changes resulted in the diversification of labour contracts and informal labour arrangements. After 2004, new credit and minimum wage policies, along with cash transfer programmes, have fostered consumption, investment and job creation,[17] while the recovery of formal employment rates has also been stimulated by government policies favouring formal employment.

The immediate impacts of the 2008 global crisis in Brazil were softened by counter-cyclical domestic policies. With private banks restricting credit growth and putting upward pressure on interest rates, public credit policies were revised and macroeconomic management directed towards the objective of maintaining stability in a situation characterized by liquidity constraints.[18] Government responses to the crisis included measures aimed at increasing liquidity and supporting fundraising in the domestic financial system; reducing exchange rate volatility; supporting credit flows to foreign trade, agriculture and civil construction (housing); and helping private companies facing liquidity constraints with the objective of preserving employment.

The Government's credit strategy was centred on the expansion of domestic credit flows by the public banks. In this respect, Banco do Brasil and Caixa Econômica Federal played an outstanding role in supporting credit flows to households, while the Brazilian development bank BNDES re-established an industrial policy aimed at encouraging investment growth. The Government also continued to increase the real value of the minimum wage, as well as maintaining the cash transfer programme (Bolsa Família). Together, the credit, income and public spending policies adopted by the Government assisted the recovery of aggregate demand and the maintenance of the employment level (as well as increasing levels of formal employment), at the same time as preserving monetary stability.

Within this scenario, infrastructure, civil construction, energy and natural resources have been defined as priority sectors in the Government's agenda in pursuit of social goals and their articulation with economic growth; at the same time, the maintenance of credit policies and income levels has favoured the expansion of the consumer goods and services sectors. Thus, expectations have been raised in connection with these sectors that are now attracting PEF managers alert to their high profit potential (table 7.3).

Where PEF managers have engaged in restructuring in Brazilian companies, their activities have been focused on the unification of financial management, planning and control; growth based on diversification and on new plants, stores (including franchising) and products; and consolidation of new

Table 7.3 Private equity funds in Brazil: Investments and capital invested by sector, 2009

Sector	No. of investments	Capital invested (US$ million)
Services	2	171
Industrial & manufacturing	3	n/a
Infrastructure	4	112
Energy and natural resources	4	232
Consumer	3	291
Banking & financial services	3	187
Media & telecommunications	1	n/a

Source: Emerging Markets Private Equity Association (EMPEA) (2010).

business lines (table 7.4). Fund managers have redefined the guiding principles of corporate management, including the pursuit of profit, according to their remit of "general responsibility" and the concomitant power it confers on them to determine investment flows and employment.

The increasing presence of fund managers and their business model, especially in buy-outs, could deepen some trends that are currently observed in the Brazilian labour market. These trends have contributed not only to the redefinition of labour contracts but also to the establishment of new priorities in unions' negotiations. The impacts of "rationalization" strategies on working conditions and workers' rights include increased outsourcing, informal employment and underemployment, among others.

The repercussions for labour of PEFs' involvement in Brazilian enterprise may be seen from the following examples of declining conditions in some of the recently acquired firms listed in table 7.4.[19]

- **Kroton Educacional:** pressure to fire professors, lack of compliance with labour contracts, difficulty in identifying managers, doubts about social protection, monitoring practices.

- **Casa do Pão de Queijo:** precarious labour, with pressure to extend working hours beyond those specified in labour contracts, including Sundays and holidays; low earnings; accumulation of tasks; increased informal employment.

- **Inpar:** outsourcing practices.

- **Georadar:** violation of workers' rights; low earnings; extension of working hours beyond labour contracts; poor living conditions in seismic research areas.

- **Azul:** general dissatisfaction of aircrew; failure to pay profit-shares until 2010; refusal to honour six-month maternity leave licence.

Table 7.4   Private equity funds in Brazil: Fund managers, companies and restructuring actions, 2009–10

Fund manager	Company: sector	Restructuring actions
Advent International*	Kroton Educacional: educational services & training	New pedagogical model; financial management unification
Axxon Group*	Mundo Verde: consumer/franchising of natural and organic food	Rapid growth based on new products and stores – 345 stores in five years (franchising and internationalization)
Standard Bank Private Equity*	Casa do Pão de Queijo: restaurants	Growth based on new products and stores (franchising); diversification
Paladin Reality Partners*	Inpar: real estate	Capitalization for future growth/new projects
Rio Bravo Investimentos**	Multdia: food & beverages	Financial management unification; capitalization for future growth/new projects
Companhia de Participações**	Pisani: industrial supplies & moulded fibreglass	Growth based on higher production; new plants until 2011
AG Angra**	Georadar: supply services to energy sector	Capitalization for growth and diversification
Green Capital Investments*	Ultracargo: logistics	Creation/consolidation of new business lines
TPG Capital*	Azul: aviation	Capitalization for growth

* Global private equity firm. ** Domestic private equity firm.

Sources: Compiled by authors from company websites.

In Brazil, fund managers are spreading a business model where the target is to sell companies on within ten years of acquisition. The 2008 GVcepe report shows that, between 2004 and 2008, the proportion of exit deals was highest in information technology and electronics, at 29 per cent of the total; this sector was followed by transport and logistics/distribution (19 per cent), medicine and cosmetics (10 per cent) and civil construction (6 per cent), many of them favoured by high liquidity in the Brazilian stock market. Of all the exit deals concluded between January 2005 and June 2008, 11 per cent were related to PE buy-outs, and 40 per cent to PE later-stage and PE expansion. Table 7.5 presents a sample of exit deals in 2009 and 2010.

Table 7.5 Private equity funds in Brazil: A sample of exit deals, 2009–10

Fund manager	Company	Sector	Exit type*
Advent International	CETIP	Banking & financial services	IPO
Axxon Group	Mills	Engineering & construction	IPO/share sale
Gavea Investimentos	Alliance Shopping Centers	Consumer	IPO
GP Investments	BR Malls	Consumer	Share sale
Decisão Gestão de Fundos	DHC Outsourcing	Information technology	Strategic sale
Great Hill Partners	BuscaPé	Information technology	Strategic sale
Pátria Investimentos	Casa do Pão de Queijo	Restaurants	Secondary sale

* IPO = initial public offering;
strategic sale = sale to investors or joint venture partners;
secondary sale = sale of an investor's interest in a private equity holding.

Source: Emerging Markets Private Equity Association (EMPEA) (2010).

The challenges to working conditions in the recently traded companies bear witness to the impact of the fund managers on social life in Brazil. It is important to point out the potential effects on labour in a context where investment trends across the world have been based on norms and practices that favour the reorganization of the labour market. The reality has been shaped by the concentration of industrial markets, leveraged by centralized structures of financial capital. The consequences for labour may include lower wages, demand for new skills and capabilities, increased precariousness of labour and homogenization of working conditions. The unequal relationship between capital and labour has been weighted even more heavily in favour of capital because negotiations between the two sides are based solely on efficiency, the only substantive criterion accepted being labour productivity, as Davidson (2009) has suggested. This rationale has no place for the social identity configured through labour by the workers (Sennet 1998).

Trade unions' responses

The investment and employment patterns underlying present conditions must be seen in a context where new practices reinforce "short-termism" in financialized business. The deregulated institutional arrangements have shaped new interactions among State, capital and labour because labour flexibilization policies favour PEFs' management of portfolio firms in a context where PE investors are especially sensitive to labour adjustment costs (Boskaya and Kerr 2009).

The global response

From an international perspective, the implications of social and economic transformations for trade unions' organization have been similar across the globe, reflecting the common tensions prevailing around the world (Gonçalves et al. 2009). In current conditions, the possibilities for workers' action through their representative institutions could include restructuring workers' organizations by means of mergers and internal reorganization; increased activism at the grass roots with mobilization of more workers; construction of alliances and coalitions to legitimize actions for social and economic change; cooperation between unions and other movements, at both national and international levels; and partnerships with employers and governments to protect and improve workers' interests (Kumar and Schenk 2006).

However, how different categories of workers understand the challenges facing them depends on their comprehension of the objective prevailing conditions, seen in the light of the recent history of union battles. The challenges now faced by workers and unions require support for universal demands of a political nature. In the context of the global crisis, the national States that intervened in the defence of institutions that were defined as national must also be called on to preserve the rights historically fought for and won by the workers.

In the face of challenges from the private equity business model, Global Unions have been defending the claim that the reregulation agenda could promote long-term productive investment growth, employment creation based on the Decent Work Agenda, employment security and protection of trade unions' rights.[20] This claim reflects a strong concern about the risks that PEFs, mainly through buy-outs, pose to the stability of the international financial system and the sustainable growth of national economies (Tate 2006).

Responses in Brazil

Recent actions by Brazilian trade unions have been characterized by adaptive resistance strategies that favour economic issues. It is worth remembering that the Brazilian trade union movement suffered an interruption in the military dictatorship period and then returned strongly in the 1980s, stimulated by the process of redemocratization. Since then, a "new" unionism has been organized and central unions have been created. During the inflationary crisis of the 1980s the new unionism concentrated on defending the workers' positions on the negotiation of economic issues. In the following decade, the institutional transformations that accompanied the rise of neoliberalism enhanced the adoption of a defensive agenda by the trade unions to meet the challenges posed by the new employment and working conditions (Gonçalves et al. 2006). From the 1990s onwards, corporations have been trying to limit the unions' power in a context where the implementation of cost and efficiency strategies has affected working conditions and workers' rights beyond the legal framework of collective contracts. The adoption of economic criteria to guide collective negotiations has threatened the trade unions' cohesion and favoured the emergence of interest groups with specific demands.[21]

The rise of neoliberalism has increased social risks, modified human relations and spread in daily life a feeling of powerlessness to transform existing conditions that has constrained the workers' capacity to organize around universal demands. The increasing participation of Brazilian pension funds in private equity investments, as the result of portfolio diversification, has become a concern of social significance beyond the workers' specific demands.[22] In 2008 private equity capital investments represented almost 1.7 per cent of Brazilian GDP; the proportion of these investments coming from domestic pension funds has grown since 2000, achieving 22 per cent in 2009 (ABDI 2009).[23]

The workers' pension funds have recently invested in PEFs that acquire companies in sectors where the investments are socially relevant and articulated with economic growth. Nevertheless, concern attaches to the relationship between these pension funds – as investors – and PEF managers. The presence of the pension funds as investors generates expectations that workers' rights will be respected.[24] International experience on this point could usefully inform the discussion in Brazil – indeed, the nature of the PEFs requires a trade union strategy that is necessarily global.

Final considerations

The 2008 global crisis revealed the close links between national States and financial capital. It also highlighted the impacts of financialization in business models, with new employment and working conditions expressing the conflict between so-called competitive growth and the prioritization of long-term social needs. Thus, the contradictions between financial hypertrophy and the expectations of society – in respect of citizenship, work and income – reflected the tensions in the relations between State, capital and society, overwhelmed by homogenization and resistance in labour markets (Madi and Gonçalves 2008). The challenges to trade unions in Brazil, under pressure from the private equity business model, could open up new perspectives in organized labour, both economic and political.

The scenario described in this chapter shows the potential for the expansion of the private equity business model to promulgate the valorization of financial wealth, which tends to reduce the participation of workers in income. The challenges to trade unions in Brazil reflect the complex reconfiguration of the labour market in conditions of fragmentation that limit the potential for organization. The future strategy for worker representation needs to be fostered through new articulations centred on the global dimension in the international market.

Notes

[1] On the social and economic transformations related to financialization, see Offe (1989); Lasch (1995); Belluzzo (1997); Chesnais (1997); Kumar (2005); Philips (2006).

[2] On the role and impact of the financial conditions on the dynamics of production, circulation and consumption, see Marx (1978a), Book I, ch. 23; Book III, chs. 30–32.

[3] Capital without locus refers to processes of accumulation and reproduction with no spatial restrictions.

[4] The reorganization of the organizations that represent workers' interests has accompanied historical changes (Hobsbawm 1984). As suggested by Kumar and Schenk (2006), the current new trends include restructuring workers' organizations by means of mergers and internal reorganization; the emergence of alliances and coalitions; and cooperation between unions and social movements.

[5] On the impact of management buy-outs on efficiency and employment, see Harris et al. (2005); Cressy et al. (2007); Jensen (2007).

[6] The idea of "vanishing" employers was raised by Rossman and Greenfield (2006).

[7] On the structural dimension of the financial crisis in a historical perspective, see Belluzzo (1997); Chesnais (1997).

[8] In 2008 there were 5.9 million formal small and medium enterprises, equivalent to 97.5 per cent of all enterprises established in Brazil. In that year, small businesses accounted for 51 per cent of the urban labour force employed in the private sector, equivalent to 13.2 million formal jobs, 38 per cent of wages and 20 per cent on average of GDP.

[9] On fund managers' practices see Klier et al. (2009); Pappas et al. (2009); Scholes et al. (2009).

[10] In this sense, the current debate is centred on the rationale of the subordination of labour to capital as a result of the contemporary transformations in business models. On the formal and real subsumption of labour to capital see Marx (1978b).

[11] Private equity investments range from leveraged buy-outs to venture capital for start-ups and other types of seed capital. Their performance has varied widely (Kaplan and Schoar 2003).

[12] Kaplan and Schoar (2003) have analysed the cyclical nature of the private equity business.

[13] In Brazil, the private equity industry includes (a) PEFs that acquire companies in the phases of restructuring, consolidation and/or expansion and (b) venture capital funds for start-ups and other types of seed capital. The portfolio companies can be traded publicly. The PEFs have been increasingly prominent in terms of fundraising and number of deals made.

[14] Most PEF managers operating in Brazil are Brazilian, though foreign fund managers have been prominent in high-volume capital investments. Domestic roots seem to be an important feature of the typical fund manager's profile.

[15] The 2008 GVcepe report divides private equity investments into three types: PE buy-out (acquisition of control of companies in later stages of development); PE expansion (capitalization of companies with growth potential); and PE later stage (investment in companies with stable and positive cashflow).

[16] This reflects Marx's understanding: "The highest ideal of capitalist production – corresponding to the relative growth of the *produit net* – is the greatest possible reduction of those living on wages, the greatest possible increase in those living of *produit net*" (Marx 1978b: 83).

[17] On the dynamics of aggregate demand and employment, see Keynes (1988).

[18] For discussion of the lessons learned in the global financial crisis, see Blanchard et al. (2010).

[19] http://www.jusbrasil.com.br; http://www.diap.org.br; http://revista.construcaomercado.com.br; http://www.conlutas.org.br; http://www.aeronautas.org.br; http://www.pstu.org.br (all accessed 16 June 2011).

[20] The main features of a regulatory reform proposal can be found in ITUC (2007). The proposal has drawn on joint efforts and activities by the International Union of Food, Agricultural, Hotel, Restaurant, Catering, Tobacco and Allied Workers' Association (IUF) and UNI, as well as cooperation with the Trade Union Advisory Committee to the OECD (TUAC), the International Trade Union Confederation (ITUC) and the International Metalworkers' Federation, among others.

[21] The current trend is mainly centred on demands that could enable the appropriation of the wealth produced by workers.

[22] One year after the crisis, the National Monetary Council modified the regulatory framework of pension funds in order to favour portfolio diversification (Resolution 792, September 2009).

[23] The main pension funds are Previ, Funcef, Petros and Valia, connected respectively to Banco do Brasil, Caixa Econômica Federal, Petrobras and Vale.

[24] Global Unions have reported challenges to pension funds' investments in private equity buy-out deals (ITUC 2007).

Resources

Agência Brasileira de Desenvolvimento Industrial (ABDI). 2011. *A Indústria de Private Equity e Venture Capital* [*The Private Equity and Venture Capital Industry*] Second Brazilian Census (Brasília).

Belluzzo, L.G. 1997. "Dinheiro e as transformações da riqueza" [Money and the transformations of wealth], in M.C. Tavares and J.L. Fiori (eds): *Poder e dinheiro* (Petrópolis, Vozes).

Blanchard, O. et al. 2010. *Rethinking macroeconomic policy* (Washington, DC, International Monetary Fund).

Boskaya, A.; Kerr, W. 2009. *Labor regulations and European private equity*, Harvard Business School Working Paper 08-043 (Cambridge, MA).

Bugra, A.; Agartan, K. (eds). 2008. *Market economy as a political project: Reading Karl Polanyi for the 21st century* (Basingstoke, Palgrave Macmillan).

Chesnais, F. 1997. *La mondialisation financière* (Paris, Syros).

Cressy, R. et al. 2007. *Creative destruction? UK evidence that buyouts cut jobs to raise returns*, University of Birmingham Business School, http://www.business.bham.ac.uk/research/eic/papers/CreativeDestruction.pdf (accessed 16 June 2011).

Davidson, P. 2009. *The Keynes solution* (New York, Palgrave).

Emerging Markets Private Equity Association (EMPEA). 2010 Available at: http://www.empea.net/ (accessed 16 June 2011).

Foster, J.B. 2010. "The financialization of accumulation", in *Monthly Review*, Vol. 62, No. 5 (Oct.), http://monthlyreview.org/2010/10/01/the-financialization-of-accumulation (accessed 16 June 2011).

Gonçalves, J. et al. 2006. "Condições de trabalho e sindicalismo no setor bancário no Brasil" [Working conditions and trade unions in the Brazilian banking sector], in J.D. Krein et al. (eds).

—. 2009. *Labour and trade unions in the financial sector: Challenges and perspectives in contemporary Brazil* (Mumbai, Global Labour University).

GVcepe. 2008. *Panorama da indústria Brasileira de private equity and venture capital*, research report [Overview of the Brazilian industry of private equity and venture capital] (São Paulo, Fundação Getúlio Vargas).

Harris, R. et al. 2005. "Assessing the impact of management buyouts on economic efficiency", in *Review of Economics and Statistics*, Vol. 87, No. 1, pp. 148–53.

Hobsbawm, E. 1984. *Worlds of labour* (London, Weidenfeld & Nicolson).

International Trade Union Confederation (ITUC). 2007. *Where the house always wins: Private equity, hedge funds and the new casino capitalism* (Brussels).

International Union of Food, Agricultural, Hotel, Restaurant, Catering, Tobacco and Allied Workers' Association (IUF). 2007. *A workers' guide to private equity buyouts* (Geneva).

Jacoby, S. 2008. *Finance and labour: Perspectives on risk, inequality, and democracy*, working paper, University of California at Los Angeles (Los Angeles, California Digital Library).

Jensen, M. 2007. *The economic case for private equity (and some concerns)*, Harvard Negotiations, Organizations and Markets Unit Working Paper No. 07-02 (Cambridge, MA, Harvard University).

Kaplan, S.; Schoar, A. 2003. *Private equity performance*, Sloan Working Paper No. 4446-03 (Cambridge, MA, Massachusetts Institute of Technology).

Keynes, J.M. 1988. *A teoria geral do emprego, do juro e da moeda* [General theory of employment, interest and money] (São Paulo, Nova Cultural).

Klier, D. et al. 2009. "The changing face of private equity: How modern private equity firms manage investment portfolios", in *Journal of Private Equity*, Vol. 12, No. 4, pp. 7–13.

Krein, J.D. et al. (eds). 2006. *As transformações no mundo do trabalho e os direitos dos trabalhadores* [The transformations in the world of labour and the workers' rights] (São Paulo, CESIT/LTr Publishers).

Kumar, K. 2005. *From post-industrial to post-modern society* (Oxford, Blackwell).

—; Schenk, C. 2006. *Paths to union renewal: Canadian experiences* (Ontario, Broadview Press).

Lasch, C. 1995. *The revolt of the elites and the betrayal of democracy* (New York, Norton).

Madi, M.A.; Gonçalves, J.R. 2008. "Corporate social responsibility and market society: Credit and banking inclusion in Brazil", in A. Bugra and K. Agartan (eds).

Marx, K. 1978a. *El Capital* (Mexico City, Siglo XXI).

—. 1978b. Capítulo VI (inédito) do *Capital* [Draft chapter 6 of *Capital*] (São Paulo, Livraria Editora Ciências Humanas).

Montgomerie, J. 2008. "Labour and the locusts: Private equity's impact on the economy and the labour market", in *Conference report of the Seventh British–German Trades Union Forum* (London, Anglo-German Foundation for the Study of Industrial Society).

Offe, C. 1989. *Trabalho e sociedade* [Work and society] (Rio de Janeiro, Tempo Brasileiro).

Pappas, G. et al. 2009. "Why private equity are restructuring (and not just their portfolio companies)", in *Journal of Private Equity*, Vol. 12, No. 4, pp. 22–28.

Philips, K. 2006. *American theocracy* (New York, Viking).

Rossman, P.; Greenfield, G. 2006. "Financialization: New routes to profit, new challenges for trade unions", in *Labour Education: Quarterly Review of the ILO Bureau for Workers' Activities*, No. 142 (Geneva).

Scholes, L. et al. 2009. "Family-firm buyouts, private equity and strategic change", in *Journal of Political Economy*, Vol. 12, No. 2, pp. 7–18.

Sennet, R. 1998. *The corrosion of character: The personal consequences of work in the new capitalism* (New York, Norton).

Tate, A. 2006. "The effect of private equity takeovers on corporate social responsibility", speech delivered to Australian Council of Trade Unions, Melbourne.

Veblen, T. 1965. *The theory of the leisure class* (New York, A.M. Kelley).

LABOUR AND THE LOCUSTS: TRADE UNION RESPONSES TO CORPORATE GOVERNANCE REGULATION IN THE EUROPEAN UNION

8

Laura Horn

Introduction

In the context of the financial and economic crisis that began in 2007, many observers have looked to the Left for alternative strategies to deal with the fallout from the collapse of finance-dominated, market-driven policies. It is commonly assumed that the crisis not only corroborates the analyses and arguments of critics of unfettered market capitalism, but that we are indeed witnessing a conjunctural "window of opportunity" for alternative policy proposals and political strategies to enter into the policy-making arena. Organized labour, in particular trade unions, perceived as "regulated representative constituencies of the Real Economy" (TUAC 2008), here represents a central node of agency in emerging networks of contestation, on the national as well as the European and international level. As John Monks, then General Secretary of the European Trade Union Confederation (ETUC), declared, "the conditions are there for a trade union counter attack" (Monks 2008). At the same time, rising job losses and unemployment levels, and pressure on real wages, have put organized labour (once again) in a defensive position. None of the bail-out plans have been initiated in response to pressure from below, that is, from trade union associations or civil society networks. Labour representation and interests are becoming more and more fragmented at both the company and the national level, while the institutional configuration of the EU has been deeply permeated by governance structures that are conducive to market-making, neoliberal policies rather than those conducive to strengthening the alleged "European social model". A leading scholar of the political economy of European integration has even gone so far as to call trade union enthusiasm about the European social model a "delusion" (Scharpf 2008).

What, then, is the role of organized labour at the EU level, and indeed, to what extent does Europe constitute an important political and institutional terrain for alternative socio-economic perspectives and initiatives? This chapter seeks to engage with the agency and strategies of organized labour at the EU level by analysing trade union responses to EU corporate governance regulation. "Corporate governance" here refers to those practices that define and reflect the power relations within the corporation and the way, and to what purpose, it is run (Van Apeldoorn and Horn 2007). Corporate governance regulation in the EU is increasingly shifting towards financial market imperatives: that is, towards a regulatory perspective focusing exclusively on the interests of shareholders (Horn 2011). Labour law, once an integral part of regulating the modern corporation, is more and more relegated to the area of social affairs and employment law, and provisions for workers' rights with regard to corporate control are increasingly marginalized. Questions of corporate control, as expressed in corporate governance regulation, go to the very heart of late industrialized capitalism. It is in this arena that contesting ideological perspectives on ownership and socio-economic organization collide most immediately. Yet whereas collective bargaining, the right to strike and working conditions have been at the centre of trade union strategies and demands, regulation of corporate governance and financial markets on the EU level has often come about outside the purview of trade unions. It is only in recent years that corporate control and corporate governance have become more politicized and contested, often in parallel with the broader debate about corporate ownership and the debate about alternative investment structures.

The chapter is structured as follows. The next section offers an overview of the conceptual and political discussions surrounding the agency of organized labour at the EU level. Subsequent sections introduce corporate governance regulation, both conceptually and as a crucial element of neoliberal restructuring at the EU level, in particular with regard to the marketization of corporate control. Here, the shift from the focus on "industrial democracy" in the 1970s to that on a "shareholder democracy" in the mid-2000s serves as a storyline. The chapter then concludes with a view on recent developments, in particular with regard to the financial and economic crisis.

Perspectives on organized labour at the EU level

International political economy analyses have long focused on the agency of transnational capital and business actors, while a focus on labour as a political actor has been fairly marginal (Harrod and O'Brien 2002: 15). A common perception is that organized labour, despite its often internationalist ideology, is still rooted at the national level and has become a conservative and inflexible force with dwindling membership, unable to adapt its strategies to the new supra- and transnational realities. And indeed, as Hyman sums up (2004: 19–20), the challenges to traditional unionism have been manifold, ranging from external factors, such as the intensification of competition across countries, regions and sectors, the internationalization of chains of production and the deregulation of the labour market, to internal challenges such as the erosion of the "normal" employment relationship, extensive social and generational changes and the consequent decline of trade union membership.

Trade unions, as the primary manifestation of organized labour in industrialized capitalism, are faced with a fundamental dilemma. While on the one hand their objective is to at least negotiate the worst social consequences of capitalism with a focus on the underprivileged, at the same time the majority of their rank-and-file membership is composed of the relatively advantaged, core section of the working class. (The pattern of course varies according to the political and confessional orientation of particular trade unions.) This dilemma raises the questions of whose interests trade unions represent, and which interests take precedence in their immediate and long-term actions (Hyman 2004: 23). *How* these interests are represented depends upon organizational and political choices made by the trade unions. Here unions often find themselves in a situation as *managers of discontent* (see Mills 1948). In order to comply with their own political and social goals, and maintain the allegiance of their members, trade unions have to articulate (elements of) class struggle at the individual, firm, sectoral or national level. Yet at the same time, in order to maintain their standing as acknowledged political actors, recognized for their intermediary role between workers on the one hand, and employers and the State on the other, they need to constrain this class struggle and channel it into manageable relationships in order to maintain the class compromises that underlie many of the advanced industrialized capitalist societies.

There are different mechanisms through which organized labour can seek to advance these objectives. Traditional union strategies have been class action at the firm, sectoral or national level, as well as close political cooperation with social democratic or other (confessional) parties. Through these means organized labour has long represented an interest group in national politics, manifest in, for example, corporatist arrangements. Increasingly, trade unions have also become engaged in "partnerships" with business at the firm level, in firm-specific agreements (which in the case of multinational corporations can take on a transnational character). International cooperation between trade unions through, for example, Global Union secretariats or TUAC has become more important for the coordination and organization of union strategies; however, the main space for action remains at the national level. As will be discussed in more detail in the following section, in recent years unions have increasingly established cooperation with social movements (see Bieler 2008). However, as Hyman points out, engaging in "contentious politics" potentially "redefines unions as outsiders in a terrain where until recently the role of insiders was comforting and rewarding" (Hyman 2004: 22). Indeed, as the next section shows, with regard to organized labour at the EU level the insider role does seem to have been more appealing so far.

In the shadow of integration? Trade union agency at the EU level

Organized labour, in particular the ETUC, has been perceived as, put bluntly, co-opted into the project of neoliberal restructuring (Bieling and Schulten 2003; see also Taylor and Mathers 2004). The ETUC and the European Industry Federations, set up as lobby organizations for worker interests at the EU level, have been incorporated into the emerging system of labour relations characterized by the European Social Dialogue and firm-level agreements. In particular, reassured by the implicit promises latent in Delors' vision of a "European social model", trade unions entered into a tacit agreement that intensified market competition and deregulation were unavoidable (Bieling 2001: 100). The institutionalization of the Social Dialogue in the Maastricht Social Chapter in 1991 has led to what Bieling and Schulten have called symbolic Eurocorporatism, incorporating trade union associations into the hegemonic bloc supporting neoliberal restructuring, while all the same "keeping alive their functionalist hopes of a slow but steady expansion of European social regulation" (Bieling and Schulten 2003: 245). The Social Dialogue channelled conflicts between capital and labour into a non-binding social partnership forum, effectively blunting the sharp edges of the antagonistic relations resulting from neoliberal restructuring.

Trade union strategies at the EU level are mainly articulated within the EU institutional framework. This, however, means that initiatives and policy objectives also remain *within* the broader political context of neoliberal restructuring, rather than posing a fundamental alternative to it. The question then remains to what extent organized labour can indeed be seen as a potential counter-hegemonic actor, and to what extent the institutional terrain of the EU would be the appropriate place for social struggles. Yet even though the space for organized labour agency is limited, there remain avenues for trade unions. As Erne points out, unions are not passive victims of the EU integration process but agents capable of politicizing its contradictions (Erne 2008: 199). While labour has, in the absence of strong uniform representation on the EU level and framed in the soft model of the Social Dialogue, acquiesced in the neoliberal programme under the promise of competitiveness and job growth, there is now increasing disillusionment with the flanking measures of the European social model.

In order to analyse the potential for contestation of and resistance to neoliberal socio-economic restructuring, the position and agency of subaltern classes in European governance have to be seen from a perspective that acknowledges the fundamental power asymmetries in the EU (Van Apeldoorn, Drahokoupil and Horn 2008). It is through the articulation of, and struggle between, concrete political projects that social forces shape European integration. Regulation here represents a juridico-political manifestation of the struggle between particular political projects, albeit one subject to political concessions and compromises. Rather than perceiving regulation as a functional outcome of the drive to improve efficiency by correcting market failures, in the understanding of this study regulatory developments are perceived as part and parcel of political projects. As Van Apeldoorn's analysis (2002: 78) of rival projects of European integration shows, the crucial question is: *what kind* of market is being promoted? The concept of the political project here serves as a starting point for the analysis, enabling its discursive and operative dimensions to be investigated empirically, while at the same time it is seen in the context of wider structural changes. As concrete, and more or less coherent, manifestations of social interests with regard to particular socio-economic issues, political projects are subject to internal contradictions as well as contestation by opposing social forces. As such, it is through an analysis of political struggle, as well as of the compromises and consensus necessary to sustain hegemonic projects, that the contours of rival political projects become most clear. Hegemony in a Gramscian sense is in fact never complete, and subordinate groups and classes may always struggle to redefine the terms of the dominant discourse and transform underlying social practices. This point, again, indicates the open-ended nature of the process of European integration, as well as the emancipatory potential within the European arena.

The transformation of corporate governance regulation at the EU level

Corporate governance here refers to *those practices that define and reflect the power relations within the corporation and the way, and the purpose to which, it is run.* This understanding of corporate governance differs from a law and economics perspective in focusing on the social power relations in the corporation, rather than perceiving corporate governance mainly as a technical solution for agency problems; for example, how "investors get the managers to give them back their money" (Shleifer and Vishny 1996: 737). At the level of the firm, this latter interpretation is expressed most clearly in the rise of "shareholder value" as the new ideological paradigm for corporate governance (cf. Lazonick and O'Sullivan 2000; Aglietta and Rebérioux 2005). The marketization of corporate control puts the corporation, its management and workers more firmly under the discipline of the capital market. In this context it is important to emphasize that the organizational form of the modern corporation did not come about as the inevitable outcome of economic processes, in which it emerged as the most efficient – that is, transaction-cost-minimizing – way of organizing production. Its organizational form, as well as its purpose (that is, in whose interest it should be run), is continuously sustained by the legal framework provided through the State. Rather than seeing corporate governance regulation in terms of de- or reregulation, as is often the case, what we need to explain is the *qualitative change* in corporate law and other regulatory domains pertaining to the social relations of the corporation. The focus here needs to be on the *political* process through which a particular regulation regime emerges, with law as a fundamental arena for political struggle.

From industrial to shareholder democracy?

In a 1975 Green Paper on Employee Participation and Company Structure, the European Commission argued that "employees are increasingly seen to have interests in the functioning of enterprises which can be as substantial as those of shareholders, and sometimes more so" (European Commission 1975: 9). Now, just three decades later, little is left of this strong emphasis on the role of workers in company-level decision-making. Rather than *industrial democracy*, the Commission has been pushing for a *shareholder democracy* (European Commission 2003). This earlier focus on industrial democracy emerged from a conjunctural shift in the power relations between (organized) labour and industrial capital in the EU, which came to an end towards the end of the 1970s (Streeck and Schmitter 1991: 139). From the late 1980s onwards, the diverging national systems of "industrial citizenship" were no longer to be harmonized; rather, the objective was to ensure that these different systems could be integrated in, and made to sustain, the single market, and that to this end a minimum level of workers' rights was guaranteed. Mandatory provisions were abandoned in favour of a more flexible approach providing national policy-makers and companies with alternative options in implementing information and consultation rights. Worker rights were increasingly relegated to the area of labour law, covered by the Directorate-General for Employment and Social Affairs (DG Social Affairs) (Streeck 1998). Company law and corporate governance regulation fell within the exclusive remit of the Internal Market and Services Directorate-General (DG Internal Market). Consequently, the focus changed towards establishing information and consultation rights, rather than participation rights with potentially redistributive consequences.

There have, of course, been several concessions to labour at the EU level, in particular with regard to the European Works Council (EWC) and the directive accompanying the European Company Statute (SE) in 2001. However, these regulatory developments provided at best *flanking measures* which served to bind labour into the emerging project of neoliberal restructuring. Instead of supranational harmonization, an increasingly complex level of coordination arrangements allowed firms to negotiate their own frameworks of worker rights. While company law directives had established several minimum provisions for companies, workers' rights had to be asserted and negotiated anew with every new legislative proposal of the Commission. With regard to labour law, corporate governance regulation is at best *defensive*, to the extent that workers are to keep acquired rights, and are guaranteed consultation rights in a process of corporate restructuring (e.g. in the formation of an SE). In general, however, with the regulatory framework granting more and more scope for firm-level arrangements and self-regulatory corporate governance standards and codes, employee protection was increasingly dislodged from the regulatory focus on corporate governance. Corporate governance was now increasingly perceived in a narrower sense, that is, pertaining exclusively to the internal and external control mechanisms between shareholders and managers. The objective of regulation turned away from protection of "stakeholders" towards a focus on creating a framework conducive to the "efficient" functioning of capital markets, relegating worker rights to the social policy domain. To be sure, labour law as a legal field is of course far broader than questions of employee participation and works councils (Zumbansen 2006). As such, however, the institutional and legal separation of employee rights and shareholder rights within the regulatory context of company law reflects, and at the same time perpetuates, the conceptual difference between the interests of shareholders and those of other stakeholders in the corporation. A narrowly conceived perception of corporate governance advances an understanding of the role of regulation that precludes the inclusion of labour in the regulatory focus. At the same time, it reinforces the institutional separation between corporate governance and labour law, as manifest at the EU level.

Corporate governance and labour: Room for agency at the EU level?

What, then, has been the role of organized labour at the EU level during this process? In particular through "symbolic Eurocorporatism" (Bieling and Schulten 2003) within the structure of the Social Dialogue, organized labour was implicated in the restructuring of social relations according to the requirements of increasingly integrated European financial markets. The transformation of corporate governance regulation was an important part of this integration process; however, as workers' rights were relegated to the arena of social policy and employment, organized labour did not concentrate to any great extent on the company law programme as such. The struggle over the Service Directive in 2004 or the right to strike has occupied labour associations on the EU level much more than the Commission's initiatives with regard to corporate governance.

When the Commission presented its Company Law Action Plan in 2003, there was no mention of worker rights at all in the policy programme. This was a turning point for the ETUC's position on the Commission's project. As a senior member of the ETUC's research institute points out, "we realized that we as a trade union didn't have anything to do with this – there is this Action Plan but we're doing Social Dialogue".[1] The ETUC strongly opposed the underlying orientation of the Action Plan, arguing in its input to the consultation that "governance is presented as a problem limited solely to the relationship between shareholders and management, as though an enterprise were a private entity that concerned the interests of shareholders alone" (ETUC 2003: 4). In May 2006, the ETUC Executive Committee adopted a resolution on "Corporate Governance at the European Level", in which it cautiously argued that the "European corporate governance framework should lay down proper institutional conditions for companies to promote long-term profitability and employment prospects, define mechanisms that prevent mismanagement and guarantee transparency and accountability with regard to investments and their returns" (ETUC 2006). The ETUC has also emphasized that Article 138 of the Treaty on European Union (now Articles 145–55 of the Treaty on the Functioning of the European Union) provides for the consultation of social partners on a range of issues concerning employment and social affairs. However, the structural separation of worker rights and company law/corporate governance regulation has put company law issues beyond the reach of social partnership for the present.[2]

There have, nevertheless, been several initiatives challenging the deep-seated hegemony of the shareholder value paradigm. There are different aspects to the agency of organized labour in this context – most importantly the question of epistemic resistance and alternatives, as well as the issue of strategic alliances. With regard to the former, in its Strategy and Action Plan for 2007–11 the ETUC stepped up the rhetoric, demanding that "it should not be left to managers and investors – nor the European Commission – alone to define what companies do for society. Workers' participation is not a private affair in the hands of employers. It is a public matter which, if need be, must be politically imposed against the wishes of employers and investors" (ETUC 2007: 79).

In expert groups at the EU level, company law experts broadly affiliated with organized labour have repeatedly made attempts to put the question of workers' rights on the legislative agenda.[3] However, the depoliticization inherent in the expert-driven process of regulatory articulation renders concrete political contestation more difficult, in particular in a discursive context in which the boundaries of corporate governance, and the regulatory debate in general, are predominantly defined according to the exigencies of capital markets. Still, there have been attempts to challenge the role of (shareholder-value-oriented) expert knowledge in the regulatory process and to provide alternative expertise (see PES 2007; Euromemorandum 2011).

In addition to challenging the discourse of shareholder value, organized labour, at the European as well as the national level, participated in broad civil society networks calling for reform of the financial system – even before the financial crisis, for example with regard to a financial transaction tax.[4] Moreover, the corporate governance programme has also been challenged by other EU-level actors. For instance, in the context of an own initiative report on corporate governance, the Parliament called on the Commission to "tak[e] the European social model into consideration when deciding on further measures for the development of company law; this also involves the participation of employees" (European Parliament 2006). In marked contrast to the Commission's programme, the Parliament stressed that "corporate governance is not only about the relationship between shareholders and managers, but … other stakeholders within the company are also important for a balanced decision-making process and should be able to contribute to decisions on the strategy of companies; … in particular, there should be room for the provision of information to, and consultation of, employees" (European Parliament 2006). In this context, there have been indications of an emerging cooperation between labour and the European Parliament (in particular, not surprisingly, the Socialist grouping).

A preliminary summary, then, would confirm that there is indeed room for agency of organized labour in the contestation of corporate governance regulation at the EU level. The next question is: what has been the impact on these developments of the financial and economic crisis that became manifest in the EU from 2008 onwards?

After the crisis? Regulatory reactions in corporate governance at the EU level

While the financial crisis has been most prominently a crisis of liquidity, it has also revealed the pathologies of market-based corporate governance. Regulatory reactions, however, have without exception adopted a problem-solving approach, focusing on "fixing the flaws" in the system rather than considering radically different policy choices. Given the firm entrenchment of the shareholder value paradigm within the regulatory domain, this does not really come as a surprise. Rather, it is a continuation of the corporate governance discourse already articulated in response to the corporate scandals of the early 2000s.

The question confronting regulators, then, is not whether marketized corporate governance regulation can (or should) be maintained, but how to find best practices to make the system work better; how to fine-tune technical issues; and, if necessary, how to insert regulatory gussets to ensure supervision capable of pre-empting market failures. This is rather well illustrated by the OECD's identification of the issues most immediately linked to financial crisis: the governance of remuneration processes; effective implementation of risk management; board practices; and the exercise of shareholder rights (OECD 2009: 2). At the EU level, following the report by the De Larosière group, a reconstruction of financial market supervision has been initiated. The Commission has also drawn up regulatory initiatives in direct response to the failure of several corporate governance mechanisms that have become central in corporate governance practices in the EU, for example with regard to executive remuneration, albeit only in the form of recommendations. Most provisions for enhanced disclosure and control mechanisms for executive remuneration, however, pertain to shareholders and the board only, rather than granting other stakeholders voice, or at least a right to consultation (beyond employer representation on boards) on these important issues. It is notable that the bulk of regulatory initiatives in response to the crisis have concerned regulations pertaining to market mechanisms which had previously been brought up by a variety of actors, including the ETUC – for instance, with regard to the regulation of credit-rating agencies – but were only taken up by the Commission in reaction to the crisis.

Is another mode of corporate governance possible?

The discussion about corporate governance has become increasingly politicized, with the European Parliament taking an ever more critical position on the Commission's policy initiatives. The Commission's decision to drop the 14th Company Law Directive for the cross-border transfer of the registered office of a company, which resulted in a resolution in the Parliament, or the debates over the Alternative Investment Fund Manager Directive, demonstrate that, in contrast to just a decade ago, corporate governance has indeed become a contested concept at the EU level. Interestingly, the European Commission seems to have developed doubts about its own policies, as a recent Green Paper by the Commission confirms:

> the financial crisis has shown that confidence in the model of the shareholder-owner who contributes to the company's long-term viability has been severely shaken, to say the least … The Commission is aware that this problem does not affect only financial institutions. More generally, it raises questions about the effectiveness of corporate governance rules based on the presumption of effective control by shareholders. (European Commission 2010)

This is quite remarkable, given that just a couple of years ago the then Commissioner McCreevy was still keen on declaring shareholders "king or queen" of the corporation. However, this tentative expression of a potential change in regulatory orientation raises several important questions. At this stage, it remains to be seen whether the by now firmly embedded marketization of corporate control will prove resilient to the regulatory changes spurred on by the immediate and mid-term regulatory responses to the crisis. Is the European Commission, situated as it is within the terrain of strategic selectivity, indeed backpedalling on its earlier programme, or is this mainly a discursive shift, a concession to assuage public criticism until neoliberal order is restored? It is important to note here that, while the Commission's statement is very interesting indeed, as argued above the "common sense" of corporate governance has not changed in its core.[5] Corporate control is still perceived as bifurcated, with control for shareholders within the corporate governance and company law domain, and all issues pertaining to "stakeholders" situated within the domain of social affairs and employment. Corporate social responsibility, environmental reporting and socially responsible investment might all be significant avenues meriting exploration within the regulatory terrain of the EU, but as long as control remains firmly isolated and exclusively allocated to owners of capital, the core of the marketization project remains intact.

However, as the financial crisis and its consequences have exacerbated the growing asymmetries in the EU, the contestation of these EU policies has also strengthened, in particular in the context of the sustained legitimacy crisis of the European Union. Both the epistemic contestation of shareholder value and strategic alliances formed by organized labour have become more prominent. An expert group commissioned by the ETUI has recently drawn together and published an edited volume emphasizing the urgency and necessity of a "sustainable company" concept (Vitols and Kluge 2011). The contributions discuss the academic and intellectual history of the shareholder value paradigm and establish the underlying principles for a sustainable company. Moreover, a range of ideas and demands that organized labour, the European Parliament and NGOs have been putting forward for a long time are now being openly discussed – who would have ever expected to see Member States' governments and the European Commission embracing the idea of a financial transaction tax?

Concluding remarks

Whether the current financial and economic crisis indeed represents a conjunctural terrain upon which opposition to neoliberal European governance can be formed remains to be seen. With regard to corporate governance and company law at least, organized labour has for the most part been struggling to maintain and defend the concessions made by capital at the EU level, rather than establishing an alternative to neoliberal restructuring. With the immediate regulatory response directed at the "obvious" culprits – that is, in the case of this financial crisis, investment bankers and credit-rating agencies – the scope for further regulatory action is increasingly limited by the established market-making regulation and the legal basis of European integration. What is more, the assumption that the crisis will be a turning point for neoliberal market integration is premature as long as the structural dominance of financial capitalism is still prevalent in the EU. However, this does not necessarily mean that trade unions have no option but to revert to mainly national strategies. Trade unions are increasingly using the EU as an alternative space for mobi - lization, and are also increasingly voicing criticism about European governance (Gajewska 2008). At the same time, the European Parliament is becoming an important ally for trade union organizations (witness, for example, the call for a Social Progress Clause in the Lisbon Treaty). However, in order to overcome the neoliberal bias of European state formation, trade unions would indeed have to participate in, or even initiate, the articulation of a counter-hegemonic project that would transcend the wide-ranging internal discussions and tensions within the labour movement. An alternative conception of corporate governance would have to be carried forward by a broader alliance of public and civil society actors.

Notes

[1] Interview with a senior researcher at the ETUI-REHS, 22 November 2006.

[2] As a member of the ETUI puts it, "we complain that they should have consulted the Social Partners under Article 138, but they tell us that employee participation wasn't concerned, and we should go and talk to DG V [Employment] about consultation information" (interview with a senior researcher at the ETUI-REHS, 22 November 2006).

[3] For example, Emilio Gabaglio and his successor Niklaas Bruun in the European Corporate Governance Forum. Perhaps not surprisingly, there has been very little interest in their arguments so far.

[4] See e.g. http://europeansforfinancialreform.org (accessed 16 June 2011).

[5] And, it should be noted, expert groups are still very much at the centre of policy formulation. The European Corporate Governance Forum has issued several statements on executive remuneration and voting, and the De Larosière group is a case in point within the financial markets domain.

Resources

Aglietta, M.; Rebérioux, A. 2005. *Corporate governance adrift: A critique of shareholder value* (Cheltenham, Edward Elgar).

Bieler, A. 2008. "Co-option or resistance? Trade unions and neoliberal restructuring in Europe", in *Capital and Class*, Vol. 31, No. 3, pp. 111–24.

Bieling, H-J. 2001. "European constitutionalism and industrial relations", in A. Bieler and A.D. Morton (eds): *Social forces in the making of the new Europe: The restructuring of European social relations in the global political economy* (Basingstoke, Palgrave Macmillan), pp. 93–114.

—; Schulten, T. 2003. "Competitive restructuring and industrial relations within the European Union: Corporatist involvement and beyond", in A.W. Cafruny and M. Ryner (eds): *A ruined fortress? Neoliberal hegemony and transformation in Europe* (Lanham, MD, Rowman & Littlefield), pp. 231–60.

Erne, R. 2008. *European unions: Labor's quest for a transnational democracy* (London, Cornell University Press).

Euromemorandum. 2011. *Confronting the crisis: Austerity or solidarity?*, EuroMemo Group, Feb., available at http://www2.euromemorandum.eu/uploads/euromemorandum_ 2010_2011.pdf (accessed 16 June 2011).

European Commission. 1975. *Employee representation and company structure in the European Community*, COM (75) 570, 12 Nov. (Brussels).

—. 2003. *Modernising company law and enhancing corporate governance in the European Union: A plan to move forward*, COM (2003) 284, 21 May (Brussels).

—. 2010. *Corporate governance in financial institutions and remuneration policies*, Green Paper, COM (2010) 284, 2 June (Brussels).

European Parliament. 2006. *Recent developments in and prospects for company law*, INI/2006/2051, 4 July (Brussels).

European Trade Union Confederation (ETUC). (2003). *Non-paper on takeovers* (Brussels).

—. 2006. "Corporate governance at European level", resolution adopted by ETUC Executive, 14–15 May, http://www.etuc.org/a/2250 (accessed 16 June 2011).

—. 2007. *Strategy and Action Plan, 2007–2011*, Seville, 21–24 May, http://www.etuc.org/ IMG/pdf_Rapport_congress_EN.pdf (accessed 26 June 2011).

Gajewska, K. 2008. "The emergence of a European labour protest movement?", in *European Journal of Industrial Relations*, Vol. 14, No. 1, pp. 104–21.

Harrod, J.; O'Brien, R. (eds). 2002. *Global unions? Theory and strategies of organised labour in the global political economy* (London, Routledge).

Horn, L. 2011. *Regulating corporate governance in the EU: Towards a marketisation of corporate control* (Basingstoke, Palgrave Macmillan).

Hyman, R. 2001. *Understanding European trade unionism: Between market, class and society* (London, Sage).

—. 2004. "The future of trade unions", in A. Verma and T.A. Kochan (eds): *Unions in the 21st century* (Basingstoke, Macmillan).

—. 2005. "Trade unions and the politics of the European social model", in *Economic and Industrial Democracy*, Vol. 26, No. 1, pp. 9–40.

Lazonick, W.; O'Sullivan, M. 2000. "Maximizing shareholder value: A new ideology for corporate governance?", in *Economy and Society*, Vol. 29, No. 1, pp. 13–35.

Mills, C. Wright. 1948. *The new men of power* (New York, Harcourt Brace).

Monks, J. 2008. "Locusts versus labour: Handling the new capitalism", speech delivered at Harvard University, 16 Apr.

Organisation for Economic Co-operation and Development (OECD). 2009. "The corporate governance lessons from the financial crisis", in *Financial Market Trends* 01/2009 (Paris).

Party of European Socialists (PES). 2007. *Hedge funds and private equity: A critical analysis*, available at http://www.nyrup.dk/cgi-bin/nyrup/uploads/media/Hedgefunds_web.pdf (accessed 16 June 2011).

Scharpf, F. 2008. "Der einzige Weg ist, dem EuGH nicht zu folgen", in *Mitbestimmung*, Vol. 7, No. 8, pp. 18–23.

Shleifer, A.; Vishny, R.W. 1996. "A survey of corporate governance", in *NBER Working Chapter*, No. 5554, repr. in *Journal of Finance*, Vol. 52, No. 2, 1997, pp. 737–83.

Streeck, W. 1998. *The internationalization of industrial relations in Europe: Prospects and problems*, Discussion Paper 98/2 (Cologne, Max Planck Institute for the Study of Societies).

—; Schmitter, P.C. 1991. "From national corporatism to transnational pluralism: Organized interests in the single European market", in *Politics and Society*, Vol. 19, No. 2, pp. 133–64.

Taylor, G.; Mathers, A. 2004. "The European Trade Union Confederation at the crossroads of change? Traversing the variable geometry of European trade unionism", in *European Journal of Industrial Relations*, Vol. 10, No. 3, pp. 267–85.

TUAC. 2008. *Reply by the Trade Union Advisory Committee to the OECD Consultation paper on hedge funds of the Commission services* (Brussels, DG Internal Market).

Van Apeldoorn, B. 2002. *Transnational capitalism and the struggle over European integration* (London and New York, Routledge).

—; Drahokoupil, J.; Horn, L. (eds). 2008. *Contradictions and limits of neoliberal European governance: From Lisbon to Lisbon* (Basingstoke, Palgrave Macmillan).

—; Horn, L. 2007. "The marketisation of corporate control: A critical political economy perspective", in *New Political Economy*, Vol. 12, No. 2, pp. 211–35.

Vitols, S.; Kluge, N. (eds). 2011. *The sustainable company: A new approach to corporate governance* (Brussels, European Trade Union Institute).

Zumbansen, P. 2006. *The parallel worlds of corporate governance and labor law*, Comparative Research in Law and Economy Network Research Paper No. 6/2006 (Toronto, Osgoode Hall Law School, York University).

TRANSNATIONAL FRAMEWORK AGREEMENTS: NEW BARGAINING TOOLS IMPACTING ON CORPORATE GOVERNANCE?

9

Isabelle Schömann

Introduction

The steady increase in the number of transnational framework agreements (TFAs) in recent years has had a marked impact on industrial relations systems, as international companies and trade unions have together developed new social dialogue mechanisms to better tackle the social consequences of globalization (European Commission 2008a). A TFA is an agreement signed between the management of a multinational corporation (MNC) and the relevant (global or European) union federation and/or national trade unions. One of the functions of TFAs is to secure the respect and promotion of core labour standards in the worldwide operations of MNCs, in particular when firms transfer production sites to countries with poor social regulation and low working standards. Furthermore, the development of TFAs constitutes a pragmatic alternative to the limits of national labour regulation of industrial relations and the lack of existing enforceable European and international legislation on transnational collective bargaining in MNCs.

Many MNCs consider the recourse to TFAs as a means to develop and improve their CSR initiatives, facing as they are nowadays the need to pay more attention to the social, environmental and societal impact of their activities as a result of pressure stemming from trade unions, NGOs and consumer groups. Following a first phase of CSR activities initiated for the most part unilaterally by MNC managements, and taking the form of codes of conduct, a growing number of trade unions and managements based in MNCs started negotiations in a more coordinated way and agreed on so-called international framework agreements (IFAs), also named global agreements or, more generally, transnational framework agreements (TFAs). These framework agreements all have in common a genesis through a process of negotiation between trade unions and MNC managements. According to the *European Industrial Relations Dictionary* (Eurofound), the term "international framework agreements" has been adopted as a means of clearly distinguishing negotiated agreements from voluntary and unilateral codes of conducts (European Foundation for the Improvement of Living and Working Conditions n.d.). These agreements embody a recognition on both sides of the need to promote basic labour standards and forms of social dialogue on an international level and apply them to MNCs' operations worldwide, as well as in general to their suppliers and subcontractors.

In recent years, IFAs and other comparable agreements have multiplied impressively. Studies have been carried out to demonstrate that IFAs may pave the way for the internationalization of industrial relations, establishing worker involvement as a benchmark for strengthening international social dialogue between labour and management in MNCs (Schömann et al. 2008). In the same vein, recent research projects have tended to focus on the European dimension of certain framework agreements in order to investigate the possibility of an institutional response to the need for a legal and/or contractual, optional framework at European level (Ales et al. 2006; Telljohann et al. 2009). Furthermore, the high proportion of EU-based MNCs involved in negotiating TFAs has had a significant influence on the parties involved, the scope and content of the agreements, and their implementation and monitoring. This has led the European Commission (Pichot 2006) and scholars (Béthoux 2008; Telljohann et al. 2009) to distinguish between international and European framework agreements. In recent documents the European Commission has suggested a new term, "transnational company agreements", with the intention of extending their coverage as broadly as possible. However, this alternative term omits reference to the "framework" aspect of those agreements, that is, the possibility at local level to incorporate TFAs into national, sectoral or local collective agreements and thereby to secure better grounding, and therefore implementation, of the TFA as well as stronger binding force. In order to include this aspect, and to cover the international as well as the European dimensions of such agreements, the chapter will refer to "transnational framework agreements" (TFAs), including within this term both IFAs (in the sense of global agreements) and European framework agreements (so-called EFAs). The first TFAs were concluded by MNCs based in Europe (France, Germany and the Nordic countries), and indeed 80 per cent of companies with TFAs are still headquartered in Europe; however, their use has now spread to corporations based in many other countries, including the United States.

All the recent studies on the topic (European Commission 2008a; Telljohann et al. 2009; Van Hoek and Hendrickx 2009) agree that international and European framework agreements are increasingly forming part of the contemporary understanding of a transnational collective bargaining process, while evolving in a legal no-man's-land. This essay will demonstrate that TFAs constitute new bargaining tools in industrial relations systems in Europe and worldwide, building on existing (European and domestic) social dialogue and collective bargaining structures and procedures. As a consequence, TFAs impact on corporate governance in terms of expanding and promoting social dialogue and collective bargaining in multinationals and their subsidiaries, crossing national and European legal boundaries. Furthermore, the coverage of TFAs contributes to improving the enforcement of core labour standards by multinationals beyond any existing legal boundaries, thus paving the way to good, sustainable MNCs (Kluge and Schömann 2008). In the same vein, TFAs bring trade unions and workers' representatives into the decision-making process on global issues within multinationals, thus giving them the possibility to become actively involved in responses to the social consequences of globalization. Their transnational nature and facilitation of bargaining intervention complements existing domestic labour standards and other means of social regulation, giving trade unions and workers' representatives the opportunity to cross the national boundaries of labour law and get access, for example, to suppliers and subcontractors in respect of their working conditions and environment. This activity can in turn lead to growing global trade union recognition by MNCs and give trade unions the opportunity to reach more workers, organize recruitment drives and improve international solidarity and support.

This chapter draws on the results of previous research, including the author's own research on IFAs as new forms of governance at company level (Schömann et al. 2008) and IFAs as new paths to workers' participation in the governance of multinational firms (Kluge and Schömann 2008). Further studies are also taken into account, such as the recent Eurofound report on "IFAs: A stepping stone towards the internationalisation of IR" and recent work on industrial relations systems (Telljohann et al. 2009). Augmenting the outcomes of previous case studies (Schömann et al. 2008), empirical analysis will focus on a small group of new case studies selected on the basis of different variables, such as the date of signature (to allow for sufficient time for implementation), representation of different industry sectors (giving particular attention to European Trade Union Federation (ETUF) and GUF policy papers, strategic positions, own guidelines in respect of negotiations, and monitoring and implementation of TFAs) in different countries, and the involvement or not of (European) works councils and/or national unions, and covering a large range of issues. This small sample brings together six TFAs:[1] the IKEA agreement between the Swedish furniture company IKEA and the International Federation of Building and Wood Workers (IFBWW) on the promotion of workers' rights at IKEA wood (1998), revised in 2001 to include suppliers; the "Basic principles of social responsibility at Bosch", signed in 2004[2] between Bosch and the International Metalworkers' Federation; the "Worldwide agreement on the principles of Arcelor's corporate social responsibility" of 2005, signed between Arcelor and the International Metalworkers' Federation; the 2005 global agreement on corporate social responsibility between EDF Energy and Public Services International (PSI), the International Federation of Chemical, Energy, Mine and General Workers' Unions (ICEM), the International Federation of Municipal Engineering (IFME) and the World Federation of Industry Workers (WFIW),[3] revised in 2009; the global agreement signed between Securitas, United Network International (UNI) and the Swedish transport unions in 2006; and finally the Telefonica agreement of 2001, revised in 2007, with UNI.[4]

TFAs as new bargaining tools in industrial relations systems

Since the late 1990s, an important trend across industry has been the spread of TFAs designed to ensure that major MNCs, wherever they operate in the world, comply with core labour standards. In most cases TFAs are quite short documents (two to three pages), making general reference to social and political rights at the workplace and including paragraphs on social dialogue at the company level, information and consultation procedures, and the obli-gations of the signatory parties. By signing such agreements, MNCs commit themselves to enforcing labour laws in their various subsidiaries and also to persuading their subcontractors and suppliers to comply with these rules.

TFAs define minimum standards and principles of industrial relations on a transnational scale. The emphasis may vary: while IFAs tend to refer to funda-mental social rights as defined by ILO principles (including bans on child and forced labour, non-discrimination, freedom of association and collective bargaining) and also broader issues like CSR or business ethics, EFAs tend to focus on more specific themes such as personnel management, restructuring, lifelong learning and environmental protection provisions.

Company-based trade unions, together with European trade union federations (and in some cases the EWC) and GUFs, are the main drivers in these developments. Interestingly, most TFAs were initiated in European MNCs using existing social dialogue structures set up at national and European levels; thus they created a dynamic of social dialogue and an impetus for negotiation at European and international levels.

A 2007 research project on "Codes of conduct and international framework agreements: New developments in social regulation at company level" (Schömann et al. 2008) analysed the influence of IFAs (in comparison to codes of conduct) on MNCs' behaviour in respect of labour conditions, social dialogue and corporate culture. The findings were interesting, in respect of both the actors involved and the procedures followed in the negotiations and signature of TFAs. Evidence shows that TFAs are developed on the basis of models of social dialogue and collective bargaining similar to those existing at national level in the country where the relevant MNC has its headquarters. Similarly, in developing TFAs parties use existing legal structures and forums such as the EWC. Recent developments also show that international and European trade union federations have developed ad hoc procedures to adapt to the development of TFAs, thus tending to "harmonize" procedures and create a "conventional" model.[5]

As figure 9.1 shows, on the workers' side, the main drivers are GUFs and ETUFs. The International Metalworkers' Federation, IFBWW, ICEM and UNI are the more active unions in this respect. In a large number of cases TFAs are initiated and co-signed by national unions. From a legal point of view, the signature of national trade unions seems to transform the TFA into a domestic collective bargaining agreement in the country where the MNC's headquarters are located (Telljohann et al. 2009). Only the International Metalworkers' Federation seems to involve EWCs up to the co-signature of the agreement. Although this function does not fall within the competence of EWCs according to EU Directive 2009/38/EC, this strategy seeks to guarantee EWCs' future involvement in the dissemination and monitoring process. By including more partners on the side of the workers, unions secure the appropriation of the IFA by labour at all levels.

On the MNC side, only representatives of the company's headquarters sign the TFA, which reflects the reality of economic power within the company. However, each subsidiary has its own legal personality, even if it is highly integrated in a group. Consequently, the fact that only a representative of headquarters signs the TFA precludes its being considered as a collective agreement as defined in labour law (Sobczak 2007). In rare cases, TFAs are the result of a joint initiative of management and labour or even a management initiative. On the management side, the negotiations closely involve the human resources department, which draws on its experience in social dialogue. In this way human resources managers reaffirm their role in CSR issues. Other departments may be involved in particular rounds of negotiation.

As for the procedures, a TFA is in all cases based on a process of negotiation and bargaining. In some cases domestic workers' consultation bodies, such as works councils and/or national unions, play an important role in the negotiation process. In other cases the EWC is the forum used to launch and sometimes carry out the negotiations, as the transnational institutional consultation body already in place by law. A related point is that legally established structures of social dialogue and of collective bargaining, which already facilitate the exchange of information between management and workforce, are used to develop TFAs or

Figure 9.1   Transnational social dialogue: A summary of interactions

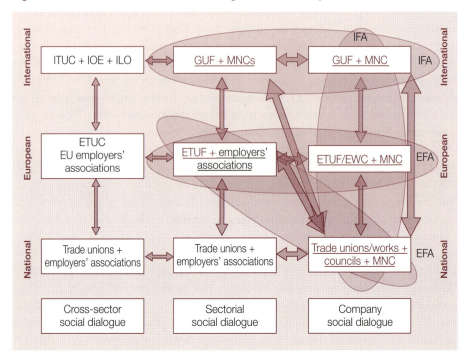

Source: ETUI.

serve as inspiration for them. These institutional platforms have resources at their disposal and access to information on the national and European activities of firms; they also have consultation rights and are part of the social dialogue structure at business level. According to Hammer (2005), the development of EWCs has influenced TFAs in recent years, in particular as some European trade union federations support EWC involvement as a facilitator in the negotiation of these agreements (Bourque 2005; Puligno 2005). In some cases, EWCs may serve as the precursor of a wider, broader information and consultation body set up by the parties to the TFA to ensure the reporting and monitoring of their agreement. A general trend seems to be that the unions are increasingly recognizing the usefulness of the EWCs as a source of information and, at times, as a forum for coordination – to the extent that in some cases EWCs are invited to sign agreements (Telljohann et al. 2009).

However, collective bargaining powers lie in the hands of trade unions. In this respect, trade unions remain the protagonists of the TFA. In recent years, some trade union federations at European and international level have developed strategies to promote TFAs by encouraging unions to take a leading role in the negotiation, signature and implementation of such agreements.

For example, model agreements have been designed to help trade unions and multinationals in the process of negotiating TFAs.[6]

Negotiation takes place with the view of reaching an agreement between the central management of the MNCs and the trade unions. Case-by-case analysis shows that negotiation may last for a couple of months or up to two years, depending on a large range of factors such as whether well-established social dialogue already exists between the MNC and the trade unions, and whether there are already transnational forums for exchange of information about the MNC's activities worldwide. Negotiations take place according to a calendar fixed by the parties and on issues that have been identified by the parties themselves. No legal obligation frames the negotiation rounds and the signature of TFAs. Once signed, TFAs are usually disseminated in the MNC headquarters and its subsidiaries. Suppliers and subcontractors are usually informed of the existence of the TFAs and they are invited to comply with the adopted provisions. However, only in rare cases do MNCs envisage applying (commercial) sanctions in the event of non-compliance. Information and training sessions may take place to make management, staff and workers' representatives aware of the TFA and its implications on a daily basis at plant level. Implementation and monitoring are usually tasks shared between the parties according to provisions included in the agreement. In some cases existing social dialogue structures composed of management and trade union representatives are in charge of follow-up to the agreement; in other cases a new body is created, such as a world works council or a transnational coordination structure.

All these characteristics lead to the conclusion that TFAs represent a formative approach to social dialogue and collective bargaining at multinational level, which contribute to accelerating the elaboration of global structures of social dialogue, information and consultation, such as world works councils. Furthermore, TFAs tend to export a certain domestic and/or European social model of employer–employee relations. In a recent report on industrial relations in Europe, the European Commission (2008b) analysed transnational negotiations between MNCs' management and workforce representatives as a form of transnational collective bargaining within developing transnational industrial relations arrangements. However, scholars (e.g. Sobczak 2007) and the European Commission agree that TFAs do not qualify as "collective agreements" as they are not generated within any legally enshrined and collectively agreed bargaining process. Indeed, TFAs are "sui generis" agreements, as they are framed neither by international or European rules of procedure, nor by domestic rules. As a consequence no power has been legally given by labour law to any actor to negotiate such agreements.

A means currently used in many cases to take TFAs out of this legal vacuum and give them a legally binding status is to transform the TFA into a series of national collective agreements. If the parties wish to do this, the signature of at least one national union and the local managers makes it possible to change the "sui generis" TFA into a national collective agreement, as long as the rules and procedure of the national labour law in the country in question have been respected. Thus the TFA will have the legal force of a collective agreement in that particular country, and will be subject to the enforcement rules of national collective agreements. This option has been used, for example, in the case of the EDF global agreement. Another alternative used by the GUFs and ETUFs is the mandate, as a legal technique to transfer negotiating power to a representative body that negotiates on behalf of (in this case) its members. The strategic choice of a trade union actor placed at the same transnational level as the MNC overcomes the main obstacles of transnational collective bargaining at company level, namely the legal personality of subsidiaries and subcontractors, and the potential conflicts between different national laws on workers' representation and collective bargaining.

In conclusion, TFAs do not qualify as collective agreements, given the limited scope of application of domestic labour law and the lack of European and international legal initiatives. However, negotiation between unions and employers regarding the terms and employment conditions of employees as well as rights and responsibilities of trade unions leads to joint private regulation. Signatory parties of TFAs consider their agreements as having a direct (conventional) binding effect on them and their contractors, providing for direct application. As such TFAs contribute to the evolution of transnational bargaining, "setting a (conventional) framework for global and European industrial relations in each company and each sector" (Higgs 2000), with an impact both on European industrial relations and on corporate governance.

The impact of TFAs on corporate governance

This section will focus on the impact of TFAs on corporate governance, drawing on a project investigating the impact of TFAs on working conditions and labour–management relations in MNCs and industrial relations systems. The project research was constructed as a follow-up, thus on a smaller scale, to the 2008 research project on "Codes of conduct and international framework agreements: New forms of governance at company level". As well as a literature review of current projects (among others, Telljohann et al. 2009), a qualitative analysis of a range of case studies has been carried out (the key actors in each are set out in table 9.1). In addition, interviews were organized with representatives of ETUFs and GUFs, EWCs and workers' representatives.

Table 9.1   Summary of case studies: Six transnational framework agreements

Sector	Multinational enterprise (date of agreement)	European industry federation	Global Union federation	National Unions	Workers' representation
Metal (steel)	Arcelor (2005)	EMF	IMF	–	–
	Bosch (2004)	–	IMF	–	EWC
Services	Securitas (2006)	–	UNI	Swedish Transport Workers' Union	–
	Telefónica (2001–07)	–	UNI	BWI	UGT, CC.OO
Retail furniture	IKEA (1998–2001)	EFBWW	BWI	Initiated by NFBWW and Swedish Wood Workers' Union	Global compliance and monitoring group
Energy	EDF (2005–09)	EMCEF	ICEM, PSI, IFME, WFIW	All five major unions in France	Consultation committee on EDF Group CSR

Notes:

– = not involved as signatory party.

BWI = Building and Wood Workers International (formerly International Federation of Building and Woodworkers, and World Federation of Building and Wood Workers); CC.OO = Confederación Sindical de Comisiones Obreras; CSR = corporate social responsibility; EDF = Electricité de France; EFBWW = European Federation of Building and Wood Workers; EMCEF = European Mine, Chemical and Energy Workers' Federation; EMF = European Metalworkers' Federation; EWC = European Works Council; ICEM = International Federation of Chemical, Energy, Mine and General Workers' Unions; IFME = International Federation of Municipal Engineering; IMF = International Metalworkers' Federation; NFBWW = Nordic Federation of Building and Wood Workers; PSI = Public Services International; UGT = Unión General de Trabajadores; UNI = Union Network International; WFIW = World Federation of Industry Workers.

According to the Eurofound definition, corporate governance refers to:

a company's mechanisms and control structures that may influence senior management decision-making. The issue of corporate governance has two dimensions. It
commonly focuses on the pattern of corporate ownership and the extent to which
the shareholders, as the owners of the company, exercise power over management
decision-making. However, in the context of decision-making in the area of employment and industrial relations, the debate also reflects a concern with the
representation of employees' interests, who, as stakeholders, have a vested interest in the company's activity.[7]

The initiatives taken by international, European and national trade unions to persuade MNCs' managements to embark on negotiating and signing TFAs represent an active involvement of workers' representatives in corporate govern - ance in order to jointly promote core labour standards in company operations worldwide. As the agreements emerge from social dialogue and collective bargaining procedures, it is not surprising that issues such as wages and working hours, training, health and safety, and more recently the social impact of restructuring are discussed.

Thus TFAs are among the key tools available to trade unions for address- ing the growth of corporate power and securing union involvement in MNCs' activities worldwide, in most cases building on existing good relationships within the company (usually at headquarters level). TFAs contribute to main- taining and developing both social dialogue between management and trade unions and employee representation at regional and local level.[8] They help to raise the legitimacy of trade union and workers' representation at lower levels in the MNC's subsidiaries, thus embedding these principles within the corporation's identity. TFAs allow for the recognition of trade union and workers' representatives as legitimate partners in the MNC and its subsidiaries, and to a lesser extent at supplier and subcontractor level. Case studies show that, if cooperation at the local management level is to be achieved, MNC headquarters needs to do more in respect of information and training on TFAs and their implications at plant level.

The impact in practice of TFAs on social dialogue and corporate govern- ance at local and plant levels may be seen by observing at one end of the process the role trade unions and workers play in the elaboration of TFAs and at the other end the role they play in almost all cases in monitoring and implementing the agreement.[9]

As mentioned earlier in this chapter, the lead in launching negotiations with a view to establishing a TFA is in most cases taken by a trade union and/or workers' representative, usually at MNC headquarters. Such initiatives are often the fruit of existing well-functioning social dialogue structures within the company, based on long-standing experience and mutual trust between management and labour. It is less often the result of a conflict between the parties, but may result from a change in activities, such as a geographical shift of production. In proposing that negotiations on a TFA are undertaken, the workers give a clear signal to management that the multinational operations are of concern to the headquarters workforce. A receptive response by manage- ment sends a signal to workers that their involvement should lead to the identification of potential human resources problems to be jointly solved.

The involvement of trade unions in monitoring the application of a TFA after signature appears to be one of the most innovative aspects of the development of TFAs in respect of their contribution to promoting core labour standards and better working conditions. In most cases, a special body is created at the level of the MNC, composed of trade union and/or workers' representatives and management representatives. This special body is in charge of regular reporting exercises; it operates as a forum for exchange of information on the TFA and promotes its dissemination within the MNC and its subsidiaries and sometimes also at supplier and subcontractor levels. According to specific procedures set out in each TFA, this special body also provides a medium for reporting on any difficulties that may be encountered in implementing the agreement and a means of consultation and jointly identifying solutions, as a form of alternative dispute resolution mechanism. The issue of conflict resolution is of particular relevance, as TFAs/IFAs tend to set rules to deal with conflicts concerning implementation at all levels, thus creating internal enforcement mechanisms (Kocher 2008). Although it appears difficult to generalize, the common model of grievance procedure provides a chain of grievance resolution, with the possibility of first dealing with the complaint at local management level on the initiative of workers' representatives. If no solution is found locally, then the complaint will be forwarded to the next hierarchical level up, usually the national level of workers' representation and management; if the grievance persists, it may be referred up to the GUF or ETUF, which can ultimately inform the MNC management if the grievance remains unresolved. The main objective is to make IFAs effective (Sobczak 2008) by creating internal (to the MNCs) grievance mechanisms that allow for internal solutions to be found through close cooperation between workers' representation and management. A common characteristic of such grievance procedures is that complaints are dealt with "in-house", so that little information is available on either resolved or pending cases. Confidentiality seems to be part of the risk management strategy of MNCs involved in TFAs. In this respect, TFAs are perceived by MNCs as a means to promote industrial peace by means of effective social dialogue with trade unions.

Conclusions

Transnational framework agreements have been promoted, mainly by GUFs and ETUFs, to address an emerging need for the internationalization of industrial and labour relations in the global context. Thus the primary function of TFAs is to reaffirm social rights and to initiate or strengthen social dialogue on an international level. Analysis of existing TFAs indicates that they are primarily aimed at regulating labour relations within MNCs, even though they sometimes include broader issues. Although they have evolved in a legal vacuum, TFAs are now a new bargaining tool, rooted in national collective bargaining traditions, social dialogue and well-institutionalized industrial relations systems. They are also inspired by existing European legal structures for workers' information and consultation such as EWCs. As such, TFAs have impacted on corporate governance in four main ways:

(1) Trade union and workers' representatives are recognized as legitimate partners in MNCs, at headquarters and in their subsidiaries, and in some cases at supplier and subcontractor levels as well.

(2) Transnational social dialogue structures and transnational bargaining structures have been extended or created to monitor the implementation of TFAs. TFAs tend to lead to further development of stable supranational structures of interest representation, information, consultation and dialogue.

(3) Trade union and workers' involvement in the decision-making processes of multinationals has been increased, in particular in respect of the treatment of the social consequences of globalization.

(4) TFAs have led to the setting up of contractual alternative dispute resolution mechanisms, involving management and trade union and workers' representatives from the plant level to the headquarters level, to solve issues related to non-compliance with TFAs.

Furthermore, TFAs strengthen cooperation between workers' representatives, nurturing and formalizing a corporate environment and culture that support the active involvement of employees and their trade unions in the MNC's operations, including its subsidiaries and reaching out to its economic partners. Finally, TFAs are usually based on well-functioning social dialogue and working conditions which thereby become established as competitive benchmarks, influencing shareholders and investors.

As global negotiated tools for promoting core labour standards on the basis of the social dialogue culture of MNCs, TFAs reflect the issues that are considered part of social dialogue at the national level (where a given multinational's headquarters is located), as well as international issues such as the promotion of core labour standards as set out in ILO Conventions. In doing so, TFAs promote the compliance of MNC operations with legal international labour standards (Ewing 2007). By establishing rules for transnational social dialogue and bargaining activities, the parties to TFAs have created the necessary contractual environment, inspired by domestic legal rules and practices and the EWCs as facilitators for negotiation and supervision, to tackle the internationalization of labour-related issues. However, to date these processes are taking place in the absence of any international or European legal provisions. The adoption of a legal framework, still much debated in Europe

(Ales et al. 2006; Van Hoek and Hendrickx 2009), would increase the security and transparency of procedures and would consequently be an incentive to companies to embark on negotiation of TFAs.

TFAs contribute to the Europeanization (if not the internationalization) of industrial relations, and one of the main issues at stake is the interaction between different levels of regulation (company, sector, national, regional, international) and between different natures of regulation (public or private). A better balance between public and private norm-setting would place such initiatives on a more secure basis, reflect the widely felt desire for this kind of response to the challenges of globalization and create a momentum for (European) institutions to act.

Notes

[1] For an in-depth presentation see Schömann (2011).

[2] http://www.imfmetal.org/files/ifa_bosch_en.pdf (accessed 16 June 2011).

[3] http://www.world-psi.org/Content/ContentGroups/English7/Focus2/Focus_articles_2005 î/EDF_signs_up_to _global_standards.htm (accessed 16 June 2011).

[4] http://www.uniglobalunion.org/Apps/iportal.nsf/3100172b0315a124c125717d005dd9bb/513a7b55742a39eec 125755100579d2a/$FILE/UNI-Telefonica-en.pdf (accessed 16 June 2011).

[5] The IMF has already developed TFAs-related policies, adopted at its Executive Committee in 2006 (http://www. imfmetal.org/files/07070311193766/IFA_recs-ec_e.pdf), as well as model agreements (http://www.imfmetal.org/files/ 0505102301487/ifamodel_total_english.pdf) (both accessed 16 June 2011).

At the European level, the European Metalworkers' Federation (EMF) "supports the development of a negotiation role in multinational companies. Through the negotiation of framework agreements both at European and international level, the EMF seeks to secure minimum standards for workers with a view to improve working conditions and avoid undercutting on social standards" (http://www.emf-fem.org/Areas-of-work/Company-Policy/Company-cases, accessed 16 June 2011).

[6] For example, the IMF as model agreements: http://www.imfmetal.org/files/0505102301487/ifamodel_total_english. pdf (accessed 16 June 2011).

[7] http://www.eurofound.europa.eu/areas/industrialrelations/dictionary/definitions/CORPORATEGOVERNANCE. htm (accessed 16 June 2011).

[8] Schömann et al. (2008), p. 77.

[9] Ibid., p. 40.

Resources

Ales, E. et al. 2006. *Transnational collective bargaining: Past, present and future*, report to the European Commission (Brussels).

Béthoux, E. 2008. *Transnational agreements and texts negotiated or adopted at company level: European developments and perspectives. The case of agreements and texts on anticipating and managing change*, http://www.anticipationofchange.eu/fileadmin/anticipation/ Logos/Documents/new_set_5509/pres/Bethoux.pdf (accessed 16 June 2011).

Bourque, R. 2005. *Les accords-cadres internationaux (ACI) et la négotiation collective internationale à l'ère de la mondialisation*, DP/161/2005 (Geneva, Institut international d'études sociales/ILO).

European Commission. 2008a. *The role of transnational company agreements in the context of increasing international integration*, SEC (2008) 2155 / COM (2008) 419 final, 2 July (Brussels).

—. 2008b. *Industrial relations in Europe 2008* (Brussels), http://ec.europa.eu/social/main.jsp?catId=575&langId=en (accessed 16 June 2011).

European Foundation for the Improvement of Living and Working Conditions. n.d. *European Industrial Relations Dictionary*, http://www.eurofound.europa.eu/areas/industrialrelations/dictionary/definitions/internationalframeworkagreement.htm (accessed 16 June 2011).

Ewing, K.D. 2007. "International regulation of the global economy: The role of trade unions", in B. Bercusson and C. Estlund (eds): *Regulating labour in the wake of globalisation: New challenges, new institutions* (Oxford and Portland, OR: Hart), pp. 205–13.

Hammer, N. 2005. "International framework agreements between rights and bargaining", in *Transfer*, Vol. 11, No. 4, pp. 511–30.

Higgs, F. 2000. "Global companies need global unions", in *Financial Times*, 2 Apr.

Kluge, N.; Schömann, I. 2008. "Corporate governance, workers' participation and CSR: The way to a good company", in *Transfer*, Vol. 14, No. 1 (Spring), pp. 13–26.

Kocher, E. 2008. "Corporate social responsibility: Instrumente zur Gestaltung transnationaler Arbeitsbeziehungen", in *WSI-Mitteilungen*, Vol. 61, No. 4, pp. 198–204.

Pichot, E. 2006. *Transnational texts negotiated at corporate level: Facts and figures*, working document, study seminar on "Transnational Agreements", 17 May (Brussels, European Commission).

Puligno, V. 2005. "EWC and cross national employee representative coordination: A case of trade union cooperation?", in *Economic and Industrial Democracy*, Vol. 23, No. 3, pp. 383–412.

Schömann, I. 2011. "Impact of transnational company agreements on social dialogue and industrial relations", in K. Papadakis (ed.): *Practices and outcomes of an emerging global industrial relations framework* (Basingstoke: Palgrave Macmillan for ILO).

— et al. 2008. *Codes of conduct and international framework agreements: New forms of governance at company level* (Dublin, European Foundation for the Improvement of Living and Working Conditions; Luxembourg, Office for Official Publications of the European Communities).

Sobczak, A. 2007. "Legal dimensions of international framework agreements in the field of corporate social responsibility", in *Relations industrielles – Industrial Relations* (Quebec), Vol. 62, No. 3 (Summer), pp. 466–91.

—. 2008. "Legal dimensions of international framework agreements in the field of corporate social responsibility", in K. Papadakis (ed.): *Cross-border social dialogue and agreements: An emerging global industrial relations framework?* (Geneva, International Institute for Labour Studies, International Labour Organization).

Telljohann, V. et al. 2009. *European and international framework agreements: Practical experiences and strategic approaches* (Dublin, European Foundation for the Improvement of Living and Working Conditions; Luxembourg, Office for Official Publications of the European Communities).

Van Hoek, A.; Hendrickx, F. 2009. *International private law aspects and dispute settlement related to transnational company agreements*, study undertaken on behalf of the European Commission, contract no. VC/2009/0157.

PART III

RESPONSES TO THE CRISIS:
NATIONAL AND LOCAL PERSPECTIVES

COLLECTIVE ACTIONS PUSH TRADE UNION REFORM IN CHINA[1] 10

Lin Yanling and Ju Wenhui

Key features of the CHAM Guangdong strike

A series of workers' strikes and protests broke out in China during late May 2010. The strike at Honda Auto Parts Manufacturing in Guangdong (CHAM Guangdong) that began on 17 May stands out by virtue of the rationality, solidarity and strength showed by the organized workers. After third-party mediation and negotiations undertaken through collective bargaining, an agreement was finally reached between employer and employees. The workers' monthly income was raised by 500 yuan renminbi (CNY) from 1,544 to 2,044 CNY, an increase of almost 33 per cent. This increase was made up of additions to the monthly wage (300 CNY), subsidy (66 CNY), and year-end bonus (134 CNY).

Certain distinctive features of the workers' collective action were instrumental in bringing about this outcome.

The location of the strike in the automobile industry

Strikes in the Chinese automobile industry have generally been significant events with considerable impact. This is because the automobile industry has such a long manufacturing chain, whereby one core factory often has more than 200 or 300 supply factories which maintain no stock. Although this modern mode of production is very efficient, it also incurs high risks, for the failure of any one parts factory will bring the whole chain to a standstill. CHAM Guangdong is the main supplier of automobile transmissions for Guangqi Honda Automobile and Dongfeng Honda Automobile: both of those factories were halted by the nine-and-a-half-day strike, resulting in losses of CNY 230 million and over CNY 100 million respectively. In all, up to 100,000 workers in the automobile industry in China suffered in some way from the strike.[2]

Another relevant aspect of the sectoral location of the strike was the low wage level prevailing in the automobile industry. It is asserted that CHAM Guangdong's wage policy does not violate China's minimum wage legislation. In this case, the workers' aim in striking was not to assert their legal right, but to fight for better economic rewards (Chan 2010). It goes without saying that the primary goal of employees is to get paid for their work and it is the employer's duty to give them that pay for work. However, the employees and employers often cannot reach an agreement on the appropriate pay level, and this becomes the core issue of contention. The general situation in CHAM Guangdong prior to the strike was that the workers had to work 10–12 hours a day, 28 days a month, for the local minimum wage. Earnings above this depended on overtime work. Curiously, CHAM Guangdong's wage level is not among the lowest in Guangdong, and in fact this plant offers its workers better pay and working conditions than many others. The macro-economic statistics show that the proportion of labour income in China's GDP dropped from 57 per cent in 1983 to 37 per cent in 2005. Other research[3] shows that 23.4 per cent of workers had no wage increase during the five years from 2005 to 2009, and 75.2 per cent of workers complain about the unfair income distribution.

In Guangdong's automobile industry, the workers have three main grievances. The first is that the wage level is too low,[4] and has not risen to reflect the industry's rapid expansion and sharply increasing employer profits. The workers complained that in the preceding two and a half years they had had only three wage increases amounting to no more than CNY 100 in total. Second, working hours are too long, and they often have to work overtime. Third, the salary structure is unfair: for example, local and foreign employees are paid differently even for the same work, and the wage gap between workers and management is too wide.[5] Since the financial crisis began in 2007, moreover, the inflation rate has been consistently rising, reducing the value of workers' pay.

The strike was organized not by the trade unions, but by the workers themselves. The fact that trade unions, especially the enterprise trade unions, played no role in the some of the strikes of May 2010 showed that the trade unions in China are becoming detached from the workers they should be protecting, an observation which reflects the unions' more general dilemma in respect of how they position themselves in the polity.[6] In fact, workers at CHAM Guangdong did complain to their trade union about their low wages before they took any action, but the enterprise trade union failed to respond. The new generation of migrant workers from rural areas, equipped with a rapidly growing consciousness of their rights and interests, are not afraid to appeal to the law, but have little opportunity to make their voices heard, a combination of circumstances that inevitably leads to labour conflict.[7]

According to the news report,[8] during the CHAM Guangdong strike no supportive interventions from the trade unions were observed; indeed, some hostile actions were noted. For example, the local union, Shishan Trade Union, even confronted the striking workers physically in an attempt to suppress the strike. Disappointed in the union's response, the young workers joined together, collectively denounced the trade union in public, and even demanded the dismissal of the enterprise trade union and the right to elect their own union in its place, by and from workers at shop-floor level.[9] This is an important indicator of the likely direction of trade union reform in China.

The Internet played a major role during the strike

During the strike, much information was disseminated over the Internet, thereby being made available to workers and the wider community rapidly and freely. Furthermore, the Internet stimulated and fostered interactive communications between the striking workers and the outside world – indeed, it provided a free communication system for the collection and exchange of opinions and the circulation of feedback from many sources, including other workers, management and government (see Lin 2009).

At the very beginning of the CHAM Guangdong strike, the news was posted promptly on some websites and blogs, along with further information about the motives for the action and, later, the progress of the strike and its outcome. By this means the workers' expectations, the employer's response and the attitude of the local trade unions were all vividly presented to the public. The workers also posted an "Open letter to social communities and all workers from delegation of strike workers of CHAM Guangdong" on the Internet, appealing for more help. In its use of the Internet, the CHAM Guangdong strike served as an example and guideline for future strike action in China.

As well as the Internet, the workers used SMS (text messaging) to communicate among themselves and to organize the strike, including discussing and deciding on its date and location.

The social background to collective action in China

Although it is hard to determine whether the strikes of May 2010 were contingent or inevitable, there are some aspects of the social background that should be taken into consideration.

The extension of marketization reforms to industrial relations

Since 1978 China has been experiencing rapid economic growth which can be attributed mainly to the success of the marketization reform programme. However, one of the obvious flaws of the reform programme is that it paid too much attention to economic growth and not enough to social development; in particular, it failed to give full protection to workers' rights and interests. Consequently, most workers did not share in the fruits of the reform's success, and indeed many, to some extent, became its victims (Chang 2009).

From the mid-1980s, the main thrust of labour system reform was towards improving the efficiency of the labour market and strengthening the power of employers. Since 2003, however, the Government has paid much more attention to improving the welfare of workers, especially migrant workers, with the aiming of building a more harmonious society. Important measures taken to this end included banning arrears of pay, setting up a standard wage-growth mechanism, and expanding the coverage of labour contract and social insurance (Qiao 2009: 312). A great breakthrough came in 2008 when China implemented three laws to protect workers' rights and interests: the Labour Contract Law, the Employment Promotion Law and the Law on Mediation and Arbitration of Labour Disputes.

Thus, over a period of 30 years that saw both the globalization of the world economy and the marketization of China's domestic economy, industrial relations in China also successfully underwent a marketization reform. The features of the new kind of industrial relations that emerged include a more reasonable balance of status in bargaining between employers and employees; a stable distribution structure of profit between employers and employees; and modern collective bargaining arrangements in place of the traditional practice of individual bargaining. In addition, it is hoped that an efficient industrial relations mediation mechanism will be created in the future.

Long-standing problems with labour conflicts and lack of redress

Labour conflicts had been a serious problem for the Chinese Government for some time (Chang 2009), provoked for the most part by the violation of workers' rights and interests – for example, through unreasonably low wages, arrears of pay and excessive working hours. The situation deteriorated from the mid-1990s onwards in particular as China's progressive economic reform strategy failed to pay sufficient attention to the situation of workers, resulting in an imbalance in bargaining power between employers and employees.

Against this background, the number of labour dispute cases in China rose steadily, year by year (figure 10.1). However, in 2008 the number of cases erupted, shooting up to 690,000, over twice the 2005 level. Within this total, the number of collective labour disputes also grew (figures 10.2 and 10.3).

After the surge of 2008, in 2009 the number of labour dispute cases decreased markedly, with an especially steep fall in the number of collective

Figure 10.1   Labour disputes in China, 1996–2009

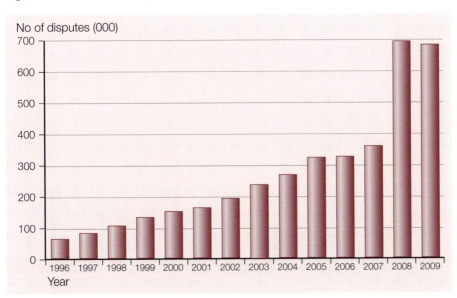

Sources: *China Labour Statistical Yearbook* (1995–2009); *Human resources and social security: Public newspaper career statistics in 2009*, http://www.chinajob.gov.cn/DataAnalysis/content/2010-05/24/content_340006.htm (accessed 16 June 2011).

Figure 10.2   Collective labour disputes in China, 1994–2009

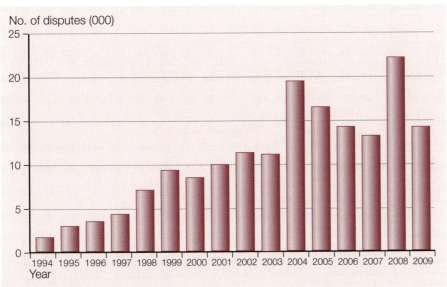

Sources: *China Labour Statistical Yearbook* (1995–2009); *Human resources and social security: Public newspaper career statistics in 2009*, http://www.chinajob.gov.cn/DataAnalysis/content/2010-05/24/content_340006.htm (accessed 16 June 2011).

Figure 10.3   Numbers of workers involved in collective disputes and all disputes in China, 1994–2009

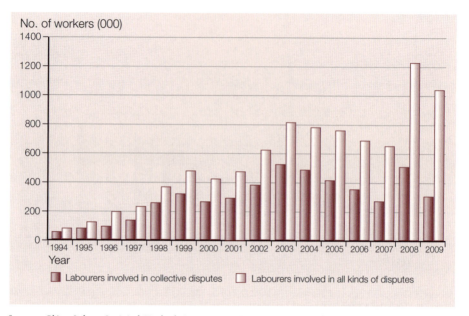

Sources: *China Labour Statistical Yearbook* (1995–2009); *Human resources and social security: Public newspaper career statistics in 2009*, http://www.chinajob.gov.cn/DataAnalysis/content/2010-05/24/content_340006.htm (accessed 16 June 2011).

labour disputes, from 22,000 down to 14,000 (a drop of about 36.4 per cent). However, much attention was given by the newspapers to workers' "group events" – the term usually used to describe protest actions in streets, or around government buildings, taken by workers as a result of labour disputes (Yang 2009). According to the statistics from Shandong Provincial Trade Union, in the first quarter of 2009 alone the number of group events reached 52, most of them prompted by arrears of pay, inadequate remuneration and other unfair treatment. The Municipal Public Security Bureau of Shenzhen reported a total of 637 group events in 2008 (a rise of 119.8 per cent on the previous year), most caused by labour disputes.

During the early stage of industrial relations marketization in China, the employers usually predominated in bargaining with their workers; in the absence of any proper mediation mechanism in enterprises, they had great freedom to set working conditions and wage levels unilaterally. In such an unbalanced labour market, employees are likely to accept unfair working conditions and unreasonably low wages up to a point in order to secure employment; however, when poor conditions and low wages reach intolerable levels, it is inevitable that workers will take some kind of action to make their voices heard. In the absence of legal and peaceful means of expressing themselves within enterprises, eventually they turned to various kinds of collective action (including group events) to bring their plight before the eyes of the Government and the wider society.

New challenges posed by the financial crisis

The new legislation of 2008 seemed to indicate a determination on the part of the Chinese Government to protect the rights and interests of labour. However, in the same year the global financial crisis brought great challenges. China's exports decreased sharply, with disastrous results for the export-oriented business sectors, especially for labour-intensive private enterprises. These employers were forced to cut workers' pay and benefits, giving rise to a new series of labour conflicts.

Confronted simultaneously by falling economic growth and great domestic controversy about the new legislation, the Government had to make a hard choice: whom should it rescue, the employees or the employers? Officials in the Department of Human Resources and Social Security insisted that the Government should preserve a balance between protecting employees' rights and helping employers to survive the crisis. This response, reflecting the Government's generally ambiguous attitude towards the protection of employees' rights and interests, was generally seen as signalling a change of direction in the wake of the new legislation.

Responses to the strike from local government and the trade unions

Since the strikes of May 2010 went ahead without the leadership of the trade unions, the question arose as to what the unions should do in response. In Guangdong, some senior officials in local government and in trade unions insisted that these strikes should be treated seriously and that appropriate action should be taken. Three such responses are considered below.

A response from the provincial Party Secretary

In a video-conference on economic transition in Guangdong held on 12 June 2010, Wang Yang, Party Secretary of Guangdong Province and member of the CPC Central Committee Political Bureau, pointed out that the economic transition should not be confined to structural adjustment in industry, the upgrading of technology, reductions in the consumption of resources and the protection of the environment, but should also encompass a change of attitudes towards people, especially within enterprises. Wang emphasized that the

Government should take prompt action to set up conflict-handling mechanisms for private enterprises and play an active role as mediator between employees and employers, paying serious and timely attention to the legal rights of both and responding rapidly to requests from both workers and employers. Wang also stated that a Democratic Management Act in Enterprises and a Collective Wage Negotiation Act should be laid down as soon as possible, and that local Party committees and trade unions should speed up the process of building up their own organizations within private enterprises. Finally, Wang emphasized that trade unions at both enterprise and sectoral level should really serve the workers, protecting their legal rights and interests.[10]

A response from the Guangdong Government through the revised Democratic Management Act in Enterprises in Guangdong

On 21 July, the Guangdong Standing Committee of the National People's Congress held a meeting to deliberate on the revised draft of the Democratic Management Act in Enterprises in Guangdong, which included a new clause on collective wage bargaining and conflict mediation to help to build up harmonious industrial relations. For example, the draft states that, where at least one-fifth of an enterprise's workforce requests it, the trade union should call a democratic meeting among workers to choose delegates who will then bargain with the employer to arrive at collective wage agreements. For those enterprises without trade unions, the local federation of trade unions should take responsibility for guiding the workers in choosing their delegates democratically (X. Lin 2010). Experts pointed out that previous laws never gave workers the right to negotiate a collective wage agreement: measures such as the Trade Union Law (1992), Labour Law (1994) and Labour Contract Law (2007) simply handed the rights over to the trade unions.

If successfully enacted, the revised draft will perform two significant functions. One is to provide a regular mechanism, distinct from the previous collective action mechanism, for the workers to demand a collective wage agreement and defend their rights and interests. The other is to restore to workers the right of collective negotiation, including the right to choose their delegates under the guidance of the trade unions, which will help workers to play a principal role in the future collective negotiations (*China Labour Bulletin* 2010).

These are not the only notable aspects of the revised Act. For example, the new draft also provides that collective negotiations should be held within the enterprises, and that the Government should play only a mediating role in the mechanism for managing labour relations.[11]

In short, the new draft represents an attempt on the part of the Guangdong Government to encourage workers to use the more peaceful forms of collective action, such as negotiation, instead of more destructive collective actions, to defend their rights. These attempts at legislative innovation also indicate that the Government needs to build up a coordination mechanism for collective negotiations to resolve the increasingly intense conflicts between employees and employers that have followed in the wake of the transition to market-oriented industrial relations (*China Labour Bulletin* 2010).

A response from the Guangzhou Federation of Trade Unions

In answer to a question from a journalist from *Yangchengwanbao*, Chen Weiguang, chairman of the Guangzhou Federation of Trade Unions, said that the union did not always have a clear idea of what role it should play in coordinating labour relations coordination, and some officials of the trade unions even unintentionally played a mediation role between employers and employees. The recent CHAM Guangdong case had raised a serious issue: which side are the trade unions on?

Undoubtedly, the Guangzhou Federation of Trade Unions has already learned some lessons. On 21 June a labour dispute arose at DENSO Guangzhou, a leading supplier of advanced automotive technology, systems and components for all the world's major auto makers. Because the enterprise trade union had lost the workers' trust, it could do nothing. When the superior Nansha trade union was asked by the Government to mediate and coordinate the negotiations, Chen clearly indicated that, if the trade union accepted the request to be coordinator, it would disqualify itself from acting on behalf of the workers. Chen therefore refused and suggested that the local Labour Bureau of Nansha District should take responsibility for mediation, insisting that the trade unions must be on the workers' side, and that the Government, not the trade unions, should play the mediation role. However, he also confessed that, within the current political framework, the position of the trade union was decided by the Party, not by the trade union itself (Zhang 2010).

Having positioned themselves clearly in relation to the conflict, in this case the local government and the trade union played active roles in successfully resolving the dispute. On 25 June the employees and the employer held a collective negotiation, and by the end of the working day had reached an agreement in a friendly atmosphere. Both sides expressed a wish to strengthen mutual communications and sustain cooperation in the future. The Labour Bureau of Nansha District eventually advised that the employees and the employer should hold a collective negotiation on increasing wages in April every year (Xiao 2010).

Along with rapid economic development, labour relations in China are becoming increasingly complicated and the enterprise trade unions are facing many new situations and challenges. In acknowledging the urgency of responding to these challenges, and in order to strengthen the role of enterprise trade unions in the future, the All-China Federation of Trade Unions (ACFTU) laid down a new resolution on 26 July 2010. This new resolution aims to promote the building of grass-roots trade unions, to strengthen trade unions' responsibilities to defend workers' rights, to direct more funding to enterprise trade unions and to strengthen the guidance on which they can draw. The new measures are strongly practical and appropriate. For example, the new resolution insists that the chairman of a trade union must genuinely represent the workers, speak for the workers, and support workers' rights (Zheng 2010).

Trade union reform in China: An inconspicuous but persistent process

Generally speaking, trade union reform is an autonomous process. However, in China it is linked to the attitude of the Party and the Government – as was clear from Chen Weiguang's acknowledgement that, within the existing political framework, the position of the trade union was decided by the Party, not by the trade union itself. Some researchers have also pointed out that the role of the local trade union in the CHAM case calls for reflection on what kinds of trade unions are actually needed in the Chinese market economy, what position they should take in labour conflicts, and what role they should play more widely (Jiang 2010). From the responses to workers' collective actions made by local Government, local trade unions and ACFTU, it appears that the trade union movement has been already undergoing inconspicuous reform in China, and that recent events, including collective action by workers, have forced the pace somewhat.

The roles and responsibilities of governments, trade unions and workers

In principle, the trade unions, as the workers' representatives, should always take the workers' side in negotiations and disputes, and it is the Government's task to set up the mechanism for dialogue between employee and employer, to promote dialogue and to mediate in cases of conflict. This division of respon-sibility was clearly set out in ACFTU's new resolution:

> When collective actions break out, the enterprise trade unions should visit the workers at the first time to gather information, report and express their demands to local and superior Party committee, and try to prevent intensification of conflict. The trade unions should be under the leadership and coordination of the Government and the Party committee to maintain the workers' rights through the collective negotiation mechanism. (ACFTU 2010)

The Party, the Government and the trade unions all acknowledge that, without clear division of responsibility among them, they would be powerless in the face of industrial conflict.

Alienation between workers and their trade unions

If strikes similar to that at CHAM Guangdong are to be prevented in the future, the trade unions must unambiguously and wholeheartedly represent and express the workers' rights and interests. This means that trade unions must send down deep roots among workers; the officials of trade unions must be chosen freely by workers, and workers must be encouraged to build up their trade unions in a bottom-up way. Previously, the trade unions were built in a top-down way, not by workers, but by themselves. Since the workers' demands and expectations were seldom taken into account by the trade unions, the unions could not win the workers' trust. Trade unions of this kind have lost credibility with the workers, and so can do nothing when conflicts break out. Fortunately, ACFTU's new resolution paid close attention to this issue, and insisted that henceforth the enterprise trade unions must be built by workers, stand for workers and defend workers' rights.

Questioned by a journalist from *Nanfengchuang*, Li Yonghai, the legal adviser to and formerly a member of the secretariat of ACFTU, said that, if trade unions failed to stand for the workers, the workers would find other ways to defend their rights and interests. He also said that, if the Party's trade unions continued to fail to represent the workers properly, eventually the workers would seek help from those "second trade unions" that are not controlled by the Party (Li 2010).

Only when workers can indeed build up their own enterprise trade unions, and when these trade unions genuinely represent the workers, will the latter trust their unions, so that at future critical moments in industrial relations the trade unions will be able to play their intended role.

Repositioning the trade unions

One of the main tasks of trade unions in representing workers in a market economy is to organize collective negotiations, bargain with employers and sign collective agreements. In China, the collective contract mechanism has been in place for over ten years; however, these contracts have been introduced and applied by the Government in a top-down way, so that the trade unions did not play their intended role in collective bargaining, and in the end the collective contract mechanism failed. Another confusion of role in enterprise trade unions is the dual role of the chairman, who is often both chairman of the union and a member of the company management.[12] In order to clarify the role of trade unions in collective negotiations, on 25 May 2010 the Ministry of Human Resources and Social Security, ACFTU and the China Enterprise Confederation jointly released the "Rainbow Programme", a three-year project to promote collective contract mechanisms, which will focus on collective wage bargaining in all kinds of enterprises that have already set up trade unions. Obviously, if the mechanism is to work, the trade unions must genuinely represent workers in the negotiation process; if they do not, the mechanism will fail again.

Li Yonghai pointed out: "It's a fact that trade unions have really done much. However, quite a number of workers are not satisfied with trade unions and what they have done, and this is also a fact. So what is the point? If trade unions failed to serve workers and voice their demands, workers will not be satisfied with trade unions, no matter how much they have done" (Li 2010). The collective wage bargaining mechanism will help to ensure that trade unions really do serve the workers and voice their demands for better pay and working conditions, which in turn will ensure that the trade unions do eventually win the trust of workers.

Conclusion

The recent collective actions have prompted great debate in China, in the course of which almost all of the problems faced by trade unions were thoroughly aired in public with the help of the Internet and other media. In a sense, the current disputes are a continuation of earlier debates; however, these discussions covered not only the embarrassing dilemmas that trade unions have faced in industrial conflicts, but also rational considerations about the future of trade unions. They have not only rehearsed time-worn historical disputes about the role of trade unions, but also disseminated successful experiences of Western trade unions.

Undoubtedly, trade union reform in China is closely related to the whole question of wider political reform. Some researchers, indeed, have pointed out that the main issue at stake in trade union reform is the resolution of the dilemma in which trade unions have had to play a double role, on the one hand to carry out the tasks set by the Party and on the other to represent the interests of the workers. The current workers' movement has already given prominence to this question. Ultimately, however, the positioning of trade unions in China will eventually be decided by the workers in the context of the fundamental social framework and the country's economic development (Xu 2010).

Notes

[1] The authors thank the Beijing office of the Friedrich Ebert Stiftung for financial support. The authors remain entirely responsible for the contents of the chapter.

[2] These data were provided by Liu Huilian, the chairman of Guangzhou Automobile Trade Union, during the authors' visit to CHAM Guangdong on 4 Aug. 2010. Liu is also the Trade Union Representative to China's 15th Congress, and he participated in the mediation and bargaining processes that led to the resolution of the strike.

[3] See Workercn.cn, 7 Mar. 2010, http://news.workercn.cn/c/2010/03/07/094212562108303_1.html (accessed 16 June 2011).

[4] One employee of CHAM Guangdong put his salary details on a webpage. These showed that his total monthly wage was CNY 1,510, made up of CNY 675 basic salary, CNY 340 job subsidies, CNY 100 attendance bonus, CNY 65 living allowance, CNY 250 housing allowance and CNY 80 commuting allowance: after the deduction of social security fees, he takes home only CNY 1,211. Taking into account the cost of food, housing and other basic living expenses, he was left with just CNY 456 every month. See also *Southern Weekend*, 3 June 2010.

[5] See also Banyuetan.org, 5 July 2010.

[6] See also Zaobao.com, 3 June 2010, http://www.zaobao.com/special/china/cnpol/pages3/cnpol100603b.shtml (accessed 16 June 2011).

[7] Lin Yanling, "The current features and trend of industrial relations in China", Banyuetan.org, 5 July 2010.

[8] See Sohu.com, 31 May 2010, http://business.sohu.com/20100531/n272472543.shtml (accessed 16 June 2011).

[9] See the "Open letter to social communities and all workers from delegation of strike workers of CHAM Guangdong", 3 June 2010, http://www.taoguba.com.cn/Article/312999/1 (accessed 16 June 2011).

[10] For Wang's speech, see http://www.sz.gov.cn/cn/sz/sz/xq/jqhd/201006/t20100613_1546822.htm (accessed 16 June 2011).

[11] Unfortunately, the revised draft generated opposition from employers, and failed to be put into discussion at the 21st meeting of the Guangdong Standing Committee of the National People's Congress on 21 Sep. 2010, which means that to date the draft has been suspended.

[12] A telephone survey in 2009 showed that it is very common for chairmen of enterprise trade unions to hold this dual role. See also Liu and Zhang (2010), p. 31.

Resources

All-China Federation of Trade Unions (ACFTU). 2010. "ACFTU's resolution on strengthening trade unions' role", No. 39, 26 July.

Chan, A. 2010. "Labour unrest and role of unions", in *China Daily*, http://www.chinadaily.com.cn/opinion/2010-06/18/content_9987347.htm (accessed 16 June 2011).

Chang, K. 2009. *Report on labour relations in China* (Beijing, China Labour and Social Security Publishing House).

China Labour Bulletin. 2010. "Review on the Democratic Management Act in enterprises in Guangdong (revised draft)", http://www.clb.org.hk/schi/node/1301271 (accessed 16 June 2011).

China Labour Statistical Yearbook. 1995–2009 (Beijing: China Statistics Press).

Jiang, Y. 2010. "Face rationally, treat legally", in *Economic Observer*, 14 June.

Li, Y. 2010. "Calls for strong trade unions", in *Nanfengchuang*, 26 June.

Lin, X. 2010. "The legislation to regulate collective wage negotiation in Guangdong", in *First Financial Daily*, 22 July.

Lin, Y. 2009. *30 years of reform and opening up: The evolution and cultivation of Chinese workers' rights awareness* (Beijing, China Social Sciences Press).

Liu, X.; Zhang, Q. 2010. "A survey on the double roles of chairmen of trade unions", in *Chinese Workers' Movement*, no. 4.

Qiao, J. 2009. "The new labour law and the status of labour in China in 2008", in Ru Xin et al. (eds), pp. 312–27.

Ru, X. et al. (eds). 2009. *Society of China: Analysis and forecast in 2009* (Beijing, Social Sciences Academic Press).

Xiao, S. 2010. "DENSO Nansha conflict satisfactorily resolved and wage raised by 800 RMB", in Xinhua.net (Guangzhou), 27 June.

Xu, X. 2010. "The double role of trade unions in China", in *Papers for the 2010 Sociology Academic Conference in China*, Institute of Sociology, Chinese Academy of Social Sciences, and China Institute of Industrial Relations, Harbin, Heilongjiang, July.

Yang, L. 2009. "Labour group emergencies would erupt", in *Liaowang*, 14 Dec.

Zhang, W. 2010. "Workers in 80 per cent enterprises will be able to bargain equally with their employers within 3 years", in *Yangchengwanbao*, 14 Aug.

Zheng, L. 2010. "A review on ACFTU's resolution on strengthening trade unions' role", in *Worker's Daily*, 29 July.

CREATING A FUNCTIONAL STATE: REDEFINING THE LABOUR–CAPITAL RELATIONSHIP IN NEPAL

11

Chandra D. Bhatta

Introduction

The global financial crisis has set new challenges for labour, capital and the State. Since 2007 we have been living through the worst economic crisis since the 1930s, and its repercussions are felt everywhere. During the 1930s the financial crisis was not experienced in the agrarian economies on the same scale as in the industrialized West, primarily because agrarian economies were not well connected at that time with a global financial system that was, to some extent, still in the making itself. The current financial crisis, however, has penetrated each and every economy around the world. In the words of the former Australian prime minister Kevin Rudd, it is a financial crisis which has become a general economic crisis, which is becoming an employment crisis, and which has in many countries produced social crisis that has ultimately turned into political crisis. Rudd further argues that it is a crisis which is simultaneously individual, national and global; a crisis for both the developed and the developing world; a crisis which is at once institutional, intellectual and ideological, and has called into question the neoliberal economic orthodoxy of the past 30 years (Rudd 2009).

For many analysts and observers, it is the Washington Consensus – already blamed for producing neoliberalism – that paved the way for a financial crisis of this gravity. Another group of commentators argue that the emergence of the crisis could also be attributed to the failure to strike a right balance in the relationship between labour and capital, as neoliberal policies placed more emphasis on profit maximization than on the overall development of society, including that of labour. This was noticed in both developed and developing countries, with majorities in many of the latter pushed below the poverty line. The lack of attention to the labour–capital relationship has led to the virtual collapse of the economic policies based on the Bretton Woods system and the

Washington Consensus – and that system now has to be overhauled if capitalism is to be saved from destroying itself.

For Nepal, the repercussions of the financial crisis are clearly visible. Large numbers of Nepalese working in foreign countries – who are better known as Lahures – started returning home, mainly from America, Europe, the Gulf, Japan, Malaysia and the Republic of Korea. Back in Nepal they have been seen as an extra burden at a time when the State is in political transition and barely produces enough jobs internally to absorb the vast number of young people, who make up more than 40 per cent of the total population. Trade unions, for their part, neither took up this issue with the manpower agencies who encouraged Nepalese to move abroad by giving false promises, even at the height of the crisis, nor put pressure on the State to expand the job market. Every year around 400,000 young people start looking for work, and most of them go abroad. In fact, people in general became worried about the job losses in those countries.[1] Remittances from Lahures amounted to 23 per cent of national GDP in 2010 – a lifeline to the national economy. The impact of the slump in these remittances was only too apparent in the real-estate business and in tourism as fewer people invested in property and declining numbers of tourists had knock-on effects throughout the country's economy.

The interesting question, however, is what forced Nepalese to become so heavily reliant on the foreign job market for their livelihoods. Many scholars take the view that the State's inability to expand the job market over the years goes hand in hand with policies that have put Nepal in this situation. One among many reasons why the Maoist insurgency gained strength during the democratic period of the 1990s is the State's failure to generate jobs and manage the large number of educated young people between the ages of 16 and 35. The adoption of neoliberal policies during that decade polarized society into haves and have-nots. The inability of the Government to strike a right balance between capital and labour contributed to one episode after another of political instability and finally pushed Nepal into the vortex of a supposedly class-based Maoist insurgency.

Against this backdrop, the overarching aim of this chapter is to shed light on the current trend of relations between capital, labour and the State in Nepal. It also emphasizes the need to redefine the labour–capital relationship as the basis for building a democratic state (Fukuyama 2004, preface).[2] The key question here is: what kind of developmental state is needed to achieve inclusive development and what is the role of organized labour in relation to the State, capital, and the rest of civil society? Citing the case of Nepal, the chapter explores the conditions under which trade unions could become active or inactive in bridging the gap between labour and capital. It asks whether trade unions are well equipped to address challenges posed by the capitalist bourgeoisie or are co-opted by it; and how trade unions could incorporate their agendas into the constitution that is soon to be drafted. Overall, then, the chapter critically analyses the current labour–capital relationship within the context of capital formation, and traces the respective roles of the employers, the State and the trade unions.

The structural problem in capital formation

Nepal has gone through multiple political transitions during the six decades from 1950.[3] This succession of changes has brought neither democratic stability nor economic prosperity. On the contrary, they are blamed for having brought more misery into the lives of working people. In this section of the chapter, I argue that there has been a structural problem in capital formation, which may in part be directly related to policy-makers who have failed to understand the needs of poor people and the basis of underdevelopment, and have misguidedly followed the prescriptions provided by the neoliberal policies that underlay the development mantras of the 1990s. This came about because, at the outset in 1990, the selection of key policy-makers, particularly the members of the National Planning Commission, was made on the basis of political affiliation rather than meritocracy, and their priority was always to seek "national development" through aid, in order to serve either their own political interests or those of the urban bourgeoisie. High dependency on "aid" for the alleged goal of national development has forced Nepal into an "AIDS"-like syndrome of underdevelopment. We could say, indeed, that in Nepal aid has become AIDS: a grave affliction that has seen mobilization of domestic resources and knowledge for development go into dramatic decline. Second, this dependence on aid has further centralized political and economic power, thereby weakening the wealth-generating capacity of the rural areas where the large majority of the population is located. This is because "aid" has been mobilized by the elites, most of whom are based in the urban centre and wish to use it to buttress their own prosperity.

The adoption of neoliberal economic policies despite a commitment enshrined in the 1990 constitution to adhere to a social market economy has generated multiple problems in society. Its most discernible effect was witnessed in the agriculture and industrial sectors. In agriculture, for example, Nepali decision-makers recommended removal of the subsidy that supported nearly 80 per cent of the entire Nepali workforce. The output from agriculture was already insufficient to support decent livelihoods; the removal of the subsidy exacerbated youth unemployment, which was already high as a result of the mistaken policies designed by the urban bourgeoisie. One scholar points out that agricultural workers are paid bare subsistence wages – just enough to keep them alive and able to produce the next generation of workers (Dahal 2007). In the industrial sector, meanwhile, the State illegally sold public industries, which used to employ large numbers of people, to private individuals for financial reward,[4] and embraced a policy of de-industrialization and de-nationalization that reduced the scale of employment in the "real economy".[5] In its place, the State has promoted a "symbolic" economy, largely based on financial capitalism and supported by the service industry, consisting of real-estate businesses, private banks, financial companies, consultancy firms, private schools, private hospitals, media organizations and insurance companies. The symbolic economy has captured a large proportion of the capital in Nepal, which has proved highly beneficial for the tiny urban elites but not for the workers at large because its benefits have not extended out to the social and geographical periphery. Financial capitalism, to the dismay of Nepalese, has been detrimental to workers and failed to provide social justice. The setting up of private educational institutions and hospitals in obeisance to the economic competitive model is another classic example of how injustice has been meted out in a society where the majority of the population live below the poverty line.[6] In social policy, too, the country faces crisis, with the State apparently following two types of policy, private and public – so that, for example, private schools and private hospitals are promoted to the detriment of public schools and public hospitals.

These fallacious policies have reduced common people's access to the resources of State and market alike by reducing their purchasing capacity. For example, workers have to be satisfied with a monthly income of 6,100 Nepali rupees (NPR) (nearly US$87 in April 2011 figures), not even enough to meet daily expenses, whereas those who work in the crony capitalist milieu – in which success in business depends on close relationships between business people, government officials and politicians – go home with huge amounts of money. Similarly, the CEOs of the private banking and financial sectors accumulate unjustifiably high salaries and bonuses.[7] The contribution made by this part of the economy to national GDP is as low as 3 per cent: it focuses on jobless growth and treats workers merely as consumers. The grand bazaar of the urban economy is largely a black economy which is thriving on tax evasion. Ghani and Lockhart (2008) revealed that over the years, particularly after the reinstallation of democracy in 1990, 120 business houses in Nepal have repeat - edly evaded tax and taken loans from banks that were never repaid. The recent resignation of the Government's Finance Secretary as a result of a row over tax evasion with the Finance Minister is the classic example of this phenomenon.[8]

The marked rise in prosperity of the urban centres through trickle-up effects – the inward movement of money and resources from the rural areas to the urban centres, from where most of it travels outside the country – has not contributed to the improvement of the rural economy. The capital surplus is recycled to generate more money, buy consumables and luxury goods, and invest in the real-estate business; it is not invested in setting up industries which could, through real production, resolve Nepal's problems of poverty, unemployment and inability to meet its people's basic needs. Many observers take the view that the structural shift from the "real" to the "symbolic" economy has transformed Nepal into a State that consumes everything but produces nothing. This can be substantiated from the latest data revealed by the Ministry of Commerce, which indicate that Nepal imports six times the value of what it exports.

The capitalistic orientation of political leaders, irrespective of their ideology, oscillates between crony capitalism and kleptocracy – a process that provides benefits to the ruling classes through organized corruption by using government machinery to augment personal wealth (Bhatta 2010). Evidence of this organized corruption, mediated through informal and formal communication channels, can be seen everywhere. The formation of the current Constituent Assembly (CA), which is massively skewed in favour of business interests, is itself a demonstration of this point. It includes influential members from all the business houses representing various political parties: these amount to 27 CA members out of a total strength of 601, representing only 10 per cent of the total population. By contrast, just eight CA members representing trade unions stand for the working classes who make up 90 per cent of the total working population; the remaining CA members represent various political parties (of which there are 31) and defend their partisan interests. This distribution of seats raises legitimate concerns about the likelihood of labour-friendly policies being adopted, because even though there are 601 CA members in all, it has always been a few influential leaders with multiple influential connections who make the significant decisions.

One could further argue that the capital formation process lacks entrepreneurship, its beneficiaries being members of an urban, non-stakeholding comprador class (Gyawali 2010) who are anti-poor, anti-labour and anti-development. As a result, the poor are becoming poorer and the rich are getting richer. The gap between the rich and poor in Nepal is such that 90 per cent of Nepalese are living lives of wretchedness, sharing among them 48 per cent of national income, while the remaining 10 per cent, who are super-rich, enjoy 52 per cent of national income. Twenty years ago Nepal had fewer poor people than it has today and more rich; today it has more poor and fewer rich. The de-industrialization policy adopted by the Government has contributed to the same disastrous state of affairs. This approach has reinforced the growth of the urban comprador political economy that now employs just 10 per cent of the people and is incapable of meeting the demands of Nepal's burgeoning workforce – primarily for two obvious reasons. First, Nepal's large workforce is either semi-skilled or unskilled and cannot compete and survive in this "symbolic" economy. Second, this economy is not deeply rooted in society.

In these circumstances, the chances of people's desire for prosperity and economic well-being being met seem small. If development is about improving the quality of life, an alteration in property and power relations is essential to create genuine space for people to participate in policy discourse. This can only be done when social solidarity is created on a basis of equality: gender equality, social equality, and equal access for all to education, health and income generation opportunities. And only a social welfare state – a state that can transform the class power of labour and capital into common citizenship and foster mutuality in society without hierarchy (Bleie 2010) – can deliver this end.

The discussion offered so far shows that capital formation in Nepal is driven solely by the philosophy of accumulating surplus capital through manipulation of policies and exploitation of workers. This philosophy needs to be countered to protect labour from structural exploitation and to introduce what Marx calls genuine democracy (Almond 2002: 136). A failure to amend the prevailing counterproductive politics and policies will compel many more to look beyond their own country for their livelihoods (for details, see Sinha 2009), and more and more people will become Lahures.[9] Those who cannot afford to travel abroad to seek work may easily become victims of radical political parties and groups that make promises that are never fulfilled. One interesting point worth making is that Lahures, too, are exploited – at the hands of labour agencies, most of which are run by the bureaucrats, politicians and their close associates. This business has again fuelled the growth of consumerism. Lahures, too, are spending their income primarily on building houses in the urban centres – very few Lahures have used their income to fund entrepreneurial activity – and this has encouraged a rentier economy that flourishes on profiteering. Nepal's rapid urbanization, achieved by converting arable lands to build houses, bears ample witness to this development. The threadbare and unfulfilled promises made by the country's leaders have led to the erosion of people's allegiance to a State whose policies merely serve the interest of urban elites,[10] widening the gap between the rich and the poor and creating a situation in which people often challenge the very *raison d'être* of the State and the political and economic system.

The role of the trade unions

Having outlined the structural problem faced by Nepal in its capital formation, the next purpose of this essay is to examine how trade unions can contribute to bridging the gap between capital and labour in order to play a constructive role in state building. Principally, the logic behind the formation of trade unions is to overcome exploitation of weak labour by strong capital. As a political agency representing the workers, trade unions have to establish their social utility by humanizing working conditions, improving industrial relations, and exerting pressure on the agencies of capital and political authority to set up a necessary framework of social justice at multiple levels of governance by reaffirming democratic practice as the source of value and political action (Dahal 2009). In Nepal, this has not happened. In many cases, workers' rights have remained just aspirations or goals whose achievement is postponed into the future.

The political process that is currently under way provides scope for the trade unions to intervene and develop a proper mechanism for setting the future course of engagement between labour, capital and the State. This represents an opportunity to put forward their vision in designing a strategy to improve the conditions of the workers, including by ensuring their rights are guaranteed in the forthcoming constitution. However, once again this process is much influenced by partisan interest, and the most important stakeholders – the workers – risk being sidelined. Nevertheless, the trade unions seem to have taken into account what Amartya Sen calls the 3Rs of engagement – Reason, Result and Reach – when it comes to fighting back against strong capital in favour of better policy formulations and effective distributional benefits.

Theoretically, almost all the trade unions in Nepal advocate a welfare state. The agreement between Government, employers and trade unions signed in April 2010 includes provision for the establishment of a national social security fund which aims to provide unemployment benefits, maternity benefits, injury benefits and sick benefits for 2 million workers. It is proposed to fund this by means of contributions of 11 per cent from employees' income, 10 per cent from employers' profit and 10 per cent from government revenue. Trade unions' plans to introduce a social security card would assist in constructing an environment in which capital and labour would work together to achieve effective post-conflict reconstruction as well as a sustainable peace. But the co-optation of unions by political parties, business houses and media organizations has reduced their capacity to put pro-labour policies into action. This is amply illustrated by the failure of trade unions to mobilize the media in 2010 when the Chambers of Commerce, with the help of the Government, flouted the principle of no pay, no work for the workers.

Historically, Nepali trade unions grew out of the political movement to install democracy, and in the process they have emerged as relatively organized actors in society. But they have not exercised effective influence, and workers' issues have not received fair attention. One reason for this is the problematic relationship between trade unions and employers, in which each side sees the other as its arch-rival and enemy. Trade unions view employers as the representatives of the capitalist bourgeoisie class, while employers see trade unions as extensions of opposing political parties. The unions do indeed seem to be heavily dependent on political parties for their recognition and indeed their survival. Many observers would in fact agree that there are no clear boundaries between trade unions and their respective political parties. There is indeed an established school of thought according to which the close links connecting both trade unions and employers with political parties have inhibited democratization of both the economic power of the market and the political power of the State. The overlapping interests among these forces have co-opted them to work independently, thereby reducing the unions' capacity for common endeavour to alter the balance of the power of the State and market in favour of labour, the poor and the powerless.

Whatever the truth of this argument, it is certainly the case that both employers and trade unions are strongly aligned with political parties. This affiliation has had an adverse impact on efforts to promote workers' rights in many areas, including capital formation and wage and benefit allocations. The direct effects can be readily seen in the failure to implement labour legislation, with measures being repeatedly drafted and amended but seldom put into action in earnest.

With rising unemployment, there is an urgent need to strike a right balance between the State, the market and the trade unions to bring labour on board. But this can only be done when trade unions ally themselves with other groups in civil society, such as the media and other social movements, to exert pressure on employers and the Government to deliver the justifiable increase in wages and develop a social market economy that will provide work also for future generations. The politics of trade unions should be geared to representing class interests, which up to now has not been the case, primarily because they have been captured and co-opted by the dominant actors in society, namely business leaders and political parties (Dahal 2009). Employers, for their part, seem not to have realized that social utility and mutual dependency apply to them too; that business exists only because society exists.

The formation of the Joint Trade Union Coordination Centre in 2009 is a positive step towards conveying the unions' demands coherently to the various constitutional committees in the Constituent Assembly. These 14 committees provide them with a vital opportunity to initiate a debate on their rights which will help them to set the future course of the State towards social transformation. This will surely help trade unions to establish the conditions necessary in order to promote the interests of workers in the productive sector. The slogans of "unity in diversity", "networking", "team spirit" and "working relationship" are sound principles on which to strive for common ground and collaborate to influence state policy in areas of common benefit (Dahal 2009).

Trade unions and the state-building agenda

State building is a holistic project. For the purpose of this study it should be understood as creating a State capable of accumulating and exercising all kinds of power (economic, political and social). Thus it is a process by which the State grows not only in economic productivity and coercive strength, but also in political and institutional power. What is important in the process of state building is how the State tries to consolidate power, how it strikes a balance between different societal actors, how it works towards distributional justice for its people and how it resolves conflicts to achieve democratic peace.

The state-building agenda has taken centre stage in Nepal since the formal end of the Maoist insurgency in 2006. A close look at the Nepali State reveals a very gloomy picture, characterized by the emergence of armed groups, the federalization of national territories, the rise of identity politics and of non-state armed actors, a crisis of governability, opaque decision-making, dominance by a small elite, loss of trust in formal state institutions and decline in economic activity (Ghani et al. 2006). For all these reasons the State has not been able to expand its authority and is often treated as weak and fragile. Moreover, there is no common understanding of "the State" in Nepal: for the poor it is everything – although they are not getting much from it, as it has been captured by the elites, for whom it is an agency to be manipulated for personal benefit.

State building is about creating a functional State that can defend the political, economic and social rights of the people and maintain its sovereignty. It is also about the democratization of economic power, which is necessary to assert political rights. The Nepali State has not worked sufficiently towards this end over the years. It allowed the cycle of financial capitalism to continue by mobilizing money again and again to earn profits without investing in the productive economy or providing a sufficient income share to the workers to enable them to create their stake in the State and defend their human rights according to the labour laws enshrined in the constitution. As noted earlier in this chapter, during the 1990s successive Governments adopted neoliberal policies that saw the market as a friend and the State as its arch-enemy; during this period the trade unions remained mere onlookers. The market, however, served only the interests of the professional elites, while promises of socio-economic transformation were left unfulfilled. The project of bidding farewell to the nation-state and welcoming economic globalization, as everywhere else, weakened the collective bargaining capacity of the unions to strike a deal in the workers' favour. The capitalist classes became influential to such an extent that they repeatedly threatened to shut down plants and industries if policies were not designed in their favour and their rights to hire and fire workers not asserted. They seem to have been more organized, through Chambers of Commerce, than the workers, who were fragmented across partisan lines. These events produced more losers than winners as time passed.

The political parties, for their part, seem to have been using trade unions as clients to serve their respective political agendas.[11] This has led to the mushrooming of separate trade unions (almost all of the 31 political parties on the Constituent Assembly have their own trade union wings); however, there was no space for them all to be productively engaged in labour work and action (Arendt 1998). During the field visits organized by the author in different parts of the country, many participants said they felt that trade unions were used by the political parties to further their interests. This suggests that political leaders have set out to identify themselves with the "masses" for political power and with the "capitalist classes" or elites for economic power. But sadly political policies are for the most part made for the "capitalist classes", not the "masses". The MNCs' reluctance to engage in dialogue with trade union representatives and the development of a new mechanism of direct communication with employees by the management of MNCs to escape national regulatory provisions have further jeopardized the future of collective bargaining in Nepal (Sinha 2009). In the past, on many occasions "profit" has been individualized and "cost" has been socialized. This has resulted in frequent industrial action in the country. In such a state of affairs, it would be appropriate to invest in the organizations that work for the poor and marginalized groups, such as NGOs, academic institutions and think-tanks. These organizations will spread the message of civic culture and promulgate the principles of corporate social responsibility across different layers of society.

Nepal is at a significant historical juncture; debates, discussions and mobilization of opinion around the new constitution-making process are interesting, contentious and promising. There are three main issues that need to be addressed urgently: first, the peace process needs to be brought to a logical conclusion addressing all social and political contradictions; second, the constitution needs to be written within the stipulated timeframe, which has now been extended for the second time, to the end of August 2011; and third, a sound environment for economic development needs to be created. If it does these three things, the State will be able to restore its legitimate claim to coercive power, taxation, and the loyalty of citizens. Trade unions, for their part, should work with the State in these processes. A dynamic role for the unions will bring nearer the achievement of noble goals such as equity, justice, poverty eradication, full employment, social cohesion and better working conditions, as well as contributing to empowering the powerless through capacity building, training and policy interventions. Towards this end, the unions should advocate a labour-friendly policy, associating themselves with it personally as well as in principle, that is conducive to equity – that is, to the wealth-creating capacity of the market and to meeting people's social needs. Achieving a balance between these decisions requires collective inputs from all social actors. In this setting, the trade unions can perform a valuable role in steering things in the right direction (Somavia 1999). The required intellectual and political leadership for the social transformation should come from the trade unions – from their "organic intellectuals", to use the terminology of Antonio Gramsci.

There are no sectoral solutions to the problems of workers, which are common to labour throughout Nepali society. Nepalese trade unions thus have to equip themselves to be seen as spokespersons for the broader concerns of society and to play the role of enlightened decision-makers, not decision-takers either for their own interests or the interests of particular groups or parties. There is an urgent need for the unified trade union movement to work in constructing coherent policies (for details, see GEFONT 2009),[12] and on this foundation to build up the necessary organizational base for gaining sufficient political support to influence outcomes at the national level. The trade unions, the largest organized group in civil society, can develop a new social contract through direct involvement with economic systems of production and distribution. Trade unions, as a critical catalytic agent, can also promote human rights and democracy – historically an important mandate of labour unions. Right through the twentieth century, unions have decisively influenced struggles either to establish or to revive democratic institutions (Somavia 1999). Civil and political rights are an essential precondition for access to labour rights, and only within a democracy can labour rights be met as human rights. All these tasks can only be accomplished through active participation of unions in a democratic political process – a precondition for the creation of a functional State.

Conclusion

The modern State is expected to protect the political, economic, social, cultural and other rights of its citizens. It is also considered the largest employer, with capacity to absorb surplus labour by creating productive capacity in industrial and other sectors as required. In Nepal, the State is the only agency that can address the demands of the returning Lahures and other workers for a welfare state by accelerating the process of industrialization. Nepalese have been becoming Lahures for more than two centuries, but this practice has not contributed much to the national economy. Industrialization would provide the nation with some sort of sustainable economy, thereby putting an end to the culture of becoming Lahures simply to achieve a means of livelihood. But even this is not enough. The State should put pressure on the private sector to generate more wealth, whereupon the State itself should engage in its rightful distribution. What is equally important, indeed necessary, is to bring a large number of capital-holding individuals, firms and business enterprises into the tax net in order to encourage them to contribute to bringing the poor and powerless out of poverty and to creating an egalitarian society. Until now it has been the poor who have paid for the rich, and this process has to be reversed.

Therefore the first and foremost task of the trade unions is to restore the confidence of poor and powerless workers in the polity by creating an environment of decent work. Another important task is to ensure that the collective bargaining process is transparent and works for labour as well as capital, which has not been the case up to now. There is also an urgent need to institutionalize the system of "codetermination", by which employees are given rights of collective representation in companies by the inclusion of representatives at board level – a practice which is not deeply rooted in Nepali culture. Such provision could encourage the realization that companies are not merely the private property of shareholders and owners; that employees too are real stakeholders with a legitimate interest in shaping corporate goals and policies. It would provide an opportunity to protect the interests of both workers and employers, and will lead towards democratic control of capital, which in turn will assist the socialization of the economy that is essential for its own survival. The underlying principle of this policy, by and large, is to establish a collective employee ownership relationship which can address intermittent tensions and disputes within enterprises. Such a process can help to counter the destructive logic of capitalism by shifting the balance of power (both economic and political) away from capital, the bureaucracy, interest groups and political parties towards the broader society.

However, as discussed above, trade unions in Nepal hitherto seem to have failed to push for the participatory development necessary to neutralize the class-based power of the State. Some critics even allege that they are too closely aligned either with the market or with political society (including political parties), and too concerned with radicalizing the labour force in pursuit of their own vested interests. The militarization of trade unions that is widely seen in Nepal has to be discouraged for the sake of industrial peace. The biggest challenge that lies ahead for the trade unions is to secure relative autonomy from the dominant groups in society in order to make a positive and independent impact. Up to now the Nepali State has been captured by dominant groups; if trade unions work collectively, they can contribute to the creation of a functional State which can translate labour rights into practice. Such a State can overcome the external challenges brought about by the financial crisis and the internal legitimacy crisis arising from its weakness. Finally, let us abandon the currently dominant mantra of the "survival of the fittest" and return to our forefathers' philosophy of the "survival of the weakest" for the prosperity of all.

Notes

[1] When the author spoke to people in rural areas of Nepal about the financial crisis, they responded that they were not worried about the Nepali job market so much as about the job market in north-west Europe, the Gulf countries, Japan, Malaysia, the Republic of Korea and the United States.

[2] State-building is a multifaceted process, but in the context of a post-conflict situation like that in Nepal, it consists primarily of the creation of new government institutions and strengthening of existing ones in order to address the challenges brought about by the changed political situation.

[3] The first took place in 1950, when Nepali political leaders launched a movement to topple the rule of the Ranas family and democracy was installed for the first time. The second took place in 1960 when a royal putsch abolished democracy and established the partyless Panchayat system, and the third in 1980 to push for a referendum against the Panchayat. The fourth one in 1990 reinstalled democracy and put an end to the Panchayat system, and the last one in 2006 abolished the monarchy and saw Nepal become a (federal) democratic republic.

[4] Thirty state-owned enterprises (SOEs) were sold to private individuals.

[5] During 1991/92 there were 4,271 organized units of industries providing employment to 213,653 people, but by 2001/02 the number of organized industries came down to 3,210 and they employed 181,695 people.

[6] According to the latest report published by Oxford University, around 65 per cent live below the poverty line. For details see OPHI (2010).

[7] The private banks pay their CEOs between NPR 0.5 million and 1.5 million a month.

[8] The Finance Secretary, Rameshwor Khanal, wanted to take action against tax evaders but was forced to resign as the line minister, Bharat Mohan Adhikari, was not willing to take action, the majority of the offenders being affiliated to the Finance Minister's party.

[9] Every day, 700 young Nepalis leave the country in search of jobs.

[10] The classic example is the recent cut made by the Nepali Government to the developmental budget that could have helped lift many out of poverty in order to give a fuel subsidy to the tiny urban elite ("Subsidy to the rich in a poor country", *Nagarik National Daily*, 20 April 2011).

[11] The UCPN (Maoist) chief Prachanda recently said that he would turn factories into barracks and appealed to workers through the trade union affiliated with the party – the All Nepal Trade Union Federation – to be ready for the revolution (reported in the *Himalayan Times*, 28 February 2011).

[12] The idea of "one union, one voice" has been proposed by Nepalese trade unions. The same issue was also raised during this author's interaction with several stakeholders.

Resources

Almond, G.A. 2002. *Ventures in political science: Narratives and reflections* (London, Lynne Rienner).

Arendt, H. 1998. *The human condition* (Chicago, University of Chicago Press).

Bhatta, C.D. 2010. "Agent of regime change or peace builders", in D.R. Dahal and C.D. Bhatta, *Building bridges of peace in Nepal* (Kathmandu, Friedrich-Ebert-Stiftung, Nepal Office).

Bleie, T. 2010. *Newsfront* weekly (Kathmandu), 11–17 March.

Dahal, D.R. 2007. "The paradox of a weak state: Distributional struggles and social transformation in Nepal", in *Readings on Governance and Development*, Vol. 9 (Kathmandu).

—. 2009. "Trade unions in the new context: An agenda of social transformation in Nepal", paper presented at a panel discussion organized by the General Federation of Nepali Trade Unions (GEFONT) in cooperation with the Friedrich-Ebert-Stiftung on "Transformation for Unity", Kathmandu, 4 April.

Fukuyama, F. 2004. *State-building, governance and world order in the 21st century* (London, Profile Books).

General Federation of Nepali Trade Unions (GEFONT). 2009. *Unity for transformation: Direction of Nepali trade union movement*, draft of policy document for GEFONT Fifth National Congress, Kathmandu, 4 April.

Ghani, A.; Lockhart, C. 2008. *Fixing failed states: A framework for rebuilding a fractured world* (Oxford, Oxford University Press).

— et al. 2006. "An agenda for state-building in the twenty-first century", in *The Fletcher Forum of World Affairs*, Vol. 30, No. 1 (Winter), pp. 101–23.

Gyawali, D. 2010. "Déjà vu politics of tragedies, farce and impunity", in *Spotlight*, Vol. 3, No. 21 (19 Mar.), pp. 5–6.

Oxford Poverty and Human Development Initiative (OPHI). 2010. *Country briefing: Nepal*, July 2010, http://www.ophi.org.uk/wp-content/uploads/Nepal.pdf (accessed 16 June 2011).

Rudd, K. 2009. "The global financial crisis", in *Monthly Review*, No. 42, Feb.

Sinha, P. 2009. "Agenda for Nepalese trade unions", paper delivered at the conference to celebrate the 20th anniversary of GEFONT, Kathmandu, 20 July.

Somavia, J. 1999. "Trade unions in the 21st century", keynote speech by the ILO Director-General, 20 Oct. 1999, http://www.ilo.org/public/english/bureau/dgo/speeches/somavia/1999/network.htm (accessed 16 June 2011).

A ROWING BOAT ON THE OPEN SEA OR IN A HAVEN FROM FINANCIAL AND ENVIRONMENTAL CRISES? NEW ZEALAND, THE GLOBAL FINANCIAL CRISIS AND A UNION RESPONSE

12

Bill Rosenberg

> Small open economies are like rowing boats on an open sea. One cannot predict when they might capsize; bad steering increases the chances of disaster and a leaky boat makes it inevitable. But their chances of being broadsided by a wave are significant no matter how well they are steered and no matter how seaworthy they are. (Stiglitz 1998)

New Zealand, an island nation of 4.4 million people in the southern Pacific Ocean, is associated with a history of social progress, including being one of the first countries in the world to give women the vote and to build a welfare state. Built on foundations laid in the late nineteenth and early twentieth centuries, the comprehensive welfare state was put in place by the social democratic Labour Party which gained power during the global depression of the 1930s, having been formed with strong trade union involvement. A high level of unionization was supported by compulsory union membership in unionized sectors, and later unqualified union preference (whereby a worker taking up a job covered by an award or collective agreement was required to become a member of the union), along with varying forms of arbitration and central wage-setting. The country's progressive image, however, tended to obscure the State's origins as a British settler colony built on the confiscation of land from the indigenous Māori people throughout the nineteenth century, which led to their widespread poverty, demoralization and threatened loss of culture throughout most of the twentieth. It is only in the last 25 years that these historical grievances have begun to be seriously addressed.

Nonetheless, by the 1950s New Zealand had one of the highest per capita incomes in the world, along with genuinely full employment. This was built on agricultural exports to its former colonial master, the United Kingdom, and a growing, highly protected manufacturing sector. Its economic structure of internationally efficient agriculture, manufacturing protected by tariffs and controls on imports, foreign exchange and capital controls, and a strong welfare state enabled successive governments to manage domestic demand, prices and wages. However, the entry of the United Kingdom into the then European Economic Community in 1973 signalled the end of New Zealand's historical dependence on British markets. As a result of this, coupled with the international oil crisis of the 1970s, the economy contracted and, after inadequate responses from a series of governments, a balance of payments crisis was used to justify radical neoliberal reforms by an administration that took power in 1984.

This chapter sketches the actions taken by this and following governments to embed neoliberalism in New Zealand's economy, public institutions and ideology, and the results for the country's economy and society. Though the grip of neoliberalism was modified in the first decade of the present century, its social and economic failure formed the basis for the development of an Alternative Economic Strategy in the New Zealand union movement through its peak body, the New Zealand Council of Trade Unions (CTU). The chapter describes the thinking behind this strategy and outlines its policies.

The coming of neoliberalism to New Zealand[1]

The neoliberal Government that came into power in 1984 was paradoxically a Labour Party Government. The neoliberal reforms it introduced were hailed by advocates as perhaps the most pure example of those policies anywhere in the world. They included a radical agenda of deregulation of many parts of the economy, including the financial sector; the creation of an independent Reserve Bank focusing solely on price and financial stability; the corporatization and eventual sale of many parts of the State in a society where large portions of industry and commerce had been built up by both central and local Government; major changes to the taxation system, including reductions of both personal and company income taxes in favour of a near-comprehensive value added tax (goods and services tax); the removal of subsidies on staple consumer goods and to farmers; and opening the economy by the removal of tariffs, import controls, and currency and capital controls, including a pure float of the currency.

As a result of the extreme deregulation, the international stock market crash of 1987 hit New Zealand worse than most countries. Over the next few years, major New Zealand companies including a major bank collapsed and unemployment rose steeply, reaching 8.9 per cent at the end of 1990.

Public splits and continuing economic turmoil led to a resounding defeat of the Labour Government in 1990. It was replaced by New Zealand's main conservative party, the National Party, which by then was also dominated by purist neoliberals. It continued the neoliberal programme, making savage cuts to social benefits and introducing new anti-union labour legislation. The programme of deregulation and increasing use of market mechanisms to provide public services and infrastructure intensified, along with further widespread privatizations and accelerated deregulation of international trade and investment.

The new National Party Government's labour legislation, the Employment Contracts Act, came into force in 1991 and represented an extraordinary attack on labour rights. It outlawed strikes over multi-employer agreements, effectively limiting the formation of collective employment agreements to a single enterprise. The word "union" appeared only once in the Act, in a transitional provision. Instead, employees would be represented by so-called "bargaining agents", which could include organizations created by the employer, or people in business for the purpose. Individual employment contracts were promoted, and all collective employment "contracts" automatically became individual contracts on expiry.

In 1990, there were approximately 720,000 workers covered by an award or a collective agreement. By 2000, only 421,400 workers were covered by collective agreements. The reduction in union membership in New Zealand in the 1990s was the sharpest in the world. Union density halved, from 43 per cent of wage and salary earners in 1991 to 22 per cent in 2000, when the legislation was replaced (figure 12.1).

Figure 12.1 Union density in New Zealand, 1970–2010

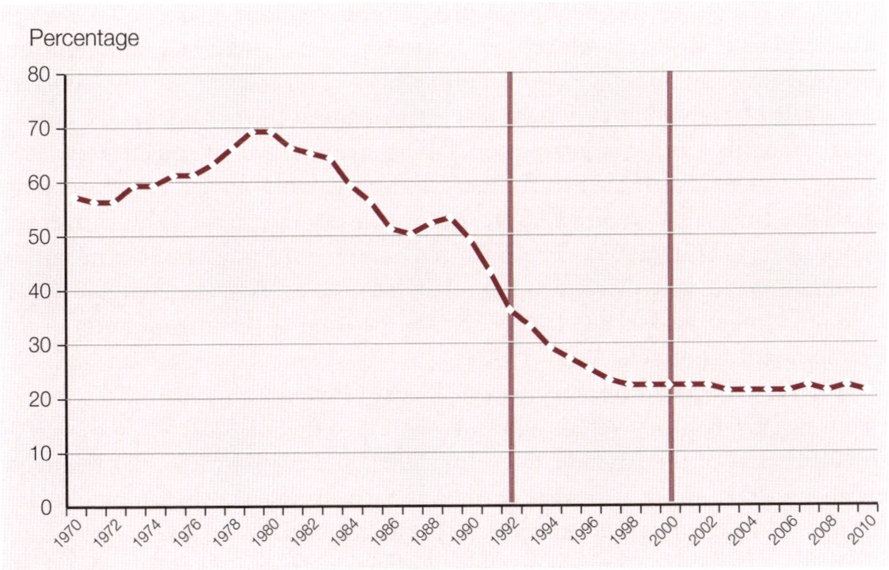

Note: Vertical lines mark recent changes in employment law: Employment Contracts Act 1991 and Employment Relations Act 2000.

Sources: 1970–2008: OECD; 2009, 2010: New Zealand Department of Labour.

Figure 12.2 Inequality in New Zealand, 1984–2009

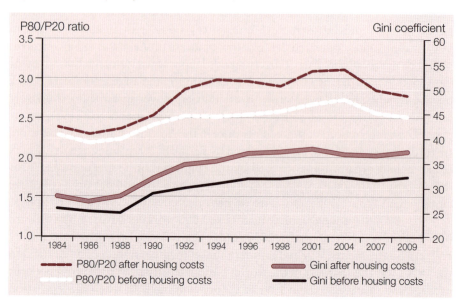

Note: P80/P20 and the Gini coefficient are measures of household income inequality.

Source: Perry (2010), p. 129.

The effects of the neoliberal programme included many job losses in manufacturing as firms closed in response to international competition, throwing large numbers of people out of work. Poverty levels greatly increased as a result of high unemployment levels throughout the period, savage cuts in social benefits, and stagnating or falling real wages as businesses used unemployment and their greatly increased bargaining power to refuse wage increases. Inequality (figure 12.2) rose at the fastest rate in the OECD over the period (see OECD 2004). The only remaining state wage intervention, the minimum wage, was allowed to fall relative to the average wage (figure 12.3). Unemployment peaked at 11.2 per cent at the time of the introduction of the Employment Contracts Act.

A New Zealand Treasury paper (Black, Guy and McLellan 2003) noted that wages fell from a level roughly comparable to that of Australia in the 1980s to 60 per cent of the Australian level by 2002, and that "with labour relatively cheaper in relation to capital than in Australia, it appears that New Zealand firms have opted for a lower level of capital intensity". In the main market segments of the economy over which official measures of productivity are available for the period 1990–2006, the compensation of employees per hour (including non-wage items) rose in real terms by only 13.6 per cent, while productivity rose 47.1 per cent (for further details see Rosenberg 2010).

Figure 12.3 Minimum wage and average wage in New Zealand, 1986–2010

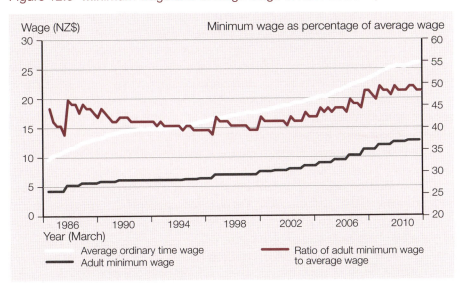

Source: Author's calculations based on data from Statistics New Zealand.

Many privatizations were disastrous failures, leading to asset stripping or expensive failed overseas adventures rather than improved services. Some were later reversed at considerable cost; others, such as those of telecommunications and the electricity system, present continuing problems of regulation.

The National Party was voted out of power in 1999. By then, Labour Party supporters had forced a change in its political programme. It turned to a "Third Way" position similar to that espoused by the British Labour Party, though with a strong aversion to privatization. In addition, the electorate had voted in 1993 to change the electoral system to a multi-member proportional representation system similar to that in Germany. From 1999 to 2008, Labour formed governments with small left and centre parties. It was voted out in the 2008 general election.

Over that period it reversed some of the damage of the 15 previous years. It was initially helped by economic growth, which was among the strongest in the OECD. It largely stopped the privatization programme, renationalized Air New Zealand and the rail system, and created a new retail bank, Kiwibank, which proved highly popular. It rebuilt parts of the public service. In 2004 it introduced a system of tax credits (in a programme called "Working for Families") which favours people in work with families. This, along with the availability of state housing at income-related rents and increases in the minimum wage which outpaced rises in the average wage, halted the increase in inequality for those in work. However, poverty among those relying on welfare benefits, including many children, remains a major problem. Benefit levels have remained largely static in real terms since they were severely cut in 1991.

In 2000 the Employment Contracts Act was replaced with the Employment Relations Act – a moderate reform and not a restoration of the earlier system. The new law recognizes union rights, acknowledges that there is unequal bargaining power between employer and employees, encourages collective bargaining, provides for voluntary union membership, is based on the principle of good faith in employer–union relationships, and promotes mediation as the preferred way to resolve problems. Nonetheless, while union membership grew in numerical terms, it failed to increase as a proportion of the employed workforce and union density levelled off (see figure 12.1).

Improvements were made to annual leave and paid parental leave entitlements, and the minimum wage was increased each year by substantially more than inflation (see figure 12.3) without damaging side-effects (see e.g. Hyslop and Stillman 2004). Labour also encouraged concepts of tripartite social partnership, with union and business representatives present in many aspects of policy development and implementation.

However, the Labour-led Government's fiscal, monetary and international trade policies were in many ways a continuation of those of its predecessors. While it had an enormous task before it in 1999 to repair 15 years of increasingly embedded poverty and damaged public services and community relationships, many were disappointed that it was not more ambitious. It maintained the independent Reserve Bank focused on price stability and continued enthusiastically to pursue preferential trade and investment agreements, locking in the liberalized international trade and investment regime.

Given New Zealand's small size and geographical isolation, international economic relationships are central to its economy. Since capital and exchange controls were removed in the 1980s, its international liabilities have ballooned and at March 2011 stood at 150 per cent of GDP in gross terms and 75 per cent in net terms. The dividend and interest income from this has driven a chronic current account deficit reaching 9 per cent of GDP in the last decade, a position which has only improved as a result of the recession lowering company profits and imports. New Zealand is still heavily dependent on lightly processed land-based commodity exports, increasingly to China.

The National Party was re-elected in 2008, and has led a coalition with a small far-right neoliberal party and the Māori Party which is based on the assertion of indigenous rights and values and is showing the tensions of trying to represent both growing Māori corporate influence and a longer-standing low-income constituency who make up a disproportionately large part of the Māori population. The new Government has not taken the austerity approach of its 1990s predecessor, but has focused so far on regressive tax changes and regulatory reform.

The National Party Government responded to the recession by bringing forward some infrastructure spending, including school building, home insulation and road-building projects, some targeted labour market programmes and tax cuts, leading to deficits which are forecast to run until the year ending in June 2015, resulting in increasing government debt levels. The OECD's estimate in 2009 was that the entire net stimulus constituted tax cuts (OECD 2009: 61). These are being used to justify severe constraints on government spending, although many welfare and pension payments are still being indexed to inflation. In its 2011 budget, the Government withdrew the remaining economic stimulus despite substantial continuing unemployment, initiated cuts to the Working for Families scheme and began a programme of several years of contractionary cuts in real terms in government spending. If re-elected in the November 2011 poll, it will partially privatize some state-owned companies, reduce subsidies for retirement saving, and attempt to substantially reduce the number of people on welfare benefits.

In 2010 the Government reversed significant aspects of Labour's industrial legislation, introducing a 90-day trial employment period without grievance rights on dismissal, and greater employer powers to oppose union access to workplaces. It also removed labour rights in the film production sector (by enabling producers to engage workers as contractors regardless of their employment relationships) in a package given to Warner Brothers to ensure a particular film was produced in New Zealand. The motivation for these changes appears to have been largely political, driven by employer groups (explicitly in the case of the film industry). Even the Department of Labour acknowledges that evidence of problems to support such changes is weak and anecdotal. Experience from the 1991 legislation provides no evidence that such changes improve economic performance.

New Zealand is now emerging from recession, but weakly. Though GDP rose by 1.4 per cent in the year to March 2011 with 0.8 per cent growth in that quarter, it had contracted (by 0.1 per cent) in the three months to September. The unemployment rate, which peaked at 7.0 per cent in December 2009 (compared to 3.4 per cent just two years previously), was still at 6.5 per cent in June 2011 and is falling only slowly. Other indicators are very mixed, with more robust recovery far from certain. A series of severe earthquakes in New Zealand's second largest city, Christchurch, has added to the country's difficulties, though in the Treasury's view these were not the major cause of the sluggish economy.

The Labour-led Governments had maintained consistent budget surpluses – a policy that put New Zealand in an advantageous position when facing the global crisis (see figure 12.4). There is therefore considerable room for stimulus programmes, and the union movement has expressed concern that the Government did not do enough in the face of continuing high unemployment, sluggish recovery in output, and the dangers inherent in the international economy, was too focused on tax cuts, and is removing what stimulus there is too early.

Figure 12.4 Net government debt, various countries, 2011

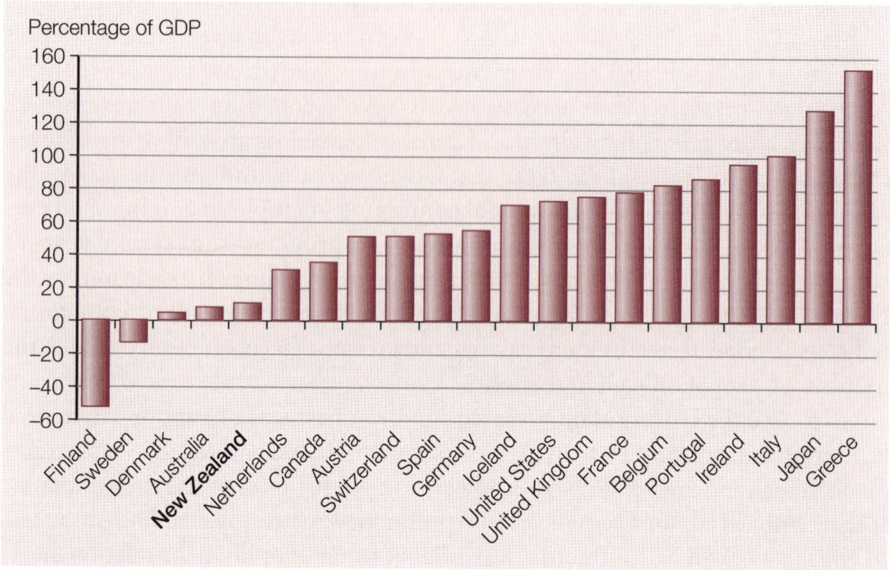

Source: IMF estimates.

Unsuccessful in its own terms

On top of the social failures issuing from the neoliberal programme, neither the radical policies of the 1980s and 1990s nor the Third Way model of the 2000s have led to economic success even in neoliberal terms. The OECD noted in its economic survey of New Zealand in 2003 that "the mystery is why a country that seems close to best practice in most of the policies that are regarded as the key drivers of growth is nevertheless just an average performer" (OECD 2004: 29). Real growth in national output (GDP) has been intermittent, and despite periods where it exceeded the OECD average, including years during the last decade, it has failed to keep up: in terms of GDP per capita, New Zealand has steadily fallen further behind in OECD rankings (see figure 12.5).

International competitiveness has been problematic: New Zealand's international goods and services trade has been in deficit for most of the last decade, and as a result of trade liberalization exports have had lower value added than prior to the 1970s, according to a recent study (Lattimore et al. 2009).

The banking system is heavily dominated by four Australian-owned banks, which together hold 92 per cent of bank assets in New Zealand. Over the last decade they have borrowed heavily on short-term international money markets in order to finance domestic loans, mainly for mortgages on residential property, to the point where in March 2011 they owed 80 per cent

Figure 12.5   Nominal GDP per capita as a percentage of OECD mean, selected countries, 1970–2009 (US$ and PPPs)

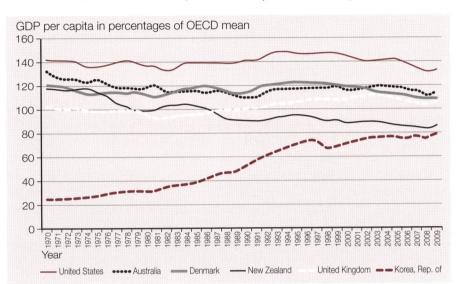

Source: Ministry of Economic Development, The Treasury and Statistics New Zealand (2011), p. 34, figure 1.5; figures from *OECD Factbook 2010*.

of New Zealand's net international debt. This international borrowing severely weakened the Reserve Bank's ability to control New Zealand's money supply, leading to its policy interest rate (the official cash rate) rising to a peak of 8.25 per cent. Exports and productive investment were choked off by the high interest rates and the consequently high New Zealand dollar in favour of speculative investment in property and leveraged buy-outs.

The banking system largely remained stable during the global financial crisis. However, when international money markets froze, the four Australian-owned banks were unable to refinance their short-term debts as they fell due, threatening their liquidity and the stability of the country's financial systems. Monetary authorities had to open up funding lines and provide them with deposit and wholesale funding guarantees.

The CTU's alternative economic strategy

Joseph Stiglitz, in the words that opened this chapter, wrote that "small open economies are like rowing boats on an open sea". Certainly this metaphor applies to New Zealand, and yet the policies of successive governments appear to have disregarded this readily apparent vulnerability in favour of the vested interests and powerful forces which benefit from neoliberalism. The events described above make this plain. "One cannot predict when they might capsize; bad steering increases the chances of disaster and a leaky boat makes it inevitable," Stiglitz continues, and this chapter has documented at least three decades of either bad steering or faulty design, along with outcomes that should have been seen as inevitable. Not only must New Zealand reduce its vulnerability to the open sea, it must be fair to all who rely on it for their livelihoods and dignity.

Affiliates of the CTU asked it to develop an alternative political economy in response to the developments recounted above. Some unions are affiliated to political parties, but all recognized that the policies being followed by the Labour-led Government, while better than what had gone before, were doing little more than stopping the situation from getting worse. The global financial crisis and the change of Government not only gave greater impetus to the project, but opened up possibilities that for many years had been closed down as valid policy alternatives.

A draft "Alternative Economic Strategy" (AES), with a substantial background paper covering the causes of the crisis and ground similar to that revisited above, was discussed by delegates to the CTU's biennial conference in October 2009. It was then sent out for further comment for six months, and workshops were held with interested union members and at workplaces. Comments were collected from external groups including a range of experts, environmental groups and political parties. The final version was approved by the CTU's executive body in August 2010 (CTU 2010). It is now available in print and on the CTU's website.

The AES is based on principles of fairness, participation, security, improved living standards, sustainability and sovereignty (CTU 2010: 4). It is structured around three "pillars": sustainable economic development; decent work and a good life; and voice: real participation in decisions in the workplace, economy and community (p. 5).

The AES begins (CTU 2010: 6) with a section which addresses the immediate needs flowing from the continuing effects of the global financial crisis. While these are shorter-term objectives, they are designed to support the longer-term development described in the rest of the policy. They include small-scale active labour market policies, strengthened public services, infrastructure development, increased access to tertiary education, support for businesses under certain criteria, publicly owned (state) house building, extended home insulation and clean heating programmes, and encouragement of local manufacturing and services through government procurement and other measures. The section also calls for immediate changes to the financial system to reduce New Zealand's vulnerability to international financial crises and the demands of overseas investors, including support for international moves to clamp down on the shadow financial economy, a Tobin (financial transactions) tax, and the recommendations of the Commission of Experts of the President of the United Nations General Assembly on reforms to the international monetary and financial system. Locally, it proposes management of international capital movements, a managed exchange rate, and an end to further concessions in trade and investment agreements which would further reduce New Zealand's policy space.

Sustainable economic development

For the longer term (CTU 2010: 8ff.), the AES responds to the central need for the New Zealand economy to develop more value added products and services, and to strengthen the tradable sector, as contributions to raising wage levels and restoring balance in external payments. It takes a strategic approach to economic development, giving priority to certain broadly defined sectors of the economy along with cross-sectoral themes such as benefiting the environment and raising productivity, and supports national and regional infrastructure plans. Economic development would include support for firms subject to strong criteria that reinforce national strategies, skill development, employment relations policies, worker participation, and improved wages and working conditions. Specific policies and projects in infrastructure development are outlined, including greater state involvement in New Zealand's problematic telecommunications and electricity markets, development of public transport, and a "human infrastructure" fund to provide long-term funding certainty to tertiary education and workplace training. Other areas covered include innovation, research and development, gaining from new technology, education and skill development, support for Māori economic development, and support for cooperatives.

As necessitated by the state of New Zealand's financial system and the GFC, considerable space is given to changes to the financial system in order to support rather than hinder economic development (CTU 2010: 15ff.). This includes closer oversight over all financial institutions in proportion to their use of leverage and systemic significance, recognizing the implicit state support for these bodies that has been revealed by the GFC. Proposals include legislation for separation of commercial and investment banking, control of executive and shareholder remuneration, a financial activities (Tobin) tax, requirements for regulatory approval for high-risk financial services, whether originating in New Zealand or abroad, reduced reliance on overseas funding, and a statutory basis for future bail-outs and deposit guarantees. Actions to reduce vulnerability to the four Australian-owned banks which dominate the New Zealand banking system include scaling up the small but very successful government-owned Kiwibank and banning offshore outsourcing of banking infrastructure. Social responsibility is addressed, and proposals are made for funding of firms that currently suffer from lack of suitable finance: these include a development finance agency which includes unions in its governance, locally raised long-term infrastructure bonds, greater local investment by New Zealand sovereign and superannuation funds, and expansion of savings through changes to voluntary superannuation schemes.

Monetary policy has caused great difficulties for productive investment and exporters, in part because of its effect on the exchange rate. The AES (CTU 2010: 17) proposes broadening the aims of monetary policy, and giving the Reserve Bank sufficient powers to manage capital flows and the exchange rate, enabling the exchange rate to be pegged (but not fully fixed). It suggests mechanisms that in addition to interest rates could be used to implement monetary policy.

Internationally, the AES (CTU 2010: 18) advocates working with others to control capital movements and to remove constraints within trade and investment agreements such as those that heighten the risk of further financial crises and limit New Zealand's ability to protect the environment or regulate important services. It seeks a "new internationalism" which recognizes that in many important areas what is required is cooperation rather than a market approach. For New Zealand this would include a new generation of trade and investment agreements with rules founded on the need to regulate and to recognize national economic development strategies rather than on concepts of market access and deregulation. The AES advocates democratization of global institutions currently dominated by the United States and the EU, and a greater role for the United Nations and the UN Conference on Trade and Development (UNCTAD) in international economic policy-making to balance social with commercial imperatives.

Given New Zealand's social democratic past and the sweeping and often disastrous programmes of privatization that the country has experienced, the role of the State is acknowledged to be a critical one. The AES (CTU 2010:19) affirms the State's role as regulator, stabilizer, redistributor and owner of parts of the economy. Government procurement and responsible contracting are identified as important tools for spreading good practice and economic development. The role of public service workers, the need for public services to meet the requirements of citizens, and the need to recognize that public organizations are different from those in the private sector in respect of governance, management, accountability and financial accounting are all noted.

Taxation is addressed (CTU 2010: 21), particularly in the light of its redistributive role given the big increases in inequality in New Zealand over the last three decades. Proposals include a tax-free band or rebate for low income earners and restoration of higher rates of income tax at high income levels. It is proposed that the regressive goods and services tax be replaced with other forms of tax, including asset taxes and commercial resource use taxes. Pollution taxes, including for greenhouse gas (GHG) emissions, are advocated, as long as there is a balancing mechanism to ensure that low income earners do not pay an unfair share of the burden.

There is a range of proposals to combat climate change, including a price on GHG emissions (CTU 2010: 22). The AES advocates support for workers and communities displaced or otherwise affected by climate change or policies to combat it, major investment in skills for a low-carbon economy, worker participation in the approaches taken in the workplace to mitigate climate change, and union involvement at all levels in decision-making on the changes required.

The AES (CTU 2010: 22) also advocates finding alternative measures of progress to use alongside GDP to guide decision-making and priorities.

Decent work and a good life

The CTU is working on a parallel strategy of "Union Change" (2010: 24) to rebuild the New Zealand trade union movement. This includes extending union coverage and collective bargaining beyond those in large and more readily unionized workplaces, a rights-based framework for workers to be covered by collective agreements, participation of unions and workers in their workplaces and industries, mechanisms for setting employment standards at national and industry level, new forms of worker organizations and a more structured approach to social partnership.

On the topic of employment, the AES (CTU 2010: 25) adopts some northern European ideas on flexicurity, including a high level of income replacement for those out of work, active labour market policies, and financial and practical support for acquiring new skills. It places full employment as a central objective of government policy.

Given the crucial role of housing not only as an essential for living, but also in investment behaviour in New Zealand, considerable attention is devoted to housing (CTU 2010: 25), acknowledging the complexity of the area. Retirement, which is important both for individuals and for the economy in terms of the savings accumulated in preparing for it, is also addressed (p. 27).

Finally (CTU 2010: 27) this "pillar" addresses equity and the need to reduce inequality (a theme which is also integrated into the rest of the policy). The former includes gender equity in pay and employment, extending paid parental leave, making more flexible working arrangements available, and increasing the minimum wage to 66 per cent of the average wage.

Voice: Real participation in decisions in the workplace, economy and community

This pillar advocates a fuller view of democracy than a vote once every few years in an election (CTU 2010: 28–29). This includes fuller consultation by central and local government with social partners (unions and business) and other groups affected by decisions. The AES proposes ways for the workplace to be seen as a place for active citizenship, and calls for more diversity and depth in the media, to be fostered through trust-owned, not-for-profit "public service" newspapers and other media, and funding for investigative journalism.

Finally, the AES proposes structures to increase worker participation. It proposes participative representative structures at the workplace level; industry sector councils to share good practice around productivity, skill development, industry development initiatives and networking of firms; and a National Tripartite Social/Economic Council.

Conclusion

Policies from the AES have been quoted by both the CTU and its affiliated unions in public advocacy, debates, media statements and internal education programmes. It has also been helpful to affiliated unions in providing a context and rationale in support of their own specific campaigns. Extracts relevant to particular policy issues such as saving and environmental sustainability have been used by the CTU in conferences and written submissions. Brief summaries of one and four pages are available, and the various policies outlined have been used in campaigning on related issues. The policies have also been taken up by activists within left political parties, and appear to have been influential in the development of those parties' own policies for the 2011 election.

The AES can be seen as a development of a range of social democratic policy strands, borrowing much from successful northern European countries, but also integrating a level of environmental sustainability and, most topically, addressing the challenges of the GFC. It is specifically designed around the situation in which New Zealand finds itself: one of dual failure. There is the failure of neoliberalism both domestically and internationally; and there is a failure of the dominant political parties and economic orthodoxies (strengthened by powerful vested interests) to consider substantive alternatives. Many parts of the strategy require long-term effort and resources, but it is presented as a coherent alternative that addresses many of the needs of working people and the problems of the crisis-ridden economic environment in which we find ourselves.

It would be unrealistic in the face of these powerful forces to expect that New Zealand could take refuge in a haven entirely protected from financial and environmental crises, but it certainly could be made less vulnerable to them. The rowing boat that is New Zealand would then be more secure and provide a better life for those who rely on it.

Note

[1] For more detail, see Kelsey (1997, 1999).

Resources

Black, M.; Guy, M.; McLellan, N. 2003. *Productivity in New Zealand 1988–2002*, Working Paper No. WP 03/06 (Wellington, New Zealand Treasury), http://treasury.govt.nz/publications/research-policy/wp/2003/03-06 (accessed 16 June 2011).

Council of Trade Unions (CTU). 2010. *Alternative economic strategy, tetahi atu ōhanga rautaki: An economy that works for everyone* (Wellington, New Zealand Council of Trade Unions/Te Kauae Kaimahi), http://union.org.nz/policy/alternative-economic-strategy (accessed 16 June 2011).

Hyslop, D.; Stillman, S. (2004). *Youth minimum wage reform and the labour market*, Working Paper No. WP 04/03 (Wellington, New Zealand Treasury), http://treasury.govt.nz/publications/research-policy/wp/2004/04-03 (accessed 16 June 2011).

Kelsey, J. 1997. *The New Zealand experiment: A world model for structural adjustment?*, new edn (Auckland, Auckland University Press/Bridget Williams Books).

—. 1999. *Reclaiming the future: New Zealand and the global economy* (Wellington, Bridget Williams Books).

Lattimore, R.; Le, T.; Stroombergen, A. 2009. *Economic progress and puzzles: Long-term structural change in the New Zealand economy, 1953–2006*, Working Paper No. 2009/6 (Wellington, New Zealand Institute for Economic Research), http://nzier.org.nz/sites/nzier.live.egressive.com/files/WP2009-06%20Economic%20progress%20and%20puzzles.pdf (accessed 16 June 2011).

Ministry of Economic Development; The Treasury; Statistics New Zealand. 2011. *Economic Development Indicators 2011* (Wellington, New Zealand Government), http://www.med.govt.nz/templates/ContentTopicSummary_45708.aspx (accessed 17 August 2011).

Organisation for Economic Co-operation and Development (OECD). 2004. *OECD Economic Surveys: New Zealand*, Vol. 2003, Suppl. 3, OECD Economic Surveys (Paris).

—. 2009. *OECD Economic Outlook 85*, Vol. 2009/1, June 2009 (Paris).

Perry, B. 2010. *Household incomes in New Zealand: Trends in indicators of inequality and hardship 1982 to 2009* (Wellington, Ministry of Social Development), http://www.msd.govt.nz/about-msd-and-our-work/publications-resources/monitoring/household-incomes/household-incomes-1982-2009.html (accessed 17 August 2011).

Rosenberg, B. 2010. *Real wages and productivity in New Zealand*, paper presented at the 14th Conference on Labour, Employment and Work in New Zealand, Industrial Relations Centre, Victoria University of Wellington, 30 Nov.–1 Dec.

Stiglitz, J.E. 1998. "Boats, planes and capital flows", in *Financial Times*, 25 Mar.

TURKEY AFTER 2008: ANOTHER CRISIS – THE SAME RESPONSES?

13

Yasemin Özgün and Özgür Müftüoğlu

Economic crises are certainly not new to Turkey. Indeed, in the global economic crisis of 2008, both government policies and the responses – ideologically differentiated – of the various trade unions reflected the impact and outcomes of ongoing class struggles and Turkey's process of adjustment to increasing marketization, insecurity and neoliberal globalization.

Turkey stepped into the 2000s in crisis. This crisis, which reached its peak in February 2001, was related to the Government's aim of embedding in the Turkish economy the Structural Adjustment Programmes (SAPs) prescribed by the World Bank and IMF, thereby furthering the "adjustment" to the free market economy which started in 1980 and gained significant momentum in the 1990s. While the Turkish economy grew by about 5.9 per cent and productivity increased by about 6.1 per cent between 2003 and 2008, real wages declined and official unemployment (not counting the many unregistered jobless) remained constant in the vicinity of 10 per cent. There have been major losses in workers' social rights, embodied most significantly in Law No. 5510 on Social Insurance and General Health Insurance (SSGSS), passed in April 2008 (Müftüoğlu and Özgün 2010: 154).

The rules of the market economy, which Governments have attempted to institutionalize in Turkey from 1980 onwards, have to a large extent now been applied, thanks to the policies implemented consistently up to 2008, but the process has not yet been completed. Lending agreements from the IMF and World Bank, reports prepared by the OECD, and the conditions imposed by the EU in the course of Turkey's application for membership have all put pressure on Turkey to complete its process of integration with the market economy. Within these exhortations, a prominent place has been given to completion of the process of marketization of public services, privatizations, and the flexibilization of the labour market to cover even employment in the public sector.[1] Opposition to regulations in this area introduced as part of the process of acquiring EU membership has been hampered by substantial union support for the goal of entering the EU. Thus, many policies eroding the employment standards and social rights of the working class could be enacted and put into effect without encountering any serious resistance (Müftüoğlu 2007: 152).

The Turkish union movement, which entered the crisis of 2001 already largely incapable of effectively representing the working class, could not resist the process of marketization that followed the crisis and slid into an even more ineffective position. As a result of the compromises made with capital and Government during this process, the unions played a substantial role in eroding the economic and social rights of the working class. This in turn undermined workers' confidence in the unions, which further exacerbated the unions' incapacity to protect workers' rights (Müftüoğlu 2007: 141).[2]

The 2008 crisis and the policies implemented in response

Up to 2008 Turkey achieved high economic growth rates, thanks to the SAPs implemented following the crisis of 2001, and the higher profit rates enjoyed by capital deferred the next crisis. However, the working classes did not share in the benefits of this growth; indeed, the very policies that fuelled the growth eroded their job security and social guarantees, reduced real wages and caused further increases in unemployment and poverty. Then, after a period in which capital accumulation increased through more intensive exploitation of the workers, yet another officially declared crisis took place in September 2008. This crisis, unlike the crises experienced by Turkey locally from 1979 onwards, affected the entire capitalist system.

Although some improvement can be observed in growth rates in the global economy in the two years elapsing since the beginning of the crisis, the deterioration in the working and living conditions of labour, particularly in respect of employment, continues. In Turkey unemployment, which stood at 10.3 per cent in September 2008 when the crisis broke out, rose as high as 16.2 per cent in February 2009 and its 2009 average was 14 per cent (TÜİK 2009). According to the statistics for May 2010, the rate of unemployment had by that point fallen to about 11 per cent (TÜİK 2010). This decline is attributable to two major factors. The first is the prominence in the Turkish labour market of sectors such as agriculture and tourism where employment is strongly seasonal. The second is that, under pressure of actual or threatened unemployment, workers accept poorly paid jobs lacking any security. Jobs offered under the rubric of "trainee" or "temporary worker", and the employment of subcontractors (encouraged by the programmes supported by governmental policies), are perceived by employers as a method of procuring cheap labour.

Production, which sharply declined as the crisis took hold, started picking up in the first quarter of 2009 and rose above the 2007 level in the first quarter of 2010. However, while production has risen rapidly, thanks to all the measures taken to lower labour costs – which meant lower and more insecure incomes for the working classes – and provide incentives for capital, the increase in employment has remained limited (figure 13.1). Although industrial investment, which is one of the primary drivers of increased productivity, has not increased during the course of the crisis,[3] and no new employment has been created, productivity nevertheless increased from the first quarter of 2009. This is because capital dismissed large numbers of workers on the pretext of the crisis and forced the workers they continued employing to work more intensively for lower wages under threat of redundancy. Thus a lower number of workers, working more intensively for lower wages and in less secure jobs, have achieved an increase in production. Capital, which has thus had the opportunity to achieve production much more cheaply thanks to this increased labour productivity, has been offered yet another major opportunity to increase profits by government incentives aimed at lightening the burden of employers' responsibility to employees. Thus, capital has not only pulled itself out of the effects of the crisis to a large extent but has also managed to turn the crisis into an opportunity.

Figure 13.1   Production, employment and efficiency in Turkish manufacturing industry, 2007–10

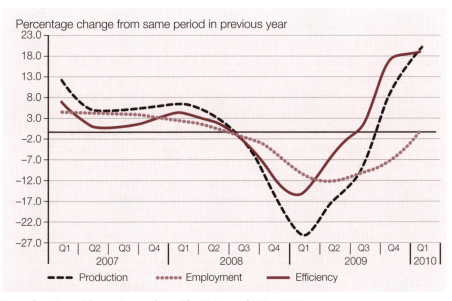

Source: http://www.tisk.org.tr/gostergeler.asp?id=528 (accessed 16 June 2011).

Turkey's economy contracted by 5.8 per cent in 2009, making it one of the countries most severely affected (World Bank 2010). Unemployment, which had remained steady at around 10 per cent since 2001, rapidly increased to 14 per cent in 2009, putting Turkey among the five countries with the highest rates of unemployment.

In Turkey, the Government responded in line with the policies determined at a global level, in particular the decisions adopted by G20 summits. Following these decisions, there has been no departure from the paradigm of the free market – to the disappointment of some analysts; on the contrary, indeed, market principles have been applied even more strictly. However, the policies implemented in accordance with the requirements of the market economy have been promulgated in public under the rhetorical banner of "solving the unemployment problem", because unemployment has become a central issue in almost all capitalist countries, with expectations of a solution to the problem becoming even more acute following the crisis. In Turkey, where unemployment was already a major issue in the pre-crisis period, the package of measures prepared by the Government in response to the crisis largely overlapped with the demands of the unions.[4] These policies have taken the form of incentives for capital through support for employment and tax exemptions, new taxes and loans, and investment promotion.

Law No. 5838 of 2009 was the first of these measures, heralded by the Government as supporting employment and combating the effects of the crisis. This new law increased the term for which worker compensation could be paid under the partial work fund allocation and raised the amount that could be paid.[5] Further legislation stipulated that wages for low-paid temporary work in both public and private sectors would be covered by the Unemployment Insurance Fund, and that employers' insurance premiums would be covered by the Unemployment Insurance Fund for a certain period of time provided that they created new employment.

These new regulations, aimed at supporting employment in the face of the crisis, may be seen as implementing the employment policies advocated by international organizations such as the OECD, the World Bank and the EU and by employers' organizations prior to the crisis. Also, as will be discussed in more detail below, given the fact that most of the unions regard incentives for capital as a means of protecting employment, it may be argued that these regulations also meet the demands of the unions. Thanks to these regulations, the burden of employment costs payable by the employers is transferred to the public through the Treasury and Unemployment Insurance Fund. In addition, the labour market is rendered more flexible by the expansion of employment under temporary and trainee statuses, with extremely low wages and minimal or no social security. The nature and extent of these developments are such as to threaten those workers who do hold permanent positions with job security.

The 2008 crisis and the unions in Turkey

As mentioned above, the unions confronted the crisis of 2008 hampered by considerable weaknesses arising from oppressive legislation and their own structural problems. The different ideologies espoused by the various unions in Turkey were reflected in the policies they adopted in the face of the crisis. Relatively left-wing workers' and public employees' unions in particular sometimes took individual positions, sometimes offered joint proposed solutions and sometimes became involved in joint action with several confederations. Some confederations even acted in collaboration with capital in combating the crisis. DİSK (the Confederation of Progressive Trade Unions of Turkey)[6] and KESK (the Confederation of Public Employees), which claim to be relatively closer to the leftist ideology and oppose the AKP (Justice and Development Party) – although they persistently advocate acquiring EU membership – have collaborated most closely in response to the crisis. On 28 October 2008, DİSK and KESK, together with other trade bodies, opposed the present Government, proclaiming their proposed solution in a joint declaration as follows: "Priority must be accorded to those measures, which promote production and employment, make the job security effective, eliminate injustice over income distribution and protect labor."[7]

Following this joint declaration, DİSK proposed an economic plan that would be mandatory for the public sector and serve as a guideline for the private sector. The same programme included support for domestic production and employment by suspending the EU–Turkey Customs Union,[8] encouragement of domestic investment, tax reform and the rescheduling of domestic debts. It also included proposals for the protection and improvement of employment, the introduction of facilities for debt payments by households, and reductions in the taxes demanded from employees through the introduction of a wealth tax (DİSK 2008).

Birleşik Metal-İş Sendikası (a union representing workers employed by the metal industries), which is affiliated with DİSK, published a declaration entitled "Programme of demands and struggle" on 3 November 2008. After emphasizing that the crisis arose within the capitalist system and was therefore a crisis of capitalism, the declaration insisted that workers must not be forced to pay for the costs of the crisis. It also voiced several other demands, such as a reduction in working hours in order to protect employment and a ban on dismissals. The most important difference between this declaration and others is that it called on all pro-labour organizations, as well as on unorganized sections of society, to collaborate in seeking the fulfilment of these demands.[9]

Protection of employment is also highlighted by a report from Türk-İş (Confederation of Turkish Trade Unions),[10] which gives the impression that it is under the guardianship of the AKP Government, in November 2008. In this report, Türk-İş defends state support for capital through incentives, on condition it protects employment, as a route out of the crisis. In addition, the report calls on the private sector to act responsibly and not to treat the crisis as an opportunity to lay off workers. It further suggests that the welfare state must be strengthened and that the purchasing power of the working class must be increased if the country is to get out of the crisis.[11]

Similarly, Hak-İş (the Confederation of Turkish Real Trade Unions), which is known for its closeness to the AKP Government as well as its conservative Islamist stance, argued in its declaration of 29 November 2008 that the crisis could be overcome through close cooperation between workers and employers. In this document Hak-İş called on the employers to consider options such as giving extra leave, paying partial wages and claiming partial work fund allocations from the State before deciding to lay off any workers. The section setting out the confederation's proposals to the Government asserts a need to raise confidence among the markets and the public and to support capital on condition that it in turn supports employment and exports. In addition, there were suggestions for attracting private foreign capital into Turkey.[12]

Türk Kamu-Sen, a union representing workers employed by the public sector, which is known for its nationalist and conservative line, made the most interesting suggestions at the onset of the crisis. Its declaration contained a number of recommendations for individual action to save money, such as not taking out loans to buy houses and cars, not using credit cards, not buying any non-essential consumer durables, not shopping from the supermarkets, and cooking meals in pressure cookers. In an apparent departure from the suggestions of other unions, this report is noteworthy for its advocacy of "an increase in the domestic market oriented production and promotion of the consumption in the domestic market" under a "national development" approach (Balta 2009: 84).

The concentration of mass lay-offs immediately after the onset of the crisis on those workers who were members of unions and enjoyed job security prompted the labour unions to focus on the protection of employment. In their statements made at the beginning of the crisis, they communicated their demands for employment protection directly to the State. However, their initial declarations – with the exception of those by Birleşik Metal-İş Sendikası and DİSK and KESK – implied a partial acceptance of the crisis as a "natural" phenomenon which accidentally broke out across the world, and not as a structural consequence of the capitalist system. Thus, as has already been noted, the demands of capital and unions overlapped on many issues, such as the encouragement of capital and the partial assumption of labour costs by the State.

In addition to making their various declarations, the unions also organized many actions and boycotts to protest against the consequences of the crisis. Most of these related to labour problems – mass lay-offs, coercion into flexible and insecure employment, failure to pay wages, and refusals to accept unionization and collective bargaining rights. Workers who were not members of trade unions also staged some unscheduled and spontaneous actions on similar grounds.[13] The issues most often cited as justification for these were accidents at work and unpaid wages.

The workers employed by TEKEL, a recently privatized public enterprise producing cigarettes, tobacco and alcohol, staged an action in Ankara on 15 December 2009 to protest at their re-employment at other worksites under Article 4/C of Civil Service Law No. 657, which eliminated their job security and cut their wages by half following the closure of their original workplace.[14] The TEKEL action, which turned into one of the most important in the history of the Turkish working class, was carried through despite the severe cold, poor conditions on the streets, and brutal assaults by forces of the AKP Government. The TEKEL workers set up tents on the streets of central Ankara and took turns to occupy them day and night for 78 days. The TEKEL resistance was supported by a wide range of different sections of the working class, and also by material and moral contributions from many unions in both Turkey and Europe. Although six labour confederations operating in Turkey declared their support for the resistance to job insecurity, this action could not be turned into a common cause. However, although the demands of the TEKEL workers were not met as a result of the resistance, some improvement was made to the wages and employment benefits of about 20,000 other workers employed under 4/C status. In addition, the regulations the Government planned to introduce in connection with severance pay and private employment offices, which had been on the agenda for a long time, could not be implemented in the face of the working-class struggles which gained momentum following the TEKEL resistance. On 22 February 2010, the confederations issued a declaration containing demands on many issues, ranging from job security, entitlement to severance pay and improvement of wages to alignment of labour laws with ILO and EU norms (DİSK 2010). This declaration, which proved highly effective in bringing the resistance to an end, was contradictory in the sense that while on the one hand it called for alignment of labour laws with EU norms, on the other it resisted the Government's effort to introduce flexible working times and private employment offices and discontinue severance pay – as required by those EU norms. Four confederations threatened to go on a nationwide strike on 26 May 2010 if the demands contained in this (contradictory) declaration were not met. However, this threat was never carried out; furthermore, in a statement on 9 August 2010 Tek Gıda-İş Union (a union affiliated with Türk-İş Confederation, representing workers employed by the tobacco, alcohol and food industry) disclosed that all the actions scheduled to support the demands of the TEKEL workers had been cancelled, and called on the workers to agree to the 4/C conditions they had been resisting for 78 days.[15]

Apart from the actions taken in connection with the problems relating to working conditions that either emerged or got worse following the crisis, many public protests were also organized over the rights to education, health, accommodation and transport. Although the unions took part in the actions over health-care rights, they did not participate in the public protests by university students over fees, the actions about rights to housing (arising in particular from the urban transformation) or the protests over city transport costs.

The union confederations Türk-İş, Hak-İş and Türk Kamu-Sen, together with the employers' organizations TISK, TESK and TOBB, jointly organized a campaign entitled "We Have a Solution to the Crisis", which aimed to overcome the crisis by increasing consumption. The basic slogan of the campaign, "Go Shopping", was designed to encourage the population in the medium income bracket to consume.[16] It is highly ironic that unions representing the working class should take part in a campaign encouraging consumption in collaboration with capital in a period when mass lay-offs and threats of unemployment were at a peak and wages were declining in real terms. Equally ironic was an initiative by DİSK Textiles Workers' Union, which placed a public notice in the newspapers asserting that TÜSİAD (the Turkish Industry and Business Association) and the capital class were the victims of the crisis, and calling for more incentives for capital.[17]

It may be argued that the Turkish unions' perceptions of the crisis and their proposed solutions largely ran parallel to those of the global union movement, which had significant influence on the Turkish unions, as noted at the beginning of this essay. For example, the ITUC, which provided a model of "governance" on a global scale, advocated solutions such as reviving overall demand, rescuing companies in the industrialized countries, providing compensation for the imbalances and inequities caused by the revival measures, and creating a new credit mechanism to offer developing countries easy access to liquidity without oppressive conditions in order to "put an end to the global economic and financial crisis" in cooperation with governments and capital so that "an effective global economy" could be developed – even at the cost of forcing workers into poverty, lack of security and exploitation at increasing rates (see ITUC 2009a, b, c). The ETUC defines the present crisis as a "structural crisis of the model of casino capitalism", not a period of "temporary vulnerability dependent on the conjunctional fluctuations" (ETUC 2009a). At a conference held in Paris late in May 2009, an agreement was reached on ITUC support for the ETUC in calling on the business community to engage in social dialogue and develop this strategy for the purpose of finding a solution to the crisis. Meetings, seminars, press conferences, marches, cultural demonstrations, lobbying activities and protests on the Internet to reach the broadest masses to the largest extent possible have been identified as potential methods of protest (ETUC 2009b).

Conclusion

The crisis of 2008 has created an opportunity for capital to demand ever more loudly arrangements to favour the supply side of the economy. In response, many arrangements have been made in order to meet the demands in particular for a flexible labour market. A large number of workers have been laid off purely on the excuse of the crisis in many countries as policies of flexible work and lower wages have become commonplace through the use of the increasing pressure of unemployment.

As Albo (2009b) has emphasized, union structures throughout the world, having compromised with governments and capital for many years, are now less combative in challenging capital and less willing to develop political agendas and alternative approaches in the face of the crisis. This in turn weakens the unions' capability to represent the working classes as well as their effectiveness in intervening in the process of capitalist development.

In parallel to the global union movement, the union movement in Turkey has failed effectively to resist the processes of marketization and the slide into increasingly precarious work. The unions' recommendations of how to deal with the crisis have come very close to supporting the economic policies prepared in line with the interests of capital; thus, far from preventing the transfer of the costs of the crisis to labour, they are contributing to the imposition of those costs on labour. However, as in many other countries, the struggle by labour has continued despite the unions and, as a result, public protests for which the unions had to claim responsibility have been carried out. In some cases a more militant attitude began to emerge among sections of the working class disillusioned with the unions because of their compromising attitudes.

Following the 2008 crisis, provoked by measures such as lay-offs, unpaid wages, increased flexibility of working conditions and pressures against unionization, workers began to carry out factory occupations and strikes in their workplaces that were not organized by the unions and indeed contravened the legal regulations on the collective bargaining process. In some cases, unions supported actions that developed independently of them. The Sinter Metal resistance in 2008, which was initiated by Sinter Metal workers who wanted to unionize, and the TEKEL resistance, which started in Ankara in 2009, are examples of resistance actions started by the workers and then supported by unions. However, the struggle of Eregli Iron and Steel Factory workers against the 35 per cent cut in wages that had been determined by collective bargaining, or the TEKEL workers' actions against job insecurity and wage cuts that started in October 2010, were seen by the unions as a reaction against themselves and were not supported.[18] Despite these efforts, as noted above, the absence of an effective union leadership and of firmly class-oriented union policies doomed most of these actions to failure; and meanwhile the Government continued to introduce new legal measures to spread flexible, insecure working conditions in an effort to lower labour costs.

Today, there are numerous struggles across the world against the working standards created by global capitalism, lack of social rights and the inadequacy of democracy – in European countries, in Latin America, and recently in North Africa and the Middle East. These demonstrate, alongside the inadequacy of the compromising line taken by unions since the 1970s, the need for a class-oriented union movement.

Putting aside the arguments about whether capitalism has overcome its crisis, for workers the crisis continues and deepens. In this process, whether the workers will finally be able to overcome their crisis by getting out of the vicious circle of unemployment and poverty depends on the power they are able to generate through class struggle; and in this class struggle, a decisive element will be whether the unions continue their compromising approaches or take a leading role in heading a "push" by the working class.

Notes

[1] On the policies aiming at flexibility in the labour market advocated by the OECD, World Bank and EU, see Müftüoğlu (2008).

[2] It is not possible to isolate the weakness experienced by the Turkish union movement from the condition of the global trade union movement. The unions, structured according to the standardized production relationships of Fordism and national labour markets, have become ineffective and weak, with falling numbers of members, in the face of globalization and the flexibilization of production systems. In this process, major issues such as union democracy, the capacity of the unions to mobilize workers and their ideological independence from the employers have come on to the agenda (Albo 2009a: 124).

[3] In 2009, imports of industrial investment goods declined by 23.5 per cent; imports of machinery and equipment, which amounted to US$36.4 billion in 2008, fell to US$29.3 billion, a decline of 19.5 per cent (Republic of Turkey 2010).

[4] For the Government's response to the crisis of 2008, see Republic of Turkey (2009).

[5] According to Labour Law No. 4857 of 2003, if, as a result of economic crisis or other emergency, employers have to make significant temporary reductions in weekly working time or stop business partially or completely for a period, a payment will be made to insured employees (not to their employers) to cover part of the working time lost on the days when they are not working.

[6] DİSK, which was founded in 1967 following the development of union rights, has taken a hard-line position on some issues.

[7] http://www.disk.org.tr/content_images/DiSKKRiZ.pdf (accessed 16 June 2011).

[8] The customs union between Turkey and the European Union came into effect on 31 December 1995, enabling goods to travel between the two entities without any customs restrictions. The EU–Turkey Customs Union is one of the steps towards full Turkish membership of the EU itself.

[9] http://www.birlesikmetal.org/etkinlik/etkinlik_2008_3.htm (accessed 16 June 2011).

[10] Türk-İş, which was founded in 1952 and has the largest membership of any union body in Turkey, has maintained its understanding of unions as existing under the guardianship of the State.

[11] http://www.turkis.org.tr/source.cms.docs/turkis.org.tr.ce/docs/file/ekonomikkriz.pdf (accessed 16 June 2011).

[12] http://www.hakis.org.tr/ (accessed 16 June 2011).

[13] For a detailed assessment of these actions, see Kaygısız (2010).

[14] What ignited the resistance was the action of the AKP Government in repudiating the workers' existing contracts and forcing them to accept part-time conditions with significant loss of pay and social rights. The 4/C contract was formulated by the Government as an interim solution to offer employment for displaced workers after privatization of state-owned enterprises. It involves redefining the employees' job status as provisional for up to one year and offers salaries tied to legal minimum wages. The new "jobs" would not necessarily be related to the displaced workers' ability or expertise, and in practice have taken various forms of simple public service such as gardening in public parks. For the TEKEL workers this move would have meant a reduction of their average monthly wages from 1,200 Turkish lire (TRY) (approx. US$800) to TRY 800 (approx. US$550) and a job contract of ten months with no guarantee of renewal (see Yeldan 2010).

[15] See http://www.tekgida.org.tr/Oku/2063/Uyelerimize-Ve-Kamuoyunun-Bilgisine (accessed 16 June 2011).

[16] See http://www.uretenturkiyeplatformu.org.tr/ (accessed 16 June 2011).

[17] See http://www.t24.com.tr/haberdetay/42446.aspx (accessed 16 June 2011).

[18] For the various workers' actions between 2008 and 2011, see http://www.sendika.org/yazi.php?yazi_no=24977 (accessed 16 June 2011).

Resources

Albo, G. 2009a. "The crisis of neoliberalism and the impasses of the union movement", in *Development Dialogue*, No. 51, pp. 119–31.

—. 2009b. "Unions and the crisis: Ways ahead?", http://column.global-labour-university.org/2009/12/unions-and-crisis-ways-ahead_3200.html (accessed 16 June 2011).

Balkan, N.; Savran, S. (eds). 2004. *Neoliberalizmin Tahribatı 2* [The devastation of neoliberalism 2] (İstanbul, Metis).

Balta, E. 2009. "Sendikaların Krizle İmtihanı" [The test of the unions in the crisis], in *İktisat*, No. 50, pp. 82–87.

DİSK. 2008. "Krize Karşı Sosyal Dayanışma Programı" [The social solidarity programme against the crisis], http://www.disk.org.tr/default.asp?Page=Content&ContentId=607 (accessed 16 June 2011).

—. 2010. "İşçi ve Kamu Çalışanları Konfederasyonlarının Ortak Açıklaması" [The Joint Declaration of Workers and Public Employees], http://www.disk.org.tr/default.asp?Page=Content&ContentId=926 (accessed 16 June 2011).

Ercan, F. 2003. "NeoLiberal Orman Yasalarından Kapitalizmin Küresel Kurumsallaşma Sürecine Geçiş: Hukuk-Toplum İlişkileri Çerçevesinde Türkiye'de Yapısal Reform" [The transition from the neoliberal law of the jungle to the institutional process of capitalism: The structural reforms in Turkey in the framework of law–society relations], in *İktisat*, No. 437, pp. 12–31.

European Trade Union Confederation (ETUC) 2009a. "From recession to depression? Downwards spirals European policymakers should take care to avoid", ETUC statement, 4 May, http://www.etuc.org/a/5972#declaration (accessed 16 June 2011).

—. 2009b. "Trade union European action days: 350,000 people in the streets", press release, 16 May.

International Trade Union Confederation (ITUC). 2009a. *Recommendation to shape a new global compromise for restructured growth, sustainable development and adequate work*, report submitted to the United Nations Conference on the World Financial and Economic Crisis and its Impact on Development, New York, 24–26 June.

—. 2009b. "Putting jobs and fairness at the heart of recovery: The role of the G8", Global Unions' statement to the G8 Summit, L'Aquila, Italy, July.

—. 2009c. "Statement to the London G20 Summit: Global Unions London declaration", April.

Kaygısız, İ. 2010. "Krizin Birinci Yılında Türkiye'de İşçi Eylemleri: İşgal, Grev ve Direnişlere Dair Gözlemler" [The labour movement in the first year of crisis in Turkey: The occupations, the strikes and the resistance], in *Praksis*, No. 22 (Spring), pp. 175–92.

Müftüoğlu, Ö. 2007. "Kriz ve Sendikalar" [The crises and the unions], in F. Sazak (ed.): *Türkiye'de Sendikal Kriz ve Sendikal Arayışlar* (Ankara, Epos), pp. 117–56.

—. 2008. "Esnekleşmenin Uluslararası Dayanakları" [The international origins of flexibility], in *Toplum ve Hekim*, Vol. 23, No. 4, pp. 269–75.

—; Özgün, Y. 2010. "Sınıflararası Mücadelede Yeni bir Dönemeç: 2008 Krizi" [A new shift in the class struggle: 2008 crises], in *Praksis*, No. 22 (Spring), pp. 151–73.

Republic of Turkey. 2009. "Küresel Mali Krize Karşı Politika Tedbirleri" [The Policies Against Global Financial Crisis], Treasury Under-Secretariat, Prime Minister's Office, 8 Oct., http://www.hazine.gov.tr/irj/go/km/docs/documents/Hazine%20Web/Konu%C5%9Fma %20Metinleri%20ve%20Sunumlar/Di%C4%9Fer%20Sunumlar/Politika_Tedbirleri.pdf (accessed 16 June 2011).

—. 2010. Treasury Under-Secretariat, presentation on economics, 15 Feb., http://www. hazine.gov.tr/irj/go/km/docs/documents/Treasury%20Web/Statistics/Econmic%20 Indicators/egosterge/Sunumlar/Ekonomi_Sunumu_TR.pdf (accessed 12 August 2010).

Turkish Statistical Institute (TÜİK). 2009. *Turkey's Statistical Yearbook 2009*, publication no. 3436 (Ankara, Turkish Statistical Institution).

—. 2010. http://www.tuik.gov.tr/Start.do;jsessionid=KNyDMwzLmp8vwn1HrhPvlkRt06 Pwly2VnjJV10fbN2QPf1L2F2m4!-1979002459 (accessed 16 June 2011).

World Bank. 2010. *Global Economic Prospects 2010: Crisis, finance, and growth* (Washington, DC).

Yeldan, E. 2010. "TEKEL workers' resistance of the proletariat in Turkey", 30 Jan., http://www.sendika.org/english/yazi.php?yazi_no=29021 (accessed 16 June 2011).

ADDRESSING COMPETITION: STRATEGIES FOR ORGANIZING PRECARIOUS WORKERS. CASES FROM CANADA

14

Maya Bhullar

The growth of precarious work is outstripping the growth of standard work relationships around the world. It is a growing component of the Canadian employment landscape as well. Since 1989 and through to 2008, contingent workers – part time permanent, temporary work, and independent contracting or self employment – comprised one third of the labour force in Canada. (Chaykowski and Slotsve 2008)

Introduction

As Canada partially recovers from the global recession, the preponderance of jobs being created are seasonal, contract and casual (Yalnizyan 2010). Year-to-year growth between 2008 and 2009 in full-time jobs has been negative, while the other four types of jobs mentioned above have all grown by over 10 per cent since 2008. It is clear that the growth of "precarious jobs" in the Canadian economy is intensifying as a response to the economic crisis (Chaykowski and Slotsve 2008).

Meanwhile, foreign investment in Canadian commercial real estate has reached unprecedented levels and will continue to increase as Canada develops innovative ways to attract foreign capital (White 2011). The Canadian federal Government has been broadcasting its astute weathering of the economic crisis. Meanwhile in each province, public sector workers, approximately 70 per cent of whom are in unions, are under attack: their benefits are being stripped and their wages frozen. The manufacturing sector, another bulwark of the Canadian labour movement, is facing lay-offs and downsizing. More of the jobs Canadians have fought to make into good jobs are under systemic attack. As Canada attracts capital for real-estate and infrastructure projects, there is job growth – but most of it is going to the private sector and is subject to competitive bidding.

The Justice for Janitors (J4J) model has been widely hailed as a successful model for organizing precarious workers. This model is sensitive to how power and decision-making in the cleaning industry are organized, and adapts organizing and bargaining structures accordingly to give power to some of the most precarious workers in the economy. The cleaning contractor (the employer) has little capital investment, most of their costs are labour costs, and contracts can shift, literally, on a dime. Therefore in this industry there is a strong need to mitigate the competitive pressures that create a race to the bottom in labour standards.

Canadian unions and workers' organizations are currently struggling to organize precarious workers and to raise standards to make precarious jobs "good jobs", while fighting back against the assault we are facing in the name of "economic crisis". In this context, the lessons learned through the adaptation and adoption by Service Employees International Union Local 2 of the J4J model to fit the Canadian context are particularly instructive.

Defining precarious work and "precarious industries"

How do we define precarious work? In 1989, in an ILO volume on the growth of atypical employment relationships in Western Europe, Gerry Rodgers disaggregated the dimensions of precariousness, relative to the "standard relationship of employment", as follows:

> *First, there is the degree of certainty of continuing work.* Precarious jobs are those with a short time horizon, or for which the risk of job loss is high ... *Second, there is an aspect of control over work* – work is more insecure the less the worker (individually or collectively) controls working conditions, wages, or the pace of work. *Third,* protection is of crucial importance: that is *to what extent workers are protected either by law, or through collective organization, or through customary practice* – protected against, say, discrimination, unfair dismissal, or unacceptable working practices, but also in the sense of social protection, notably access to social security benefits (covering health, accidents, pensions, unemployment insurance and the like). *A fourth, somewhat more ambiguous aspect is income* – low income jobs may be regarded as precarious if they are associated with poverty and insecure social insertion. (Rodgers 1989, emphasis added)

With deregulation and outsourcing, supply chains have lengthened, and work is increasingly subcontracted out to firms, employers or companies that are responsible for producing a component part or component service for the delivery of the end product. This could be manufacturing one part of a car, or delivering a service like security or cleaning. Contractual relationships between firms to deliver these services, or components, are made through competitive bidding and can be revoked at any time. This means that firms, too, experience the first and second dimensions of precariousness.

The contracting firm outsourcing the work often stipulates what the contractor companies must produce, how much, and in what timeframe. The contracting firm may also stipulate the way in which the product must be produced. The differential margin (profit) of firms operating in the same industry segment is often based upon lowering the cost of production relative to other competitors in the industry segment. This, of course, is what we call the "race to the bottom". Firms are not as vulnerable as workers; however, organizations that are engaged in raising standards for workers employed by these firms must understand how these dynamics operate in industries and how firms structure their businesses and competitive capability in the face of this "precariousness".

Precariousness is generally spoken about in the context of "globalization" – but, as the Workers' Action Center's study on precarious work in Toronto found, workers' experiences show that outsourcing, indirect hiring and misclassifying of workers take place in sectors with distinctly local markets: restaurants, business services, construction, retail, warehousing, trucking, janitorial, home health care and manufacture of goods consumed locally (Workers' Action Center 2011).

Therefore, for the purposes of definition, precariousness in this chapter focuses on workers who meet the criteria defined by Rodgers and extends the ideas of lack or control, and uncertainty about whether work will continue, to industries and to firms as well.

Union density, labour law and employment law

In Canada, union density started to increase during the post-war productivity boom, peaking in the 1980s when unions represented approximately 38 per cent of the labour force. Since then, union density has been falling gradually, hovering around 30 per cent of the labour force since the 1990s and slipping below 30 per cent in 2007 (Kumar 2008). Despite an increasingly anti-union environment, union membership in Canada actually increased by 19 per cent or 660,000 from 1997 to 2007, the largest increase since the 1970s. Notwith - standing recent surges, however, the growth in unionization has not been able to keep pace with the growth in the number of people joining the labour force, so union density continues to decline slowly (Kumar 2008). In 2006, in Canada over 70 per cent of public sector workers, but only 17 per cent of private sector workers, were in unions (British Columbia Business Council 2006). The private sector employed 84 per cent of the Canadian non-agricultural labour force (nearly 14 million workers). Thus 12 million private sector workers were not in unions in 2006.[1]

Another disturbing fact is the low union density in small businesses. Currently, 98 per cent of the businesses in Canada are classified as small businesses, namely those having fewer than 100 workers. Small businesses employ 48 per cent of the Canadian workforce that is registered as employed with the Canadian Revenue Services (Industry Canada 2010). These small firms make up 98 per cent of service-producing and 97 per cent of goods-producing sectors – so small businesses are not concentrated only in the service sector, as some would suggest (Industry Canada 2010). For small businesses with one to 20 employees, union density was only 13 per cent in 2006 (British Columbia Business Council 2006). For small businesses with 20 to 99 employees it was still below average at 29.7 per cent in 2006. Union density statistics for small businesses are, however, deceptive: 1,209,435 firms (more than half of all small businesses) are listed as "indeterminate", because the owner did not pay taxes for any employee at the business. Many of these firms are where precarious workers reportedly work (Workers' Action Center 2007). Some of these firms exist on paper only, and workers misclassified as "independent contractors" are in fact the "owners" of these "indeterminate" small businesses; in others workers are working "under the table" (Industry Canada 2010; Workers' Action Center 2007). Therefore, the large number of "indeterminate firms" and the growing trend of misclassifying workers means that the real union density in Canada may actually be lower than the figures suggest, because the statistics are not capturing workers who are "misclassified" or hidden and so are not registered as employees.

"Labour law" in Canada means the laws and regulations which apply to collective bargaining and unionized workers; "employment law" sets standards for workers whether they are unionized or not. Labour law in Canada, with the exception of Quebec,[2] is based upon the Wagner Act principles, similar to those that apply in the United States. In Quebec workers can have a say at the industry level through the "decree process", wherein industry-level association bargaining is established for all workers, union and non-union, in an industry with unions that are dominant in the sector. In the rest of Canada, union members are certified and bargain at the company level.

Both labour law and employment law in Canada are highly decentralized, and only about 10 per cent of Canadian employees are regulated by federal labour law and employment standards. Approximately 90 per cent of workers are covered by ten different provincial labour laws and employment standards (Bernard 1995). These provincial laws are far more responsive to political realignments than the much more centralized labour regime in the United States. As progressive elements – generally in the form of the National Democratic Party, which is strongly linked to labour – gain control there is pressure on Governments at federal, state and provincial level to adopt policies that make certification and bargaining easier, and when the political pendulum swings in the opposite direction, contested elections and other policies that limit the power of unions are introduced (Logan 2010). This provincial system and the political power of unions together explain why the strong anti-union animus evident in the Taft–Hartley Act, "right-to-work" bills and other similar legislation from the United States has not taken hold in Canada (Bernard 1995).

Since the 1990s, increased economic integration with the United States, the stipulations in international trade agreements, and the increasing dominance of the political discourse by neoliberal and conservative elements in Canada have been important factors behind the erosion of many of Canada's labour standards. When the provincial labour laws were originally drafted, most Canadian provinces had automatic certification, what is called "card check recognition" in the United States. Automatic certification means that, if a threshold of signed union cards (union cards that can be signed privately) is met, these are submitted to the appropriate labour board, which verifies that the threshold has been met, and the union is certified as the bargaining agent. Over the years, in most provinces, *automatic certification* has been replaced with provincially regulated mandatory representation votes, where submitting union cards triggers a labour board election. Only in the jurisdictions of Manitoba and Quebec (the provinces where union density is highest in Canada), and in federally regulated industries (and, with more restrictions, in New Brunswick and Prince Edward Island), do workers still enjoy card check.[3]

Under employment law, most workers in a standard employment relationship have access to employment insurance (unemployment benefits), pension benefits, mandated statutory holiday and sick pay, unpaid but job-protected family and parental leave, and workers' compensation if injured. There are relatively strong provincial health and safety acts mandating a safe workplace and employment standards protections. In Ontario, approximately 18 per cent of a full-time permanent worker's pay is deducted to pay for statutory benefits.

All employees are eligible for these benefits. However, part-time and temporary employees have a more difficult time qualifying for benefits such as employment insurance because of work-hour thresholds, and get smaller payments from the Canada Pension Plan because of the way in which contri-butions and payouts are calculated, even though all employees are de jure covered (Fudge, Tucker and Vosko 2002; Vosko 2002). Workers who are misclassified as "independent contractors" and "own-account self-employed" are not eligible for employment insurance; to protect themselves in case of unemployment, they must make their own contributions to pooled funds like workers' compensation funds or the Canada Pension Plan (Fudge, Tucker and Vosko 2002; Vosko 2002). Because of how responsibility is legally structured, independent contractors and own-account self-employed are covered by most of the provincial health and safety acts – but again the question is one of enforcement, and home-based workplaces are not covered by most of the health and safety acts (Edwards 2000).

De facto enforcement of these standards for "all workers" is another story. The capacity of ministries of labour to inspect small workplaces and enforce protections for precarious workers is limited, and time and again it is up to the worker to wage a protracted fight to gain access to statutory benefits and protections (Workers' Action Center 2007).

If precarious workers are generally those working as part-time, temporary or contract workers, or as "independent contractors" and "own-account self-employed", then these workers are often de facto, and sometimes de jure, working without the protections and benefits afforded by employment law, including the right to work in a safe environment. This is a key part of the competitive edge that is gained by companies which increase precarious employment in Canada.

The Justice for Janitors model in the United States

The Service Employees International Union (SEIU) was initially chartered as the Building Services Employees International Union (BSEIU) in 1921, representing mainly elevator operators, window cleaners, janitors and other maintenance employees in commercial buildings.[4] By the 1950s, institutional investors had started purchasing commercial buildings and an industry based on the contracting out of building maintenance started to emerge. The innovative strategy of the BSEIU, in both Canada and the United States, was that throughout their history they negotiated collective bargaining agreements with a group of employers through association bargaining, rather than with just one employer, attempting to mitigate the downward pressure on wages as cleaning contracts were awarded through competitive bidding (Waldinger et al. 1998).

However, by the 1980s, anti-union cleaning companies had severely eroded the capacity of SEIU to bargain and raise standards in unionized companies. Roger Waldinger et al. produced an instructive case study on Justice for Janitors in Los Angeles, published in 1998, which discussed why this happened in the Los Angeles market. According to Waldinger et al., SEIU was the dominant union representing cleaners where they were organized in the United States, with established relationships with the large companies that had controlled the cleaning industry through the 1980s (Waldinger et al. 1998). In Los Angeles, SEIU began to push to improve conditions and compensation for cleaners, and initially this push was successful. However, the inherent precariousness of the industry motivated property owners and managers to explore non-union options for cleaning. To understand why, one must look at the decision chain or power dynamic in the cleaning industry as outlined in

Figure 14.1 Primary relationships in the cleaning industry

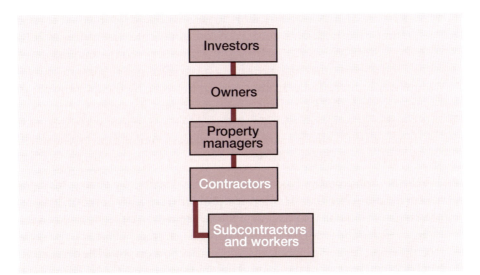

figure 14.1. The cleaning contractors are "straw bosses"; the real power lies with the property owners and managers.

Waldinger et al. pointed out that cleaning is highly labour-intensive, with direct labour making up the single largest part of a company's expenses. While there was a small advantage to gaining a certain size/asset threshold, because owners and property managers of high-value assets will invite larger companies to bid on maintenance contracts, it is easy for companies to enter the market with little capital investment, and the previous drift away from owner-management of buildings had made for increasingly fragile relationships. Since contracts were written so as to permit very short notice of termination, union members could lose work almost overnight if a building owner switched from a union to a non-union service.[5] Therefore, as the cost differential between using union and non-union contractors grew, this created an incentive to use non-union companies. The preferential systems that currently exist between the financialized owner, property manager and cleaning contractors are not strong, and can easily be subverted if the cost differential is high enough.

One of the major principles in Justice for Janitors in Los Angeles, as discussed by Waldinger et al., was an antipathy towards the normal "board election" process and an active decision to circumvent the Government as a mediator in certifying the union and in bargaining. This decision was based upon the two factors outlined below – taking into account as an additional underlying factor the fact that national labour policies in the United States are difficult to change:

(1) *Certification*: In the United States, the union is generally certified through a mandatory representation vote, not automatic certification. The average lag time at the National Labor Relations Board (NLRB) between requesting a certification vote and the date of the vote was 38 days in 2010 (Trottman and Maher 2010). During the time between the submission of cards and the vote, the employer often actively campaigns against the union. Employer intimidation is against the law; however, by the time the union is able to get the NLRB to issue a sanction against the employer, the union organizing drive has often been thwarted. Also, precarious workers have little job security and it is easier for an employer to intimidate these workers without resort to illegal activity.

(2) *Prohibition of secondary boycotts*: In the United States, the Labour Management Relations Act (Taft–Hartley Act) prohibits secondary boycotts, limiting the right of labour unions to engage another employer, either up or down the supply chain, who is not the target of an organizing campaign, to put pressure on the employer being unionized. A secondary boycott would be declared an unfair labour practice by the union, if the union were to use the NLRB process. However, if the union does not engage the primary decision-makers, the owners and property managers, there is no way to raise standards for cleaners, because the owners and managers would award contracts to non-union contractors as the standards for union contractors increased.

A recent study analysed the 22,000 petitions for an election filed under the current NLRB certification system between 1999 and 2004. From start to finish, only one-fifth (4,592 out of 22,382) of all organizing drives that filed election petitions ultimately reached a first contract (Ferguson and Kochan 2008). This statistic further affirms the decision to circumvent the traditional board election process.

It must also be noted that in the United States the majority of the cost of providing health care and other benefits is borne by the employer.

The J4J model in the United States is based upon six key stages of action:

(1) Map and understand the cleaning industry in a city.

(2) Engage in strong corporate leverage campaigns, focused on mobilizing workers, community allies and politicians, to put pressure on companies to recognize the union.

(3) Build and support community initiatives to strengthen workers' rights and benefits in the city.

(4) Unionize the companies predominantly through agreements achieved by using the corporate campaigns to achieve "employer neutrality" (that is,

the employer must agree not to campaign against the union). At the stage of company-by-company agreements, wages are not increased but a grievance procedure and other non-cost measures are implemented with a clause in each agreement that triggers market-wide bargaining when a certain proportion of the city is organized.

(5)   Engage in city-wide bargaining that raises wages and standards.

(6)   Utilize a system of "responsible contracting" to engage property owners and managers, so that the property owners and managers are respecting prevailing wages in unionized cities.

Organizing in Canada: Justice for Janitors and city-wide campaigning

In Canada, the BSEIU established its first two locals (branches) in Montreal and Vancouver in 1943. Members of these locals were mainly elevator operators, window cleaners, janitors and other maintenance employees in commercial buildings. Following a similar timeline to that described above, the cleaning industry in Canada structured itself similarly to its counterpart in the United States. When J4J campaigns were launched in Canada in 2006, most of the major cleaning companies in Canada were Canadian companies, not multinational firms as in the United States. This, however, is changing: for example, Compass Group PLC recently acquired the largest cleaning contractor in Canada (Hurley Brothers and Compass Group 2010).

The cleaning industry and SEIU before Justice for Janitors

In Montreal, in October 1975, SEIU Local 800 and the Quebec Building Service Contractors' Association requested that the Government of Quebec issue a decree which granted to the cleaning employees of public buildings, whether union members or not, the working conditions agreed to between the union and the employers.[6] Basic wages and benefits for the nearly 20,000 cleaners working in the province of Quebec are established by two separate decrees, one anchored in Montreal and one in Quebec City. The approximately 7,000 of these workers who are members of Local 800 have a grievance procedure and additional benefits above those provided for in the decree through company-based collective bargaining. This industry-wide model has meant that the lowest-paid workers in commercial cleaning companies make C$13.90 (Quebec decree) with regular wage increases. Under the Montreal decree, cleaners working for commercial cleaning companies make C$14.95/hr. The wages for non-union cleaners in the rest of Canada hover around the minimum wage, at C$10/hr.

The largest group of cleaners excluded from coverage under the decree are franchisers and "contractors", a "contractor" being defined as "a self-employed worker doing business alone who contracts directly with the owner, tenant or administrator of a public building and who carries out himself, or with his spouse, the children of either one, his father, mother, or the father or mother of his spouse, maintenance work in public buildings for his own benefit".[7] The employers on the Parity Committee have consistently expanded their use of franchising and cleaning franchises and currently most of the large cleaning contractors in Quebec run franchising operations. Currently there are no protections in Quebec formulated for franchisees, only the civil code, which treats the franchises as independent businesses (Whittaker 2006). While Quebec has better labour laws than most of the other Canadian provinces, it is important to note that loopholes exist through which precarious work enters and undermines the sector. Local 800 is aware of the threat posed by franchising; however, to date it has not been able to address the problem through the Parity Committee and these workers have not been unionized.

In Vancouver, in the 1970s and 1980s, SEIU Local 244 engaged in organizing drives without recourse to the decree process. By the 1980s, SEIU 244 represented the workers at most of the large commercial office cleaning contracting companies in Vancouver through company-level contracts. By 2006, however, inter-local strife and other issues had eroded SEIU 244's share of the commercial cleaning sector so that only 200 cleaners remained in its membership, and the workers working for the largest cleaning contractor in Vancouver were represented by the Canadian Auto Workers.

Market-wide organizing of cleaners had not been undertaken by SEIU, or any other union, in any of the other major cities in Canada. Cleaners working for cleaning contractors in some of the commercial buildings in Toronto were unionized predominantly by building trades or construction sector unions. The union was certified at and bargained at the building or worksite level. If the union tried to increase wages at a worksite, the cleaning contractor feared it would lose the contract as the majority of the cleaning contractors were non-union. Therefore, despite being unionized, both union and non-union cleaners' wages hovered around the minimum wage, which in 2006 was C$7.75/hr.[8] However, some cleaners did get access to supplementary health-care and benefit plans. In the other large Canadian cities, outside Quebec, most cleaners working for cleaning contractors were not in unions.

Justice for Janitors in Canada

In 2006 there were approximately 77,000 cleaners working in the ten largest cities in Canada, and 47,000 were not represented by a union. SEIU represented the nearly 20,000 commercial cleaning contractors in Quebec through the decree process, and approximately 500 cleaners in the rest of Canada outside of Quebec. Other unions represented approximately 2,000 cleaners. SEIU Canada undertook to build a national J4J movement in Canada outside Quebec, and SEIU Local 2 is the lead union in this initiative.

Most of the cleaners in Canada were precarious workers, generally making the minimum wage, which (outside Quebec) averaged C$7.75 an hour in current dollars and C$7 in constant dollars (Kerr 2008). Cleaning has been a first job for many immigrants in Canada (Clifford 2020). From the 1950s through to the 1970s the nascent cleaning industry was developed and dominated by Irish, Greek and Portuguese cleaners in Ontario and Quebec. By 2006 the industry was more established, with large national cleaning companies dominating the market. Temporary immigration policies, or "guest worker" programmes, have been expanded in Canada since 1996. By 2008 the number of people working in Canada on temporary Canadian work visas had increased by 118 per cent over 1996 numbers (Clifford 2010). An increasing number of these workers are deemed low-skilled by Immigration and Citizenship Canada (Clifford 2010). Many of these new immigrants are working as cleaners.

According to a seminal study by the Workers' Action Center in Toronto, the cleaning industry is by definition precarious, as it is based on outsourcing work that is considered low-skilled and labour-intensive to intermediaries operating as contractors (Workers' Action Center 2007). Furthermore, through J4J and Workers' Action Center's fieldwork with cleaners, it has become apparent that within the cleaning industry many companies make use of nominal subcontracting, that is, using intermediaries to "payroll" existing staff who overnight become employees of subcontractors, and/or misclassify workers as independent contractors so that they can be deemed exempt from labour laws. Thus these companies shift the costs of doing business to misclassified workers, franchises and nominal subcontractors, and tell the cleaners themselves, who have no control over their work, that they have to be incorporated as a company and must pay a fee to get work as well as paying for their own cleaning supplies and equipment (Workers' Action Center 2007). Finally, in Alberta, SEIU J4J campaigns have exposed the abuse of temporary foreign workers, whereby foreign workers with precarious immigration status are employed by cleaning contractors, and then denied overtime pay and statutory benefits and threatened with deportation (CBS 2010).

According to reports from industry specialists, the cleaning industry in Canada has been consolidating since the 1990s, and the cleaning of most office and industrial space is now done by a handful of large, professionalized companies (Garland 2008). A dozen large national companies, with approximately 40 regional and local competitors, dominate the cleaning sector in the ten large metropolitan areas of Canada. These companies then employ legitimate subcontractors and misclassified workers from the 17,622 registered janitorial firms in Canada (Aguiar 1999). The structure of the cleaning industry in Canada is very similar to that in the United States. It is an industry defined by "flexibility" and competitive bidding, dominated by "straw bosses" who are consolidating market share; it is also an industry which is by definition precarious and where the race to the bottom is especially pernicious. SEIU Local 2's goals were twofold: to organize cleaners and raise their employment standards; and to find innovative ways to raise standards in the new forms of work, defined by contract and temporary employment, that are challenging workplace standards for workers across the country.

The J4J campaigns in Canada have not bargained a master agreement as yet, although Ottawa is nearing this stage. However, owing to the differences in strategies adopted by the campaigns in Canada (compared with the United States), the impact of the J4J campaign in Canada has been significant.

Certification strategy

SEIU Local 2 has been engaged in corporate campaigning similar to that undertaken by J4J in the United States; however, in Canada the campaign has also relied on labour relations boards, when possible, to certify the union. The province where this is most difficult is British Columbia, because of significant barriers, built into labour precedent and regulations, to organizing contract employees in multiple locations. In the other provinces in Canada, outside Quebec, the labour board has been engaged in the certification process.

The rationale for this was to establish jurisdiction and insulate the campaign, as much as possible, from inter-union competition. Unions in Canada are highly competitive. Sometimes, when faced with an intractable union organizing drive by a militant union, a company will bring in another union to undermine the campaign. To challenge the status quo, where the few unionized workers were making approximately the minimum wage, SEIU had to engage in a strong campaign. Therefore, it was important to establish through board certification that the local was engaged in an active campaign to organize cleaners in key markets, and to establish an organizing protocol with unions in the markets where other unions already had a presence.

Ontario does not have automatic certification; however, in Canada, during the certification vote process, the lag time between the labour board mandating a vote and the vote is generally between five and ten days (Logan 2010). While it is true that during that gap the employer often actively campaigns against the union, Canadian Governments have tended to be more interventionist in their approach to industrial relations than those in the United States (Bernard 1995). This does mean that it is easier to file and win legitimate complaints on unfair labour practices and intimidation in a timely fashion in Canada. In 2007 an organizing protocol was signed with the other large union in the Toronto cleaning sector, facilitated by the Change-to-Win labour federation in the United States.

By using the labour relations boards for certification during the J4J campaigns in Canada, SEIU Local 2 has set precedents for establishing company-wide bargaining units that are sensitive to the turnover of contracts in sectors where the business model is based upon outsourcing and competitive bidding with constant changes in the employee's worksite.[9]

Engaging the owners and property managers

In Canada there is no prohibition on secondary boycotts, which means that the companies that actually control the race to the bottom can be engaged. Trusteed pension funds, which manage the direct benefit pensions of union members around the country, are some of the largest property owners in Canada; however, the "capital stewardship" programme in Canada is nascent at best. There are some firms that have been funded by unions to help union trustees on these powerful funds understand and manage their responsibilities and to help with proxy voting and move responsible investing. The Shareholder Association for Research and Education (SHARE) based in British Columbia is a small organization, but has been one of the key players in this emerging field.

In 2007 the Atkinson Foundation, a large charitable foundation, engaged SHARE to ensure that its investment portfolio met the social and environmental criteria that the organization supported. On the back of this project, SHARE and Atkinson brought together property managers, investors, real-estate advisory and ancillary companies and unions and other stakeholders and drafted a Responsible Property Services Code for property managers to adopt. To date, most owners and managers have not adopted the code; however, SEIU and SHARE and others now have a document that can be put to owners and managers as part of an on-the-ground campaign. Working with owners and managers on a code for responsible investment was also a strategy used in Australia as part of the Clean Start campaign to organize janitors in that country.

Furthermore, thanks to the corporate leverage campaigns and the strategies to target the property assets of pension funds, successes in persuading pension funds to consider more responsible management of their assets are helping to bring SEIU into the enterprise of building the Canadian version of capital stewardship.

Engaging the politicians

As Elaine Bernard has pointed out through her scholarship, the structure of the Canadian political system makes political engagement a much more viable strategy in Canada than it is in the United States (Bernard 1995; Logan 2010). Although Canada is changing and becoming increasingly anti-union, and in particular anti-public sector unions, there is still some appetite for protecting temporary foreign workers, precarious workers and workers who are working outside the statutory protections and other protections that most Canadians enjoy.[10]

In 2006, J4J in Canada started to bring together workers who had been largely invisible to give them a voice. Around that time unions and community activists in Ontario were working on a campaign to raise the minimum wage, which had been frozen for nine years and was still among the lowest in Canada, to C$10. In 2008 these activists won, and for many cleaners this was the first significant wage increase they had seen for nearly a decade.

Since 2008 J4J has become active and has won the changes it recommended to different regulatory and advisory panels of the provincial Government concerning contracting out, procurement and health and safety. As a result of hard work by many people across Canada, the Ontario Government has expressed an interest in taking some steps to help precarious workers. The political opportunities available in Canada are becoming more scarce as the political environment becomes less propitious, but there is capacity to make change through political action – though admittedly the major changes that would really improve the lives of all workers will take a great deal more work.

Conclusion

On 17 January 2011 *The New Yorker* published a piece by James Surowiecki that argued, in essence, that unionized workers are now a tiny percentage of the US workforce and the benefits they win are no longer percolating down to the rest of the workforce; thus "it is easier to just dismiss [them] as another interest group, enjoying perks that most workers can't get" (Surowiecki 2011). As precarious work grows, the gulf in terms of "perks" or standards widens, and this is currently being used to attack unionized workers with increasing ferocity.

In Toronto, a right-wing ideologue was elected mayor and is dismantling municipal services. On 2 May 2011, the Conservative Party finally gained a majority in the Canadian parliament and has the public service squarely in the cross-hairs. The assault on unionized workers is becoming more and more intense in Canada and precarious work has become a key feature of the employment landscape. Precariousness has an impact on most middle-class and working-class Canadians, whether as workers or as owners of small businesses, and it is changing the way in which unions must conceptualize their relation - ships with "workers" and "employers". The downshifting of risk without proper supports, the increase in productivity without wages that keep up, the growing income gaps – all are fundamental threats to our way of living, and have become entrenched.

One way to react to these shifts – and it is a valid way if we have the power to win – is to try to fight for an end to "precarious work". However, the experience with cleaners in Toronto and across Canada leads to a recognition that labour "flexibility" has become a way to organize labour that will be difficult to end in most of the private sector. In fact, many of the members in each of these groups do not disparage "atypical contracts". Their goal is to create stability in their industries to fight the insecurity inherent in precarious work and fight to raise standards.

In order to create good jobs, the arrows in our quiver must include ways to organize precarious workers, and to push for legal and institutional supports and bargaining structures which make this task easier in each of our particular political environments. The J4J model in Canada attempts to do just this.

Notes

[1] Environics Analytics, Demographic Estimates and Projections, 2010, and Statistics Canada 2006 statistics, reproduced by the Toronto Region Research Alliance; HRSDC (2009).

[2] Often termed "English Canada", admittedly a highly imperfect term, which means all the Canadian provinces except Quebec.

[3] Card check matters. In 2008, the provinces with the highest union density were the provinces that still had "card check" certification. Quebec (with card check) has been buoying up the Canadian union density rate, while in Ontario (mandatory elections), the province with the largest percentage of workers in Canada, the union density rate is consistently below the national average. See HRSDC (2008).

[4] For the history of the BSEIU, see http://www.seiu32bj.org/au/history.asp (accessed 16 June 2011).

[5] In the United States, by the 1970s, cleaning was dominated by African Americans due to the class dynamics and history of segregation; by the 1980s the cleaners were mostly new immigrants from Central America. See Waldinger et al. (1998).

[6] Website of le Comité Paritaire de l'entretien d'édifices publics, http://www.cpeep.qc.ca/pages/historique/ (accessed 16 June 2011).

[7] Website of le Comité Paritaire de l'entretien d'édifices publics, Decree, http://www.cpeep.qc.ca/files/pdf/EN_DECRET.pdf (accessed 16 June 2011).

[8] Ontario Ministry of Labour, minimum wage, http://www.worksmartontario.gov.on.ca/scripts/default.asp?contentID =1-3-2 (last modified 16 June 2011; accessed 16 June 2011).

[9] See Service Employees International Union Local 2. *ON Brewery, General and Professional Workers' Union v. Hurley Corporation*, 2006 CanLII 24988 (ON L.R.B.), Date 07, 07, 2007, Docket 0597-06-R, http://www.canlii.org/en/on/onlrb/doc/2006/2006canlii24988/2006canlii24988.html (accessed 16 June 2011).

[10] See Shareholder Association for Research and Education, http://www.share.ca (accessed 16 June 2011).

Resources

Aguiar, L. 1999. "The 'dirt' on the contract building cleaning industry in Toronto: Cleanliness and work reorganization", D.Phil. thesis, Department of Sociology, University of York (Toronto), July.

Bernard, E. 1995. "The Canadian experience: Labor, the NDP and the social movements", in *New Politics* (Winter), pp. 44–52, http://www.law.harvard.edu/programs/lwp/people/staffPapers/bernard/1995%20Labour%20NDP%20%20Soc%20Movts.pdf (accessed 16 June 2011).

British Columbia Business Council. 2006. "Trends in union density across Canada" (Executive Comment), in *Industrial Relations Bulletin*, Vol. 38, No. 9 (Sep.), pp. 1–2.

CBS. 2010. "Janitors allege deportation threats, withheld cash", CBC News, 1 Oct., http://www.cbc.ca/news/canada/edmonton/story/2010/10/01/edmonton-bee-clean-janitors.html (accessed 16 June 2011).

Chaykowski, R.P.; Slotsve, G.A. 2008. "The extent of economic vulnerability in the Canadian labour market and federal jurisdiction: Is there a role for labour standards?", in *Social Indicators Research* (Ontario Federation of Labour), Vol. 88, pp. 75–96.

Clifford, L. 2010. "Number of temporary foreign workers in Canada rises drastically", Canadian Immigration Report, 17 June, http://www.cireport.ca/2010/06/temporary-foreign-workers-have.html (accessed 16 June 2011).

Edwards, C.A. 2000. "Delegating safety?", special section in *Contractor Safety* (OHS Canada), July–Aug., http://www.ohscanada.com/lawfile/contractor.aspx (accessed 16 June 2011).

Ferguson, J-P.; Kochan, T.A. 2008. *Sequential failures in workers' right to organize*, MIT Sloan School of Management, Institute for Work and Employment Research (Cambridge, MA), Mar.

Fudge, J.; Tucker, E.; Vosko, L. 2002. "The legal concept of employment: Marginalizing workers", report for the Law Commission of Canada, Sep.

Garland, B. 2008. "Policies to temper a harsh business climate: Unscrupulous labour practices undermine operational efficiency", in *Canadian Property Management*, Feb./Mar.

Human Resources and Skills Development Canada (HRSCDC) 2008. *Union membership in Canada – 2008*, http://www.hrsdc.gc.ca/eng/labour/labour_relations/info_analysis/union_membership/index.shtml (accessed 16 June 2011).

Hurley Brothers and Compass Group. 2010. *Compass Group Canada acquires the Hurley Group*, press release, 5 Feb., http://www.hurley-group.com/hm/inside.php?id=131 (accessed 16 June 2011).

Industry Canada. 2010. *Key small business statistics*, special edition: *Growth map of Canadian firms*, Jan., http://www.ic.gc.ca/eic/site/sbrp-rppe.nsf/eng/h_rd02440.html (accessed 16 June 2011).

Kerr, K.B. 2008. "Federal minimum wages and low-income workers in Canada", Parliamentary Research and Information Service PRB 08-39E, 5 Nov., http://www2.parl.gc.ca/content/lop/researchpublications/prb0839-e.htm (accessed 16 June 2011).

Kumar, P. 2008. "Is the movement at a standstill? Union efforts and outcomes", in *Our Times*, Vol. 27, No. 5 (Oct.–Nov.), http://www.ourtimes.ca/Talking/article_94.php (accessed 16 June 2011).

Logan, J. 2010. "Union recognition and collective bargaining: How does the United States compare with other democracies?", Labour and Employment Relations Association, *Perspectives Online Companion*, Spring 2010, http://www.leraweb.org/publications/perspectives-online-companion/union-recognition-and-collective-bargaining-how-does-unit (accessed 16 June 2011).

Rodgers, G. 1989. "Precarious work in Western Europe: The state of the debate", in G. Rodgers and J. Rodgers (eds): *Precarious jobs in labour market regulation: The growth of atypical employment in Western Europe* (Geneva, International Institute for Labour Studies, ILO).

Surowiecki, J. 2011. "State of the unions", in *New Yorker* magazine, 17 Jan.

Trottman, M.; Maher, K. 2010. "Labor Board's recent decisions tilt in favor of unions", in *Wall Street Journal*, Business Section, 11 Nov.

Waldinger, R. et al. 1998. "Helots no more: A case study of the Justice for Janitors campaign in Los Angeles", in K. Bronfenbrenner et al. (eds): *Organizing to win: New research on union strategies* (Ithaca, NY, Cornell University Press).

White, S. 2011. "Real estate market braces for TMX–LSE merger", in *Globe and Mail*, 5 Apr.

Whittaker, S. 2006. "Franchisees get perks", in *Montreal Gazette*, 17 Apr., http://www.droitdespme.com/documents/Franchisees_Perks.pdf (accessed 16 June 2011).

Workers' Action Center. 2007. *Working on the edge*, http://www.workersactioncentre.org/!docs/pb_WorkingOnTheEdge_eng.pdf (accessed 17 August 2011).

Yalnizyan, A. 2010. "The temporary recovery", Progressive Economics Forum, http://www.progressive-economics.ca/2010/04/11/the-temporary-recovery/ (accessed 16 June 2011).

PERILS AND PROSPECTS: THE US LABOUR MOVEMENT'S RESPONSE TO THE ECONOMIC CRISIS

15

Jason Russell

The American labour movement, like progressive movements across the world, attempted to mount an effective response to the economic crisis that began in 2008. American unions and their allies have tried to promote a social and economic agenda that has emphasized the role of the State in protecting domestic jobs and social programmes. This includes promoting state intervention to protect the manufacturing sector and social programmes. These efforts have often been pursued through the labour movement's traditional political alliance with the Democratic Party, and within the context of substantial political upheaval in the United States. Labour's agenda in response to the crisis has so far yielded mixed results.

The American labour movement in 2011

When considering how American unions responded to the economic crisis, it is important to emphasize that it is difficult to refer to a single large, collective American labour movement. The movement operates within a particular structural framework that has shaped the manner in which American unions have responded to the crisis. American unions are divided between two major federations: the American Federation of Labor–Congress of Industrial Organizations (AFL-CIO) and the Change-to-Win Coalition (CTW). This division is further complicated by the fact that CTW, created in 2005, is slowly disintegrating as a result of conflict between and within some of its founding unions. The Union of Needletrades, Industrial, and Textile Employees–Hotel Employees and Restaurant Employees (UNITE-HERE) split into two unions in 2009, with approximately 150,000 joining a new union called Workers United. The Labourers' International Union of North America (LIUNA), another CTW affiliate, chose to return to the AFL-CIO in 2010.

Divisions between unions and federations are further accentuated by geography. Each American state has a labour federation that is chartered by the AFL-CIO. However, those federations have widely differing levels of influence. Variations in regional influence and membership levels have particularly influenced the response of American unions to the economic crisis, and dramatically shaped their ability to operate in the political arena. At the end of 2008, when the economic crisis began, approximately 12.4 per cent of American workers (about 16.1 million) belonged to unions (BLS 2011).

It is important to note that nearly half of all American union members, 7.4 million people, live in just six states: California, New York, Pennsylvania, Illinois, New Jersey and Ohio. New York State has the highest union density at 24.2 per cent, while North Carolina has the lowest at 3.2 per cent. Unions are virtually absent across the Southern and Midwestern states. This means that American unions essentially comprise a regionally based movement that tries to exercise a national mandate. This demographic reality has circumscribed organized labour's ability to mount a broadly effective response to the economic crisis. Furthermore, the American labour movement is increasingly a public sector movement: 36.2 per cent of public sector workers belong to unions, while only 6.9 per cent of private sector workers are unionized (BLS 2011).

Its regional concentration notwithstanding, the American labour movement is often able to influence national elections through its highly effective political apparatus. Indeed, if someone who had never visited the United States travelled directly to Washington, DC, she would likely get the impression that American unions are politically powerful. Political action committees abound in American politics: the CIO created the first one in 1944, and the AFL-CIO, CTW and their affiliates continue to be politically active today. American unions devoted both money and volunteers to electing Democrats in both the 2008 presidential election and the 2010 mid-term elections. AFL-CIO president Richard Trumka announced in early September 2010 that the federation would launch a "Labor 2010" campaign to mobilize workers across the country in anticipation of the mid-term and state elections (*Huffington Post* 2010).

The 2010 congressional mid-term and state elections

The 2010 mid-term congressional and state elections were initially portrayed as a major loss for both the Democratic Party and organized labour. The Democrats emerged with a reduced majority in the Senate, the loss of their majority in the House of Representatives and control of only 20 governors' offices (Democratic Governors Association 2011). Organized labour stayed with the Democratic

Party through the mid-term elections, even though unions have not been entirely supportive of the party's response to the economic crisis. Unions and other progressive groups had high hopes that the Obama Administration would implement policies that would favour them, while also countering the effects of the economic crisis. While there has been considerable criticism in progressive media sources about the Administration's policies, there is nonetheless evidence that some of them worked. For instance, organized labour was bitterly disappointed that Congress did not pass the Employee Free Choice Act (EFCA). This law would have made it easier for workers to join unions and given greater protection to those trying to organize. It would have also made it easier for unions to conclude collective agreements in newly organized workplaces. A voluminous body of writing on this act has appeared in the popular press, progressive blogs and academic journals. Most analyses conclude that the EFCA would provide a useful regulatory method of making unionization easier (Nissen 2009).

The EFCA did not pass, but the Obama Administration has made significant pro-labour appointments to federal government agencies. For instance, Craig Becker was appointed to the NLRB in the face of determined opposition from the Republican Party and business lobby groups. Becker is a former counsel for the SEIU and AFL-CIO. His appointment caused conservative groups and the business community to go into a state of near-hysterics, with the pro-business *Wall Street Journal* referring to Becker as "labour's secret weapon" (*Wall Street Journal* 2009). Hilda Solis, a pro-labour former member of Congress from California, became Secretary of Labor. Those were both important appointments for the labour movement.

American unions support government intervention in the economy, although many union leaders argued for more economic stimulus spending than was actually provided by Congress and the Obama Administration. Unions also wanted a so-called "public option" in the federal health-care legislation passed early this year. On the other hand, the Administration successfully pushed through a series of unemployment benefit extensions for displaced workers, which was a policy decision strongly supported by unions. President Obama and Secretary Solis both appeared at a Labor Day rally in 2010 with the AFL-CIO leadership to motivate union voters. The Administration and the labour movement thus hoped to cooperate fully as they went into the November elections, and otherwise continue to pursue policies that will mitigate the effects of the economic downturn. Pursuing a mutually beneficial policy agenda will now be much more difficult in the face of emboldened Republican opposition (*The Hill* 2010).

A tale of three states

The discussion so far has focused on broad national trends, but it is important to consider also how the economic crisis has been handled at the level of the individual state. The states are, in many ways, the "laboratories of democracy" described by the late US Supreme Court Justice Louis Brandeis (Politico 2011). I will discuss here in some detail events that show how American unions have responded to the economic crisis on a regional basis. These events illustrate both the American labour movement's weaknesses and its strengths. I will first discuss the public sector in New York – the state with the highest union density. I will then turn to union responses to the impact of the economic downturn on the domestic automotive industry, which is primarily based in Michigan. Finally, I will review how the newly elected Governor of Wisconsin has sought to strip public sector workers of the right to collective bargaining.

Every state in the United States (with the exception of Nebraska) has a lower and an upper legislative chamber. There is considerable variation between states when it comes to how their legislatures interact with their state executive branches. The nature of New York State's political environment helped set the parameters of a long debate over the state's budget. The state is dominated by Democrats: the party controls the state assembly and executive branch, and has a large minority in the state senate. New York State is currently led by a new and politically skilled Democratic Governor named Andrew Cuomo, who has previously been State Attorney-General and was a federal Cabinet secretary during the Clinton Administration.

The previous New York Governor, David Paterson, also a Democrat, indicated in autumn 2009 that the state budget would have to be cut owing to a US$13.7 billion deficit (New York State Department of Budget 2011). This concern about budget deficits has been evident around the world, and has become a topic of increasing policy debate across the United States. For instance, there are numerous websites that show that the total US national debt is approximately US$14.1 trillion (US Debt Clock 2011). The Republican Party, which presided over a massive expansion of public debt during the George W. Bush presidency, has become fixated on that number. Republicans have invariably called for cuts to social programmes and reductions in government spending rather than any type of tax increase. Remarkably, they continue to suggest that cutting taxes – particularly for the wealthy – will actually increase government revenues. In fact, the tax structure in the United States is now such that 47 per cent of Americans either pay no federal income tax or pay negative taxes and receive rebates (Tax Policy Center 2010).

Many Democrats have also become fixated on debt levels, and it was this concern about mounting debt that led Governor Paterson to suggest the need for significant spending cuts across the state budget. Many Democrats in both the state assembly and the senate opposed those reductions and supported some tax increases, although the Republicans uniformly opposed any more taxes. The resulting legislative impasse led to the state's 2010 budget being approved 125 days late (*New York Times* 2010b). The new budget included spending reductions, but also included US$1 billion in new revenue that would be partially derived from new taxes. The fact that the budget included some tax increases, and did not lead to massive public sector wage reductions, was partially attributable to the effective response of New York unions to the crisis.

Governor Paterson proposed to renegotiate union contracts and freeze wages. The state legislature actually approved furloughs, or unpaid time off, for state employees in May 2010 (*New York Times* 2010a). A coalition of public sector unions, including the Civil Service Employees Association (CSEA) and the New York State Union of Teachers (NYSUT), sued the state Government and overturned the furlough legislation (New York State Union of Teachers 2010). Wage increases were restored, and early retirement provisions were instead introduced to help reduce the need for redundancies. The state budget was consequently not balanced on the backs of public sector workers.

Governor Cuomo, despite being a Democrat, has taken a harder approach on the state budget. He proposed a budget for 2011/12 that would reduce overall state spending by US$10 billion, but would also lead to substantial reductions in services such as education and health care. New York unions were uncomfortable with Cuomo during the election, but still supported him and other Democratic candidates. The new Governor invited unions to help identify cost savings, which is perceived by labour as meaning the acceptance of concessions. Otherwise, Cuomo threatened to eliminate up to 9,800 public sector jobs. New York State's public sector unions thus find themselves facing demands for economic concessions from a Governor whom they supported (New York State Department of Budget 2011).

The second issue that I wish to examine here is the restructuring by government of General Motors (GM) and Chrysler, and the impact this action has had on the state of Michigan. Many American states are synonymous with certain industries. Florida conjures visions of oranges and Walt Disney, Texas of oil and natural gas, Nevada of gambling and entertainment. Michigan is principally known as the birthplace of the American automobile industry. Detroit, the state's main city, was described as a "city of homes" by historian Thomas Sugrue and had over 1.5 million residents in 1970 (Sugrue 1996: 23). In 2010 its population was just 713,777 (United States Department of Census 2010).

Michigan, particularly Detroit, could not bear the further industrial job losses that would result from GM and Chrysler going out of business. Both of those firms went into bankruptcy protection in 2009. The American auto mobile industry has changed markedly since the late 1960s, and there are now many automobile factories in the United States that are operated by firms based in other countries. Honda and Toyota have assembled cars in America for many years, and have been joined more recently by firms such as Volkswagen and Hyundai. Not coincidentally, many European and Asian car manufacturers chose to build their facilities in "right-to-work" states in the South and Midwest. Section 14b of the 1947 Taft–Hartley Act enables states to ban the mandatory deduction of union dues, which in turn grants the so-called "right to work" without having to support organized labour. "Right-to-work" states invariably have weaker unions, and are more likely to have Republican governors and legislatures (Millis and Clark-Brown 1950).

Jefferson Cowie and William Adler have both shown how states in the South and Midwest used their non-union, low-wage status to attract business from the 1960s onwards (Cowie 1999; Adler 2000). By 2008, many of the politicians who opposed the aid package for GM and Chrysler were from those states. Alabama senator Richard Shelby, whose state is home to plants operated by Honda, Mercedes-Benz and Hyundai, was described as "Detroit's leading nemesis" during hearings on the aid package (*New York Times* 2008). Shelby, like most Republicans, opposed any support for the domestic automobile manufacturers. The Bush Administration appeared willing to let GM and Chrysler slide into bankruptcy without government intervention. By contrast, the Obama Administration, in conjunction with Democrats in Congress, essentially nationalized GM and Chrysler in 2009, in a move widely denounced as "socialism" in the American right-wing media (*New York Times* 2009). Conservative think-tanks such as the Cato Institute referred to GM as Government Motors (Cato Institute 2010).

The Obama Administration's decision to assist GM and Chrysler was shaped by a range of factors, principally the impact that further massive job losses would have had on states such as Michigan and Ohio. These are two of the states that have higher union density. The state Government in Michigan, which in 2008 was led by a Democratic Governor named Jennifer Granholm, lobbied the Obama Administration and Congress in order to get financial support for GM and Chrysler. The federal Government in Canada and the Government of the province of Ontario also committed to helping the two companies. The United Auto Workers (UAW), a union which is now a much diminished version of what it used to be, also lobbied governments at all levels to provide assistance for GM and Chrysler.

Unemployment in Michigan, currently at one of the highest levels in the United States at 12.5 per cent, would almost certainly have been even worse had GM and Chrysler not been able to continue operating without government assistance (BLS 2011). The UAW, which is now down to 390,000 members from a peak of over 1.5 million in the early 1970s, would probably not have survived the loss of GM and Chrysler in its current form (UAW 2010). Both companies, particularly GM, are now in much better financial shape and are beginning to hire more workers. The Obama Administration has claimed that assisting GM and Chrysler was indeed the correct decision to make. On 30 May 2010 President Obama told an audience in Hamtramck, Michigan, that "it's estimated that we would have lost another million jobs if we had not stepped in [to help GM and Chrysler]" (*USA Today* 2010).

In supporting GM and Chrysler, the Obama Administration was supporting a key Democratic Party constituency – organized labour – while also maintaining jobs. On the other hand, the UAW survived at the price of accepting major bargaining concessions. UAW members are now covered by two-tier wage agreements at GM, Chrysler and Ford (White House 2010). This decision to accept two-tier wage scales led to revolts among rank-and-file members – who were not consulted during the union's negotiations with the Government and the auto-makers. Delegates to the UAW's 35th convention in Detroit challenged the decision by then union president Ron Gettelfinger to accept these drastic concessions. A new worker hired at GM will now make half of what a long-service worker is paid, and will not have either health insurance or access to a company pension plan. Wages and benefits for new domestic auto-maker employees are now similar to those earned by workers in plants in right-to-work states (*Labour Notes* 2010a).

The UAW national leadership also made the unusual decision to support the Obama Administration's efforts to conclude a free trade agreement with the Republic of Korea. New UAW president Bob King was initially considered a reform candidate, but supported the trade deal because he believed that it would lead to greater exports of American cars to the Republic of Korea. The UAW was joined by the United Food and Commercial Workers (UFCW) in supporting the trade deal, but the AFL-CIO and most other unions vociferously opposed it. Possibly the UAW supported the deal in return for Obama having saved GM and Chrysler. Whether this is so or not, the American domestic auto industry has survived, but at a material cost to unionized workers (*New York Times* 2010d).

The final case of how labour has responded to the economic crisis involves events that have occurred in the state of Wisconsin since the 2010 mid-term elections. Wisconsin is home to both conservative Republicans and liberal Democrats. Republicans recently won control of both houses in the state legislature and the election for state Governor. This happened largely as a result of support from the Tea Party movement that emerged after Barack Obama's election in 2008. Wisconsin's new Republican Governor, Scott Walker, is a favourite of right-wing Tea Party supporters and began to attack the state's unions immediately following his election. Republican legislators in Florida, Ohio and Indiana also began pursuing similar objectives. They claim that changing collective bargaining laws is necessary to help states cope with budget problems precipitated by the economic crisis.

Wisconsin Republicans introduced Senate Bill 11, which denies University of Wisconsin employees the right to collective bargaining, requires public sector unions to re-certify every year, and limits public sector unions to negotiating over wage increases up to the rate of inflation (Wisconsin Legislature 2011). Unions in Wisconsin, and across the United States, quickly went into action to oppose this law. Wisconsin senate Democrats, who are in a comparatively small minority, left the state so that senate business could not proceed because of the absence of a voting quorum (*New York Times* 2011b). Tens of thousands of union supporters from across the United States streamed into Wisconsin to protest against Scott Walker's effort to weaken collective bargaining rights. The Wisconsin controversy led Barack Obama to suggest that what was happening in the state was "an assault on unions" (*Washington Post* 2011).

Assessing the responses

There are both similarities and differences between how the UAW responded to the auto industry crisis, how public sector unions in New York State responded to government efforts to reduce their wages and benefits, and how Wisconsin's public sector unions responded to Governor Walker. These were responses to the loss of unionized wages and, in the cases of the UAW and unions in Wisconsin, they were also reactions against threats to labour's survival. However, the UAW accepted concessions that New York's public sector unions did not accept. The resistance of the New York unions can be attributed to the fact that New York has the highest unionization rate in America, and that its unions are politically influential. On the other hand, we see the Wisconsin labour movement fighting to protect basic labour rights; and in New York we also see the challenges that unions can face even when negotiating with governments led by Democrats rather than Republicans.

Unions in all three cases nonetheless supported the capitalist free market framework that dominates social and economic discourse in the United States. They also did so within the boundaries of the post-war labour relations system – a framework that many historians have suggested disproportionately favours business (Dubofsky 1994; Lichtenstein 2002). American labour leaders have not actively attempted to remake the free market system, and have instead sought to ensure that the material rewards of capitalism are more equitably distributed. For instance, unions and progressive groups are now preparing to oppose possible changes to the social security system that provides supplementary retirement benefits to Americans (*Labour Notes* 2010b). The fact that the UAW and UFCW supported a free trade agreement with the Republic of Korea shows the extent to which free market ideology is accepted in the American labour movement.

After the crisis

The American labour movement faces many perils, but also has some positive prospects. The main problem clearly confronting American labour is the fact that one of the two main political parties – the Republican Party – is now mounting a major assault on collective bargaining rights. The American labour relations system already favours business, but now Republicans and corporate interests are seeking to unravel it completely. In contrast, Democrats like Andrew Cuomo may want to push unions for concessions, but are not attempting to undo the labour relations system. As Kim Phillips-Fein revealed, corporations and wealthy business owners have been funding right-wing, often anti-union agendas since the 1930s (Phillips-Fein 2009). As she further showed, people like the Koch family have long been involved in right-wing conservative causes (Phillips-Fein 2009: 130). Koch money poured into Wisconsin in 2010 to help elect Scott Walker, and the family continued to help Republicans in that state pursue an anti-union agenda after the election (*New York Times* 2011a).

Regardless of what has happened in Wisconsin, and may also happen in other Republican-dominated states like Indiana and Ohio, the outcome of the 2010 mid-term elections is not as politically negative as what occurred when Republicans took control of both houses of Congress in 1994. Democrats control the White House and US Senate. They lost control of many state legislatures, but nonetheless enjoyed some successes. Most notably, they are in complete control of the California Government – the largest state Government in America. Prior to the 2010 mid-term elections, commentators such as the economist Paul Krugman argued that Republicans were preparing for a repeat of their challenge to the Clinton Administration in the 1990s (*New York Times* 2010c). Such predictions have not come true in their entirety, although confrontation over the federal budget is continuing. Republicans have instead chosen to attack unions at the state level because they are still politically effective and can have a significant influence on economic and social policy.

The main prospect for renewal and expansion of American organized labour involves workers who are not yet in unions, but who are still forming a workers' movement. As Dorothy Sue Cobble recently argued, there is an "other" labour movement that exists in America outside the bounds of collective bargaining. It is found in places like immigrant worker centres, which have multiplied across the United States from five in 1992 to 140 in 2006 (Cobble 2010: 18). The established labour movement has also begun reaching out to workers who are not in unions. For example, more than 2 million people now belong to Working America, a community affiliate established by the AFL-CIO in 2003 (Cobble 2010: 19). As Cobble observed, most of the "other" labour movement exists outside the AFL-CIO and CTW. Unions will perhaps find their future, and ways of responding to the ongoing economic crisis, through alliances with community groups such as immigrant worker centres and through finding more ways for non-union workers to join with organizations like Working America.

The American labour movement in 2011 is thus at a new crossroads. It has responded to the economic crisis through its link to the Democratic Party, and through various campaigns to promote social justice such as advocating health-care reform and the protection of social security. It has faced setbacks: the EFCA was not passed in the Senate; health-care legislation did not include the public option that unions wanted; and organized labour would have preferred stronger regulatory reform of the financial industry. Conversely, Democrats successfully implemented a significant economic stimulus package, made important pro-labour appointments to federal agencies, and at least began the process of improving access to health care in the United States. Indeed, Barack Obama signed the Lilly Ledbetter Fair Pay Act shortly after being sworn in as President. This law made it easier for workers to file equal pay lawsuits (White House 2009).

Looking ahead

Confrontation with conservative Republicans will continue, but there are reasons to be optimistic that unions will continue to be an effective voice for working Americans, and will retain the ability to influence economic policy in the aftermath of the 2008 recession. The Democratic Party will continue to be successful in states with higher union density. The political situation is much more fragile in states with lower union density. There is a clear correlation, because states with lower density are more likely to elect Republican candi-dates, while states in which the Democrats are successful are more prone to have higher union density. Republicans at the federal and state levels emerged emboldened from the 2010 elections, and the divide between the two main political parties is greater than ever. Nonetheless, organized labour will still have a strong regional base from which it will continue to try to exercise a national mandate. A disproportionate number of American union members may be concentrated in just six states, but those states account for one-third of national waged and salaried employment. Labour's regional base is thus still significant (BLS 2011).

The labour movement endures as a key Democratic constituency, regardless of its sometimes strained relations with the party. It is possible that the AFL-CIO will work more closely with CTW, even if such efforts do not lead to all of the CTW unions returning to their original federation. For example, SEIU and the AFL-CIO joined other organizations in sponsoring One Nation Working Together, a progressive coalition pursuing social change. National union leaders such as Gerald McEntee, president of the American Federation of State, County and Municipal Employees, have argued that the labour movement is re-energized in the face of attacks from the political Right (*New York Times* 2011c). The stakes are high for American workers and their organizations. It will take a determined effort that involves unions, other social movements and left-leaning political groups in order more fully to counteract the long-term effects of the economic crisis.

Resources

Adler, W. 2000. *Mollie's job: A story of life and work on the global assembly line* (New York, Touchstone).

Bureau of Labor Statistics (BLS). 2011. "Union members summary", http://www.bls.gov /news.release/union2.nr0.htm (accessed 16 June 2011).

Cato Institute. 2010. "Government Motors", http://www.cato-at-liberty.org/government-motors/ (accessed 16 June 2011).

Cobble, D. 2010. "Betting on new forms of worker organization", in *Labor: Studies in Working-Class History of the Americas*, Vol. 7, No. 3 (Fall), pp. 17–23.

Cowie, J. 1999. *Capital moves: RCA's seventy-year quest for cheap labor* (New York, New Press).

Democratic Governors Association. 2011. http://www.democraticgovernors.org/governors/ (accessed 16 June 2011).

Dubofsky, M. 1994. *The state and labour in modern America* (Chapel Hill, NC, University of North Carolina Press).

The Hill. 2010. "Obama to appear at Labor Day rally with AFL-CIO president", http://thehill.com/blogs/blog-briefing-room/news/116435-obama-will-appear-labor-day-alongside-afl-cio-chief (accessed 16 June 2011).

Huffington Post. 2010. "AFL-CIO launching Labor Day political blitz", http://www. huffingtonpost.com/2010/09/01/afl-cio-labor-day-tea-parties_n_701713.html (accessed 16 June 2011).

Labour Notes. 2010a. "Auto worker convention fiddles while union burns", No. 376 (July).

—. 2010b. "Retirees rally to save social security", No. 378 (Sep.).

Lichtenstein, N. 2002. *State of the Union* (Princeton, NJ, Princeton University Press).

Millis, H.; Clark-Brown, E. 1950. *From the Wagner Act to Taft–Hartley: A study of national labor policy and labor relations* (Chicago, University of Chicago Press).

New York State Department of Budget. 2011. "Governor Cuomo's 2011–12 executive budget provides transformation plan for a new New York", http://www.budget. ny.gov/pubs/press/2011/pressRelease11_ eBudget1.html (accessed 16 June 2011).

New York State Union of Teachers. 2010. "Unions successful in blocking furloughs", http://www.nysut.org/mediareleases_15156.htm (accessed 16 June 2011).

New York Times. 2008. "Foreign auto makers say little in aid debate", 10 Dec., http://www.nytimes.com/2008/12/10/business/10transplants.html?adxnnl=1&adxnnlx=1298348700-rtD0Hl1Vm19ITJ/MtLEvJg (accessed 16 June 2011).

—. 2009. "Socialism then vs. socialism now for General Motors", 3 June, http://economix.blogs.nytimes.com/2009/06/03/socialism-then-vs-socialism-now-for-general-motors/ (accessed 16 June 2011).

—. 2010a. "New York legislature approves 1-day furloughs", 10 May, http://www.nytimes.com/2010/05/11/nyregion/11furlough.html (accessed 16 June 2011).

—. 2010b. "125 days late: A state budget with new taxes", 3 Aug., http://www.nytimes.com/2010/08/04/nyregion/04albany.html (accessed 16 June 2011).

—. 2010c. "It's witch-hunt season", 20 Aug., http://www.nytimes.com/2010/08/30/opinion/30krugman.html?scp=5&sq=krugman&st=cse (accessed 16 June 2011).

—. 2010d. "US union backing boosts Korea trade pact", 9 Dec., http://www.nytimes.com/2010/12/09/business/global/09trade.html (accessed 16 June 2011).

—. 2011a. "Billionaire brothers' money plays role in Wisconsin dispute", 21 Feb., http://www.nytimes.com/2011/02/22/us/22koch.html?src=ISMR_AP_LO_MST_FB (accessed 16 June 2011).

—. 2011b. "Missing Democrats continue Wisconsin budget stall", 22 Feb., http://www.nytimes.com/2011/02/23/us/23wisconsin.html?hp (accessed 16 June 2011).

—. 2011c. "Countering the siege", 12 Apr., http://www.nytimes.com/2011/04/13/business/13mcentee.html?_r=1&scp=5&sq=wisconsin%20protests&st=cse (accessed 16 June 2011).

Nissen, B. 2009. "Would the Employee Free Choice Act effectively protect the right to organize? Evidence from a South Florida nursing home case", in *Labor Studies Journal*, Vol. 34, No. 1, pp. 65–90.

Phillips-Fein, K. 2009. *Invisible hands: The making of the conservative movement from the New Deal to Reagan* (New York, Norton).

Politico. 2011. "Republican governors strike hard at unions", http://www.politico.com/news/stories/0211/49852.html (accessed 16 June 2011).

Sugrue, T. 1996. *The origins of the urban crisis: Race and inequality in postwar Detroit* (Princeton, NJ, Princeton University Press).

Tax Policy Center. 2010. "Why nearly half of Americans pay no federal income tax", http://www.taxpolicycenter.org/publications/url.cfm?ID=412106 (accessed 16 June 2011).

United Auto Workers (UAW). 2010. http://www.uaw.org/node/39 (accessed 16 June 2011).

United States Department of Census. 2010. http://www.census.gov/newsroom/releases/archives/2010_census/cb11-cn106.html (accessed 16 June 2011).

USA Today. 2010. "President Obama drives Chevy Volt and touts job gains", http://content.usatoday.com/communities/driveon/post/2010/07/president-obama-drives-chevy-volt-and-touts-job-gains/1 (accessed 16 June 2011).

US Debt Clock. 2011. http://www.usdebtclock.org/ (accessed 16 June 2011).

Wall Street Journal. 2009. "Andy Stern's go-to guy: Meet Craig Becker, labor's secret weapon", http://online.wsj.com/article/SB124226652880418035.html (accessed 16 June 2011).

Washington Post. 2011. "Obama: Wisconsin budget fight seems like 'an assault on unions'", http://voices.washingtonpost.com/44/2011/02/obama-wisconsin-budget-fight-s.html (accessed 16 June 2011).

White House. 2009. "President Obama signs the Lilly Ledbetter Fair Pay Act: January 29, 2009", http://www.whitehouse.gov/video/EVR012909 (accessed 16 June 2011).

—. 2010. "Remarks by the President at the General Motors Hamtramck auto plant in Hamtramck, Michigan", http://www.whitehouse.gov/the-press-office/remarks-president-general-motors-hamtramck-auto-plant-hamtramck-michigan (accessed 16 June 2011).

Wisconsin Legislature. 2011. "Senate Bill 11", http://nxt.legis.state.wi.us/nxt/gateway.dll?f=templates&fn=default.htm&d=billhist&jd=top (accessed 16 June 2011).

MEETING THE RIGHT'S ATTACK ON PUBLIC SECTOR UNIONS IN THE UNITED STATES: ARE THERE EFFECTIVE STRATEGIES?

16

Lee Adler

Introduction

This essay was prompted – indeed, provoked – by the rapid turn to the political Right in domestic US politics. It is not a traditional academic undertaking, but rather an effort to inform our international colleagues of what this worrisome shift looks like and what at least one union, the United Federation of Teachers in New York City, is doing to counter this attack.

The numbers describing the unionized public sector[1] in the United States' workforce over the last two years are not pretty:

- More than 200,000 workers have been laid off in the past year,[2] with 48,000 state and local government workers laid off in July alone; many hundreds of thousands more experienced "furloughs", that is, compulsory days off without pay.

- A July 2010 government report filed by leaders of city, municipal and county agencies predicts that total lay-offs (including non-union employ - ees) are likely to approximate 500,000 workers by the end of 2012. Unions represent 37 per cent of the public sector workforce in the United States, although nearly one half of those workers are in the states of New York, New Jersey, California, Illinois and Pennsylvania.

- Eligibility for excellent health-care coverage at modest or affordable cost is rapidly disappearing, especially for retired people.

- Wage decreases between 3 and 7 per cent, ostensibly to avoid lay-offs, are on the increase throughout the country.

- Historic job security for public school teachers is threatened by sharp decreases in funding for public schools and for publicly subsidized, non-union "charter schools", and by statutory changes in "tenure" definitions often making it easier to get rid of so-called "underperforming" school teachers; 26 states have already laid off public employees and five more have used the furloughs mentioned above.

This essay will describe certain aspects of this economic and political reality, and then show through case studies the efforts of New York City's education union,[3] the United Federation of Teachers (affiliated with the American Federation of Teachers and the AFL-CIO), as it struggles to blunt the harshest effects of the crisis that are affecting so many of our friends, families and neighbours.

Why are public sector unions blamed for this governmental crisis?

It is helpful to begin answering this important question with some more numbers. In the United States, barely 7 per cent of private sector workers belong to unions, while 37 per cent of public sector workers do. In 2009, for the first time, unionized public sector workers exceeded those in the private sector in absolute numbers.[4] The federal government agency that annually monitors these statistics also found that the density of public sector membership actually increased during 2009, despite the recession, lay-offs and furloughs.

This resilience of the public sector unions alarms the US Right,[5] which has resorted to vilifying the growing strengths of the labour movement by referring to the UFT's "cozy" relationship with Mayor Bloomberg of New York City as a "cartel", and the public sector as having "become so powerful as to threaten the Madisonian system set up to constrain any one faction from overwhelming the public interest".[6] Websites[7] are filled with salary tables of every public school teacher, firefighter and police officer. Newspapers are fed stories about the "gross" earnings, often through overtime, of public safety officers, as exemplified here:

> In New York City, where public sector union benefits have grown twice as fast as those in the private sector since 2000, fire-fighters may retire after 20 years at half pay. Pension benefits for a new retiree averaged just under $73,000 (all exempt from state and local taxes) ... To top it off, they receive a health insurance policy that is worth about $10,000 annually...

> ... According to the *Boston Globe*, 225 of the 2,338 Massachusetts state police officers made more than Governor Deval Patrick's $140,535 annual salary in 2006. Four state troopers received more than $200,000, and 123 others were paid more than $150,000. California teachers are represented by one of the country's most powerful teachers' unions and earn 25 per cent more than the national average. Forbes has reported that there are California prison guards making $300,000 a year.[8]

Reports like those shown here leave the relatively uninformed citizenry with the dual impression that public sector unions wield naked power, and, worse, that they use it to increase the average citizen's tax burden – how else, after all, are these sums paid to police officers, teachers and other public workers? Even moderate national publications print incomplete stories and exploit these concerns by telling America that government workers make 20 per cent or more than their counterparts in the private sector; but they seldom mention that their statistical "conclusions" do not take into account the educational levels of the workers compared, or their years of experience.[9]

This broader anti-tax, anti-union and thus anti-government sentiment has risen in many quarters in the United States since the onset of the recession. The fact that many banks, financial houses and auto companies like GM have paid back considerable sums of the monies they were lent is not a key part of the public conversation. It is in this context, too, that the attack on the unionized public sector in the United States must be understood. With unemployment remaining very high, taxes still being raised, at least locally, and schoolchildren's performance in most major cities stalled again, support for unionized public workers continues to sag. The ability of the right to control the public dialogue so skilfully, and to develop this distorted narrative, is also helped by the very fact that public employees are often among the few who have good health care and a pension, paid for by their neighbours, who are likely to have neither.

Fighting this blame game and its demonization of public sector workers is increasingly difficult as the US economy struggles, and stubborn long-term unemployment magnifies so many families' frustrations. While the stories of excessive overtime and ballooning earnings jeopardize the credibility of fire-fighters and police officers and thus erode their support among the citizenry, public education professionals and their unions find themselves undermined by President Obama and his educational advisers, who reward "winning"[10] states with significant monetary infusions if they change their educational systems to an untried, more free market model. Unions have not succeeded in offering different explanations to counter this disturbing narrative created by the Right; and, as a result, their bargaining and political strengths are slipping.[11]

Given these developments, has the United Federation of Teachers been able to create a different trade union narrative?

Although New York City is often thought to be among America's most liberal cities, since 2002 its public education system has embodied a classic neoliberal design. New York's mayor, billionaire Mike Bloomberg, seized control of the 1 million student system by legislative action, and through his education tsar,

Chancellor Joel Klein, has tried one free market change after another, the latest being the installation of nearly every school principal as an entrepreneur, meaning her/his yearly evaluation will in part depend on the success of an economic "report card".

Corporate friends and allies of Bloomberg have poured hundreds of millions of dollars into the city's public education efforts, enhancing "innovation" in teaching and learning, nearly always sidestepping, ignoring and disrespecting the voice of the education professionals and their union, the UFT. A stated objective of the Administration's policies – a laudable one – is to close the educational achievement gap between white and Asian children, on the one hand, and other children of colour, on the other. For years they claimed success at this – only to find the discrepancy as great as ever when the State of New York announced in July 2010 that the tests for previous years were both too easy and too easily graded, resulting in brown and black children being once more, and perhaps all along, behind white and Asian children.

But these pieces of reality do not help the UFT in its battles with the City. After all, the children most needing educational aid are still in the same situation, and the question remains: what can an educational workers' union do in an environment like this to remake its image and reshape its influence to help New York's most needy families and children, and, hence, themselves?

The pursuit of innovative strategies, including those that struggle with the complexity of race, has characterized the UFT's political arm for decades. It does seem, however, that in 2004 and 2005 a more decided and determined community-based strategy emerged. What is meant by this is that leaders and decision-makers in the organization, or at least some of them, began to see their fate as tied intimately to the well-being of the communities where they worked. Instead of thinking primarily of teachers and union grievances and objectives in various undertakings and campaigns, locally or city-wide, they began to listen more carefully to and act more in consonance with the needs of the communities they served, principally those of colour.[12] In order to be successful in these efforts, the UFT has looked more to young women and men of colour to lead these campaigns. I will describe some of the specifics of the UFT's strategy in detail in the following pages.

The childcare campaign

One of the UFT's most unusual efforts has been the decision to join an upstate/downstate alliance with AFSCME's state-wide local, CSEA,[13] and through this to organize childcare workers throughout New York State. Under their agreement, CSEA received jurisdiction to organize all the childcare workers outside New York City, while the UFT had responsibility for those within the five boroughs that comprise the City. Both unions were not just assisted but actually directed in their organizing efforts by the remarkable ability of the now largely discredited ACORN community organization.[14] ACORN somehow, and miraculously, went through the five boroughs of this city of 8 million people, discovered and surveyed more than 28,000 different childcare workers,[15] many of whom worked from their homes, and explained to them why it made sense to join the UFT and fight for reimbursement and credential improvements in their difficult work.[16]

Tammie Miller, the chapter chair of the organization (formally known as UFT Providers), explained that the UFT did not have the practical ability or the political credibility to go to these "worksites" and organize these low-wage workers. She praised the determination, focus and skill of the ACORN and UFT organizers, who worked closely with the rank-and-file day-care workers. These efforts made success possible, but it only became likely when thousands of rank-and-file women accepted the constant organizing messages – "Everybody must be a leader", "You take control of this organization" and "This will only work if you decide your own fate" – as the core of their commitment. This messaging created an unmistakable flattening of the fledgling union's structure from the outset, and told interested workers that membership requires involvement and accountability, often key missing attributes in most US union members' relationships to their organizations.

Besides lining up tens of thousands of historically isolated workers into one organization, the childcare workers drive required the legislative clout of the UFT (and also of CSEA, which is a political powerhouse outside New York City), and ultimately was "legally" successful only because of an executive order signed by the then (and only briefly) Governor, Elliot Spitzer.[17] After a difficult struggle over two years, and in the midst of this awful recession, they succeeded in obtaining a decent first contract that improves the lives of nearly all of their members.

Much remains to be done and fought about, but the UFT's commitment to this new class of worker means it now has members in nearly every neighbourhood in every corner of New York City. In the conservative Borough of Staten Island that presence resulted in the ability of the UFT Providers to offer prompt and critical assistance to a family suffering from one of its children killing several other family members. Providers' members were on the scene shortly after the police and played a key supportive and compassionate role that was prominently acknowledged by the police and other community organizations. Actions such as these lend the union considerable credibility in the community when in fact UFT members are simply acting consistently with who they are and what they believe their work and responsibilities as community leaders are.

The campaign against school closures

Numerous legislative criteria are involved in any mayoral decision to close "failing schools", including educational viability, safety, educational outcomes, and impact upon the community served and other communities affected. The law requires considerable notice, ample opportunity for public involvement, an educational environmental assessment, and then a final assessment based upon what was learned.

In late 2009 the City's Chancellor announced the likely closure of 19 schools, for a variety of shortcomings. The UFT felt that, while several were poor performers, many non-targeted schools were considerably worse, and believed that politics played a key role in the selection of schools. Closing a school often has a wrenching impact upon families and children: it forces students to travel much further than their own communities to pursue their education, and affects childcare arrangements, local businesses and their commerce with children and faculty, as well as the resources inherent in the building as a place to convene and work on community issues. Closure can also burden neighbouring schools with excessive overcrowding and demographic changes that they are not prepared to meet. In short, the issue was and is significant enough for very specific, restrictive legislation to have been passed earlier in 2009 that required the City to go through a very careful and thoughtful decision-making process in these matters.

In this case the UFT, through its parent liaison officers in each borough,[18] and two specially assigned, highly skilled central headquarters staff members, actually set up a war room and went to work coordinating the community opposition that existed in many of the areas slated for school closing. It met with a number of community-based organizations, policy groups and city council members whose districts included the targeted schools, and built an effective and formidable city-wide coalition that established that the Chancellor had failed to comply with the law.

Key alliance members included the National Association for the Advancement of Colored People (NAACP), a leading national civil rights organization, and New York's leading independent educational advocacy group, the Alliance for Quality Education, a key contributor to the 2009 legislation that made it much harder for New York City to close any of its schools without presenting detailed findings to the affected communities. The UFT and its allies discovered that significant parts of the statutory requirements that the Chancellor needed to meet had been overlooked or ignored. The notice of public hearings which required the City education officials to gauge the community's sentiment was often too short, and the Chancellor's assessment of the "environmental impact" of the closures was not undertaken with the rigour the law required. When the coalition saw that even the near-universal public and community opposition to his decision had failed to force the Chancellor to conform with what the law required in cases of prospective school closure, the UFT and its manifold community and political partners sued the City of New York, seeking a negation of the Chancellor's decision to go ahead with closing the selected schools. Interestingly, the UFT's ability to make a transnational union connection with the German Metal Workers, IG Metall, resulted in the latter placing pressure on BMW, one of the sponsors of a technical high school that trained students to be auto mechanics – and the Chancellor removed that school from the closure list!

The judge who heard the case agreed with the union and its coalition partners, ruling that the Chancellor could not proceed with the closures, for many of the reasons mentioned above. The decision was a clear-cut victory for the communities and their schools, and it also strengthened the UFT community coalition strategy. Success had been achieved by building a meaningful and fully endowed campaign with partners to advance the educational needs and interests of the community of colour. A considerable amount of goodwill was generated by this effort, which was part of the UFT's endeavour to demonstrate that a city-wide educational union has a lot more in common with its citizenry than do the right-wing attackers who drone on about teachers' salaries, access to health care and pension rights.

Fighting for smaller classes and technical education

The next two cases differ from the previous examples in that they do not involve extensive community-based organizing on the same scale as the child-care and school closure campaigns. Nevertheless, they demonstrate the UFT's identification of key issues that not only have very strong community support but foster considerable, long-term coalition building in which the partners, the UFT and community-based organizations, have similar strong interests.

The class size struggle

For more than 15 years a number of community and educational groups throughout New York waged a constitutional battle, alleging that the funding for New York City and New York State schools was unconstitutional. This complicated litigation posited, among other things, that the "maldistribution" of monies between City, rural and suburban school districts was especially harmful to poor students in New York City. The harm suffered, so went the argument, resulted in poor pay for teachers, insufficient resources (such as paper, pencils and textbooks for the children) and overcrowding of classes to such a degree that children were simply unable to learn. A number of New York charitable foundations and private litigants provided the monies to fund this effort.

After its successful conclusion in 2006, in 2007 the new Governor, Elliot Spitzer, proposed, and the legislature passed, a US$7 billion commitment to address a number of the most pressing court findings. Implementation would occur, in part, through the state's signing contracts (Contracts for Excellence or C4E) with local school districts. In fiscal years 2007 and 2008 contracts for nearly US$300 million, earmarked for the reduction of class sizes, were signed by the state and the New York City Department of Education (DOE).[19]

For more than a year prior to the signature of these contracts, the UFT had been running a community campaign in the attempt to force the City's DOE to reduce class size. It was an effort to raise citizens' awareness of the critical relationship between class size and the ability to learn. Rallies were held, leaflets were handed out at subway stops, and testimony was given at City Hall. Although the depth of community coalition-building that was apparent in the childcare and school closing campaigns was not present here, the UFT signalled to concerned parents and organizations that this was also their fight; and when the state-level negotiations about how to spend the monies that Governor Spitzer ultimately allotted got under way, the UFT, along with its community allies, stressed expenditure on class size reduction.

Remarkably, and despite the express earmarking of several hundred million dollars to reduce class size in New York City, and considerable community and political activity by the UFT and its new coalition partners, class sizes in New York City public schools actually *increased* in the years immediately following the receipt of these hundreds of millions of dollars. Exasperated, the UFT and its educational partners[20] brought suit against the City DOE for failing to use the monies distributed by the state education department for the reduction of school class sizes. The UFT has used the lawsuit to educate parents and citizens in New York City about the City Administration's failure to use taxpayers' funds properly, taking an opportunity created by nearly 15 years of litigation. The early rulings in the case, through to midsummer 2010, were promising.

Perhaps more importantly, the UFT is beginning to explain that the City's failure to improve educational opportunities and test results for children of colour, and to narrow the so-called achievement gap between white and Asian children and children of colour, reflects the maladministration of the City's educational system by Mayor Bloomberg and his Chancellor, Joel Klein. As the high-stakes educational wars are ratcheted up in New York and elsewhere across the United States, with teachers increasingly the subject of blame and scorn, the UFT's efforts in educating the public on issues like fiscal impropriety, class size and apportionment of educational blame take on increasing importance. The union's ability to deepen its true and honest engagement with community-based organizations is clearly the most effective way to dispense its views and have its message heard.

The UFT's advocacy of technical education

Career and technical education (CTE), that part of New York's public, "vocational" education comprising high-school training for such occupations as graphic art, automotive repair, beauty, health care, tourism and public safety (among many others), is often thought of as the blue-collar side of New York City's educational offerings. The schools that offer these courses are not the high-performing high schools that graduate their students into Harvard or Yale, but rather community colleges whose students go on to jobs all over the city. Too often they are overlooked, and their value underestimated. That is not the UFT's view, however: its new president, Michael Mulgrew, taught in one of those schools and was a UFT vice-president of the CTE schools.

Before becoming president, Mulgrew launched an effort to build a city-wide coalition of city workforce development agencies, women's and civil rights groups, educators and building trades organizations to recast the CTE schools as major engines of economic development, targeting the city's 300,000-plus families who are among the working poor. This was a difficult and amorphous group to coordinate, but Mulgrew learned a lot from the experience and tasked his new vice-president for the CTE schools, Sterling Roberson, with the responsibility to "get this thing going".

Roberson – who has since moved to the state-wide level, where the audience is friendlier to ways of strengthening technical education and using the schools in an effort to promote workforce development – has maintained the relationships Mulgrew developed with community groups, while deepening the UFT's credibility with the state education department leaders. At present, the effort is not primarily one of coalition work and community organizing, but successful grants from the state could put the UFT in a very strong position with its historic workforce development partners not only to ensure CTE's critical role in training future New York City workers, but also to expand its role as an income-elevating force in the communities of the working poor.

This vision is what drove Mulgrew and now his successor, and success can only be realized by taking into account the progress the UFT has made over the last decade in the city's communities. In a sense, the restructuring at head - quarters and in the five boroughs, where new, young, critical-thinking and energetically organizing women and men, mostly of colour, have led these campaigns, has created a certain credibility that the UFT lacked earlier. It is this new "look" and "effort" that will, hopefully, cause the state education department to set goals for and fund the union's CTE work in a manner that advances the lofty vision shared by Mulgrew and Roberson. And, should this even partially take place, it will remind public sector union observers that, when important union players in the sector look to deepen their *real* ties to the communities they serve, some of the toxic bluster that passes for political debate in the United States evaporates.

Conclusion

This is a difficult and frightening time in America. Workers' strongest institutions, public sector unions, are maligned, ridiculed and threatened daily, simply because they are viable politically and maintain a public vigilance that thwarts the political Right's ambition to turn back to or "restore" what they imagine is America. For the most part, these unions are slow in responding to the attacks, in part because historic allies such as the Democratic Party and President Obama provide at best tepid support – and, with regard to education, actually undermine the unions' efforts to fight back.

What I have shown in this essay is that New York City's educational union has turned to community allies and developed political approaches to important issues that have a critical impact both on families of colour and on the union itself. Focusing upon these issues, expending considerable resources and engaging in shared decision-making are gradually changing the perception of the UFT in the city's communities as New York's citizens struggle to fight for the important issues that they have in common. Advancing these objectives on many fronts, and often having men and women of colour leading the offensives, is a good start in building a different kind of political power.

Knowing that the UFT truly cares about improving their children's expe - rience by professionalizing and improving the economic well-being of tens of thousands of childcare workers is a significant development. So is pursuing high-level negotiations with state officials in Albany to expand workforce opportunities for the more than 300,000 New York City families who are the working poor. These reinforce a developing perception of change and long-term UFT sincerity.

This is just a beginning, but it does mean that there is a significant part of the UFT dedicated to blunting the reactionary forces unleashed by this economic crisis by rededicating itself to doing real things and creating real power by building meaningful relationships with the citizens and the communities it serves. If this continues, and if it becomes contagious in the public sector labour movement in the United States, the Right's attack on this part of the country's labour movement will ring increasingly hollow and insincere.

Addendum

In September 2010, this writer presented a wary but hopeful perspective about the ability of at least some public sector unions to meet America's right-wing attacks upon them. Then, two months later, came the mid-term congressional elections, since when every public sector trade union in America, from the "heroic" to the ministerial, has experienced derision, disrespect and in most cases brutal political attacks upon its sense of meaning and economic well-being.

This brief addendum, then, augments the main body of the essay that precedes it with an attempt to account for these worrisome changes in the political environment. In doing so, the model of hope and real public sector union change, evidenced by the UFT's efforts to link with the communities it serves, continues to be of great importance.

The stunning rise of the Right in the United States is better explained by others, but the warning signs were certainly visible to many. Just as the Obama Administration had sat out the health-care debate, allowing conservative Democrats and the Tea Party to define its terms, its failure to address the needs of those adversely affected by the US economy's slow recovery in 2010 persuaded large numbers of Americans to move in a different political direction.

Mixed with the economic malaise was a sense, across the political spectrum, that the country was heading in the wrong direction. The Right skilfully played these social and economic uncertainties in various ways, but clearly the dominant strategy was to take on politically and severely damage the one force in American society not controlled by capital – the public sector unions. This was especially important because of these unions' ability to spend monies in national and local elections to achieve their members' economic and political goals.

The election results were stunning. Republicans regained control of the lower house of the US Congress, took several Senate seats, and won control of a majority of state legislatures and governorships, where most legislation about education and all about non-federal public sector workers' rights originates. In particular, they gained firm control of the legislative apparatus in Pennsylvania, Michigan, Ohio and Wisconsin, all critical for President Obama, who will seek re-election in 2012.

Flushed with their success, and in many cases on the pretext of respond - ing to economic crisis in their respective states, the Right brought forward legislation to end or not contribute to public sector pension funds; end or severely abridge teachers' ability to gain tenure; restrict unions' ability to have dues deducted from their members' pay cheques (a key funding source); force unions, yearly, to hold a referendum in public workplaces to "make certain" that their members still want their representation; permit, unilaterally, local government control to be outsourced to a corporation (Michigan); and, of course, end collective bargaining in the sector altogether.

Many of these legislative offerings are now law in many states. Rights have vaporized so quickly that Massachusetts, America's most Democratic state, is just now debating whether to end public sector collective bargaining over health care. The bill passed the lower house of the state legislature, which Democrats control by a ratio of 3:1.

These developments have forced powerful, innovative unions like the UFT to circle the wagons as they face the constant threat of more than 7,000 lay-offs of teachers in New York City. While millions watched with hope the bold actions of Wisconsin's police and firefighters, not targeted for collective bargaining extinction, they also learned, just a month later, of the passage of laws in Wisconsin, Ohio and elsewhere that tore apart hundreds of thousands of workers' rights gained over 50 years of struggle.

What's next? Neither political commentators nor academics or union leaders really know. The AFL-CIO just now pursues a tepid legal strategy of fighting back through special autumn elections, but the stalled economy and the silent White House suggest that this is a doubtful strategy. Democratic Party operatives range from "wondering" to advising the unions to make further concessions, when there is little room left to do so. In our labour education outreach, we urge the UFT to continue its neighbourhood power-building, and counsel the police and fire unions to form meaningful, long-term, strategic relationships with those in American society who are powerless or historically treated as pariahs. For now it seems that many in power are willing to treat public sector unions in just that way; and only by changing the syntax of struggle, and who is partner with whom, and what trade unions are *really* willing to fight for, can these shocking developments be righted.

Notes

[1] When this chapter mentions the "unionized public sector", it refers to city, municipal, county and state workers. This essay was essentially written in September 2010, but events in early 2011 throughout the United States only strengthen its observations.

[2] Federal Reserve Chairman, Ben Bernanke, in *Washington Times*, 9 Aug. 2010.

[3] Actually, the fact that the UFT represents and seeks to represent public day-care workers, nurses and school-related personnel, among others, and not just teachers, is what makes it effective in these difficult times.

[4] According to a report of January 2010 from the Bureau of Labor Statistics, US Department of Labor, there were 7.9 million public sector workers versus 7.4 million unionized workers in the private sector.

[5] The "Right", for present purposes, includes press and blogging critics, Tea Party activists and substantial segments of the Republican Party, many of whom put most of the blame for the massive state and city budget deficits in the United States on what they consider excessive salary and benefits and pension promises that public sector unions have achieved through collective bargaining and legislation.

[6] The quotes are from an article, "The New Tammany Hall", published in the *Weekly Standard* on 12 Oct. 2009, co-authored by Fred Siegal and Daniel DiSalvo, who wrote an admiring biography of former NYC mayor

Rudolph Guiliani. Madison was one of the key creators of the US Constitution, considered by many a key architect of the "inherent fairness" in the balance of power reflected in that document.

[7] A good example of this "blasting" of public sector salaries is the website of the conservative think-tank Empire Center: see http://www.empirecenter.org (accessed 16 June 2011).

[8] Siegal and DiSalvo, "The New Tammany Hall", p. 4.

[9] See, among many, many other examples, *USA Today*, 10 Aug. 2010.

[10] The President calls this contest a "race to the top", but its criteria involve heavy reliance on testing, very controversial in the United States, as the measure of "school and teacher success".

[11] An article in the *New York Times* of 27 June 2010 (Steven Greenhouse, "Labor's new critics: Old allies in elected office") wrote about how former allies of unions in New York, New Jersey, Los Angeles, Oregon and elsewhere were challenging or rejecting key public sector union legislative and political concerns, a surprising and unexpected development.

[12] A bit of NYC history is helpful here. In 1968 the UFT was seen by many as disregarding community concerns in the explosive racial aftermath of the late 1960s, and for decades it was treated, not universally, but significantly enough, with suspicion in many communities with considerable populations of black and/or brown people.

[13] AFSCME is the American Federation of State, County and Municipal Employees, the union that organized the sanitation truck workers in 1968 in Memphis, Tennessee, where Dr Martin Luther King was killed. CSEA, its mostly upstate New York affiliate, is the Civil Service Employees Association.

[14] In this regard, the UFT learned what other unions have learned across America – they need Worker Centers and other community organizations if they are to succeed in reaching poor or immigrant workers.

[15] In the literature about this campaign, the number of childcare workers in the City has been variously given as both 28,000 and 32,000 prospective UFT members.

[16] "Reimbursement" refers to the years-long fight by childcare workers to get the full value of what they contracted for, which, in essence, is their daily wage. Promising to address and solve this problem was critical to the UFT's success in organizing these workers.

[17] Since then, Spitzer's successor, Governor Paterson, has signed legislation that formalized, by statute, the rights that Ms Miller's organization won by the considerably less durable executive order signed by Spitzer. This action clearly strengthens the UFT Providers organization under US law.

[18] These parent liaison officials, as official UFT representatives, had responsibility to work with parent groups on educational and community issues of importance. They acted as de facto UFT community organizers, particularly in the Bronx and in Brooklyn, meeting with parents affected directly or indirectly by the school closures, and their community organizations, and forged quite meaningful community and personal ties. This was, like the childcare campaign, a further expression of the union's intention to deepen its ties to underserved communities on an issue of great importance to the citizens who lived there.

[19] Much useful information on this topic may be found on the web page for one of the UFT's litigation/coalition partners in its class size lawsuit, a community non-profit organization called Class Size Matters: http://www.classsizematters.org (accessed 16 June 2011).

[20] In this litigation, the UFT again teamed up with the civil rights organization NAACP, along with the Hispanic Federation, a service-oriented, progressive community non-profit organization that encompasses 90 different Latino organizations in the north-eastern United States, and the non-partisan educational entities Alliance for Quality Education and Class Size Matters.

INDEX

Note: Page numbers in bold refer to tables; those in italics refer to figures. Numbers in subscript refer to endnotes.